THE MODERNIST CORPSE

THE MODERNIST CORPSE

Posthumanism and the Posthumous

ERIN E. EDWARDS

University of Minnesota Press

Minneapolis

London

Excerpts from Mina Loy, "The Sacred Prostitute," in *Stories and Essays of Mina Loy*, ed. Sara Crangle (Champaign, Ill.: Dalkey Archive Press, 2011), 199, and excerpts from Mina Loy, "Letters of the Unliving," in *The Lost Lunar Baedeker*, ed. Roger L. Conover (New York: Farrar, Straus and Giroux, 1997), 129–32, are reprinted here courtesy of Roger L. Conover, Mina Loy's literary executor and editor. "Her Lips Are Copper Wire," "Portrait in Georgia," and "Reapers" from *Cane* by Jean Toomer; copyright 1923 by Boni & Liveright, renewed 1951 by Jean Toomer; reprinted by permission of Liveright Publishing Corporation. "Tender Buttons," words and music by James Cargill and Patricia Keenan, copyright 2005 Warp Music; all rights administered by BMG Rights Management (US) LLC, all rights reserved, used by permission, reprinted by permission of Hal Leonard LLC; copyright 2005 Warp Music.

A portion of chapter 1 previously appeared as "Extremities of the Body: The Anoptic Corporeality of *As I Lay Dying*," *Modern Fiction Studies* 55, no. 4 (Winter 2009): 739–64.

Copyright 2018 by the Regents of the University of Minnesota

Published by the University of Minnesota Press
111 Third Avenue South, Suite 290
Minneapolis, MN 55401-2520
http://www.upress.umn.edu

ISBN 978-1-5179-0127-1 (hc)
ISBN 978-1-5179-0128-8 (pb)

A Cataloging-in-Publication record for this book is available from the Library of Congress.

The University of Minnesota is an equal-opportunity educator and employer.

FOR CRIS

The corpse is a new personality.

GANG OF FOUR

CONTENTS

ACKNOWLEDGMENTS

One of the central premises of this book is that human activity only occurs through interactive participation in complex networks of human and nonhuman agents and actants; it seems particularly fitting, then, to begin this book by acknowledging the many people who enabled me to write it.

I am grateful to Danielle Kasprzak, my editor at the University of Minnesota Press, for her work in bringing this project to fruition and for placing my manuscript in the hands of careful readers whose insights helped me develop the work.

At Miami University, there are many colleagues and friends who helped create the social and intellectual communities that supported my writing, including Madelyn Detloff, Katie Johnson, Cindy Klestinec, Andrew Hebard, Anita Mannur, Jonathan Strauss, Stefanie Dunning, Margaret Luongo, Yu-Fang Cho, Michele Navakas, and Cathy Wagner. I am particularly grateful to LuMing Mao and Keith Tuma, who provided guidance and support at critical moments; Tim Melley, who read and offered incisive feedback on parts of this book; and Mary Jean Corbett, whose mentorship has helped me more than she knows. I feel fortunate to have taught graduate and undergraduate seminars on posthumanism while planning and writing this book; the students' investment in the topic amplified my own, and affirmed my sense of posthumanism's relevance.

This book had its beginnings in my graduate work at Berkeley, and I am fondly indebted to the friends and professors who formed the fabric of my experience there, including Sophia Wang, Karen Leibowitz, Erika Clowes, Amy Jamgochian, John Binder, Carol Clover, John Bishop, and D. A. Miller. I am profoundly grateful to my dissertation director, Dori

Hale, who read and discussed my earliest writing on this topic with generosity, fierce intelligence, and good humor; the many hours of discussion with her enlarged my thinking. This project has evolved since then, but I would never have been in a position to write this book without her influence.

I am forever grateful to cris cheek, who met each of my corpses with me and who pulls me, beautifully and continually, toward life.

INTRODUCTION

A Modernist Body Count

THE DECOMPOSING CORPSE of Addie Bundren in *As I Lay Dying*. The radically dehumanized, lynched bodies in *Cane*. The defenestration of Clare Kendry in *Passing*. Tea Cake Woods, infected with a zoonotic disease in *Their Eyes Were Watching God*. Vicente Girones, gored by a bull, "All for sport. All for pleasure," in *The Sun Also Rises*.[1] Myrtle Wilson, hit-and-run victim in *The Great Gatsby*, and Gatsby's own corpse, leaving only the strangely geometric trace of "a thin red circle" in his West Egg swimming pool.[2] The self-organizing "crowd" of corpses flowing ethereally through the city in *The Waste Land*. The corpses of Bessie Mears and Mary Dalton, reported and circulated by the news media in *Native Son*. The "nothing at all" corpse of William Carlos Williams's bluntly titled "Death," which offers no consolation, only the pragmatic advice: "just bury it."

The corpse occupies a prominent place in American literary modernism, but it also acquires a new cultural visibility across a range of early-twentieth-century technical media. Photographs of World War I corpses gave U.S. subjects visual access to transatlantic battlefields and subterranean trench cities of the dead, graphically materializing the impossible calculi of "body counts" through which the gains and losses of war are measured.[3] Lynching photographs perpetuated and made visible the dehumanization of American racism, circulated both as grotesque "souvenirs" of killing and as human rights documents bearing witness to the continuing atrocity of American slavery. More generally, the early twentieth century's increasingly capacious media archives provided ways to reanimate the voices and images of the dead, troubling the boundary not only between the living and the dead but also between the human and the technical media forms that reproduced the voice and image with such fidelity.[4] Exemplifying this troubled boundary, early Hollywood's zombie, vampire, and *Frankenstein* films repetitively reanimated the corpse both thematically and formally, through the sequel, the adaptation, and the remake. Often set in distant locations, these filmic depictions of the corpse posed questions about the status of the human and the nonhuman that were nevertheless central to early-twentieth-century American culture, as zombie films depicted the "walking dead" status of industrialized workers and racialized "others," and the reanimated corpse in *Frankenstein* represented the vertiginous possibilities of a technologically produced posthuman "life," famously articulated in Colin Clive's exclamation, "It's alive!"

The Modernist Corpse argues that the corpse in American modernism is involved in a trenchant reexamination of who—and what—counts as human and as "alive" in the early twentieth century. As this opening "body count" seeks to illustrate, American modernism foregrounds the corpses of those who have been defined and treated as expendable forms of "bare life," and, in doing so, figuratively exhumes the techniques by which racialized others, gendered others, queer others, and an array of "other others" have been systematically dehumanized, condemned to social death, "buried" from cultural view, and otherwise regarded as less than "fully human." Yet the goal of this project is not to recuperate the "humanity" of these subjects but to problematize the categorial privileging of the human that has made such dehumanization possible. My discussion maintains a radical skepticism toward the concept of the "fully human," which paradoxically implies that there are degrees of infrahumanity to be adjudicated and claims a homogeneously "human" quality predicated upon its difference from, and frequently its dominion over, nonhuman life. Seeking to undo this autonomous human subject, this book regards the corpse as a site of "becoming-earth," to use Rosi Braidotti's Deleuzo-Guattarian term,[5] through which the human decomposes and becomes part of the larger ecological network of natural and technological forces within which it is embedded. While the corpses in American modernism thus comprise a "body count" of life reduced to its most dehumanized, such corpses are also surprisingly vivified, giving rise to a seemingly uncontrolled production of forms: bodies verging upon animality, acephalous bodies divorced from volition, corpses that seem to live, living bodies depicted cadaverously, and euphoric systematizations not easily assimilated to the category of the human. Examining such unfamiliar forms of life, my project suggests that modernism anticipates many of the questions that currently occupy posthuman studies. Positioned at the intersection of past atrocities and the possibilities ushered in by modernity, the corpse is engaged in a retrospective unraveling of the exclusionary category of the humanist subject, even as it imagines what comes "after" this traditionally defined human form.

My focus on the corpse also contributes to an emergent area of inquiry for posthuman studies. While posthumanism has considered relations between the human and its various others, such as the animal, the machine, and the thing, the corpse provides a significant but thus far underexplored nonhuman "other" that is intimately yoked to the human as its inevitable fate. *The Modernist Corpse* intervenes into the work of cultural critics who are currently rethinking, as W. J. T. Mitchell notes, "a whole set of nonhuman entities that seem to take on organic, lifelike, or 'autopoietic' characteristics—intelligent machines, of course, but also systems and swarms, viruses and coevolutionary organisms, corpses, corpora, and corporations, images and works of art."[6] Far from signifying the mortal limits of the human, the corpse in modernism functions "autopoietically" as a generative site from which to rewrite the living body and its relations to putatively dead or lifeless things.[7]

Posthumous Posthumanism

The posthumous is literally *post*human in that it follows human life, but how might the posthumous also exist along a continuum with the living, entailing a reconceptualization of what counts as "life"? For much of its history (and the corpse, too, has a history that intertwines with that of the living), the corpse has represented a "naturalized" conception of the body. Its fate dictated by enzymes and colonies of bacteria, the corpse marks the cessation of rationalist control over the body, the moment when the socially defined person is given over to biological forces, and the molar form of the human yields to the molecular processes of decomposition. Just as the living body in modernity is the site of technological intervention, enhancement, and refashioning, however, the modern corpse, too, is a technological product. Modern embalming practices evacuate and reconstruct the body, arresting the "natural" processes of decomposition so that the corpse has its own technologically dictated temporality.[8] Given its radical interpenetration with technology, the modern embalmed corpse is a prosthetic body, even a cyborgian body. The corpse thus uniquely occupies the intersection of biological and technological forces that posthumanism is currently interrogating—and it perhaps does so in ways that are productively defamiliarized, allowing us to pose new questions about the fate of the living body.

In claiming the corpse as a posthuman body, however, I want to distinguish my approach to *post*humanism from contemporary discussions of *trans*humanism. Led by theorists such as Hans Moravec and Ray Kurzweil, transhumanism embraces the technological enhancement of the human and looks toward a technologically enabled evolution of consciousness away from the body.[9] The finality of the corpse is in some sense the teleological boundary toward which transhumanism aims, as it seeks not only to overcome illness and debility but, more optimally, to "offload" human consciousness onto technological structures so that the frailty of the human body and the eventual demise represented by the corpse are transcended altogether. In this way, transhumanism posits a binary between the biological and the technologically engineered postbiological. Moravec, for example, claims a human *"essence"* defined by "pattern-identity" rather than "body-identity," such that the patterns of consciousness and life could be replicated in postbiological forms:

> Body-identity assumes that a person is defined by the stuff of which a human body is made. . . . Pattern-identity, conversely, defines the *essence of a person*, say myself, as the pattern and process going on in my head and body, *not the machinery supporting that process*. If the process is preserved, I am preserved. The rest is mere jelly.[10]

Modeling the *"essence of a person"* upon "say myself," Moravec describes a transhuman iteration of the Cartesian subject defined by a traditional binary between masculinist forms of reason and feminized and racialized forms of "mere jelly." This transhumanist aspiration toward disembodied consciousness thus has a surprising alliance with the long history of mind-body dualism that characterizes the liberal humanist subject; as N. Katherine Hayles points out, the transhumanist understanding of the body as "the original prosthesis we all learn to manipulate" can be regarded as an extension of the liberal humanist subject's treatment of the body "as an object for control and mastery rather than as an intrinsic part of the self."[11] By focusing on the enhancement, perfectibility, and transcendence of the body, transhumanism, as Cary Wolfe and others have noted, paradoxically replicates many of the central tenets of humanism, which understand the human as an exceptional entity who exists apart from a world of animals and things and whose fate can be directed by the rationalist will.

In contrast, my discussion of modernism's various corpses pursues an understanding of posthumanism that is emphatically terrestrial and embodied, interpenetrated with both nature and technology, rather than motivated by the technological determinism of transhumanism. In this way, the posthuman corpse is not evolutionarily "after" the human but is post*humanist*, representing a significant reconfiguration of the human-ist discourses that define the human's hierarchical relation to natural and technological worlds. While transhumanism seeks to transcend the boundary of death in pursuit of (post)anthropocentric goals, my project seeks to erode the boundary between vitalism and mortalism in order to position the human along an embodied continuum of newly vivified things. My approach to posthumanism is thus aligned with Hayles's cri-tique of transhuman disembodiment, but this erosion of the boundary between vitalism and mortalism marks a departure from Hayles's call to "celebrate finitude as a condition of human being."[12] Hayles seeks to reclaim the horizon of death from a transhumanist aspiration toward material transcendence, but defining the human through its finitude has significant political, ethical, and psychological implications; as Braidotti notes, philosophical conceptions of the subject's finitude "fuel an affec-tive political economy of loss and melancholia at the heart of the sub-ject" and support "the constitutive vulnerability of the human subject, which sovereign power can kill."[13] Reconceptualizing death as part of a vitalist continuum rather than as a cessation or punctuated finality entails reconceptualizing the political, social, and psychological subject not as a bounded entity but as similarly constituted through productive exchanges and transfers with the nonhuman. *The Modernist Corpse* thus takes a vitalist approach to the corpse in order to challenge the liberal humanist subject who has traditionally defined itself against a world of inertly reified matter but who, in doing so, risks being conceptualized as "bare life" itself.[14]

In what way, however, do corpses have their own "afterlives"? How do corpses function as actants not only in the bounded subject's experience of mourning but also in larger biological, social, and political spheres? Emptied of traditional forms of agency, the corpse is nevertheless not without its own powers of moving, and even organizing, the world.[15] If we consider the scene of funeral processions, for example, it is hard to deny that the corpse is the central actant—drawing crowds, disrupting flows of traffic, and evoking profound emotion from the people who surround it. From an actor-network point of view, there is a "corpse-power" that moves the living world.[16] Emphasizing the particular *doings* of a body rather than its categorization through organs, functions, or species characteristics, Deleuze and Guattari claim, following Spinoza: "We know nothing about a body until we know what it can do, in other words, what its affects are, how they can or cannot enter into composition with other affects, with the affects of another body, either to destroy that body or to be destroyed by it, either to exchange actions and passions with it or to join with it in composing a more powerful body."[17] While the corpse is indeed *human* from a species point of view (although here I am questioning my own tendency to presume that "the" corpse is necessarily a human corpse, rather than another kind of corpse), "live human" and "corpse human" part ways, not according to a more traditional divide between vitalism and mortalism but according to different modes of *doing*.

Each of the following corpses, for example, has not only its own ontology but also its own form of "corpse-power" that moves and shapes the living world: the impossible blind spot of one's own future corpse, the corpse of the beloved, the erotic object of the necrophiliac, the suicide's corpse that often "speaks" the pain that was silent in life, the mutilated remains of the victim of violence, the unidentified "John" or "Jane Doe" who inaugurates a criminal investigation, the medical cadaver used for pedagogical purposes, the sacred bodies of spiritual leaders, the sacralized bodies of celebrities, and the corpses of political leaders or martyrs who inaugurate regime change or revolution.[18] In each of these instances, how are the categories of the living body escaped or reinscribed in death, such that the privileges of class, for example, fall away or persist? In what way is a corpse raced or gendered, and for what period of time? (In one of my own mortuary experiences, for example, I was informed that husbands are conventionally buried to the left of their wives "because people read from man to lady, just like they read from left to right.") We might also ask how we "access" corpses. Burial rites and practices both performatively present and conceal the corpse. Jani Scandura and Michael Thurston argue that the often unseen corpses produced on the national and international stage serve as the focal point for historical events, functioning as "an allegory for all we have not been permitted to see, but have been induced to desire to see."[19] Corpses also have their own temporalities, such that the newly dead body, still seemingly expressive and bearing the bloom of life, is markedly different from the long-buried body, decomposing or leaving only the skeletal trace of that which has returned to the surrounding ecological network. And what of those who leave very different kinds of "remains," such as the cremated body, or the body devoted to scientific experimentation or organ donation, destined not only to die but also to "live" in the bodies of others?

In theorizing the vitalism of the corpse, my project often draws upon Deleuze and Guattari, whose work has been important for posthuman studies more generally. While Foucault and Derrida both anticipate post-humanism through the pronouncement of the discursive "erasure" of man "like a face drawn in sand at the edge of the sea"[20] and the philosophical "ends of man,"[21] Deleuze and Guattari attend to the materialist unity of human, nature, and technology whereby "man" is no longer an exceptional or central entity. Turning back to Spinoza, Deleuze and Guattari recuperate a form of vitalism, claiming "a unity to the plane of nature, which applies equally to the inanimate and the animate, the artificial and the natural."[22] Their conception of vitalism nevertheless undoes the traditional binary between vitalism and mechanism; "the real difference," they argue, "is not between the living and the machine, vitalism and mechanism, but between two states of the machine that are two states of the living as well."[23] These two states, molarity and molecularity (which are understood not in binary opposition to one another), sub-tend Deleuze and Guattari's theoretical approach to a range of contexts—cultural, psychological, material, aesthetic, and political among them. From a molar perspective, for example, we can understand the human through its visible, functional, anatomical, and taxonomical difference from animals, but from a molecular perspective, human and animal continually enter into composition with one another through becomings that deterritorialize both. Molecularity has a basis in biology, but it also describes exchanges and transformations in contexts that are, if not biological, no less "real"—microaggressions that perpetuate racism and sexism, for example, or local engagements with technology that problematize the subject's singular agency.

Deleuze and Guattari's reconception of the human who exists along a vitalist "plane of consistency" significantly informs much of this book. Rather than defining the human as the product of progressively linear evolutionary processes, Deleuze and Guattari position the human as part of a relentlessly connective, trans-specied ecology of material assemblages, a-centered rhizomes, and localized intensities: "Not man as the king of creation, but rather as the being who is in intimate contact with the profound life of all forms or all types of beings . . . who ceaselessly plugs an organ-machine into an energy-machine, a tree into his body, a breast into his mouth, the sun into his asshole."[24] Deleuze and Guattari emphasize the material, extrinsic, prosthetic, and boundary-transgressing properties of psychic life rather than the oedipal subject for whom the material world becomes symbologized within a circumscribed psychic arena. Distributed across a flat ontology, matter is, far from being dead, engaged in the imperceptible, molecular processes of becoming and deterritorialization: "There are only relations of movement and rest, speed and slowness between unformed elements, or at least between elements that are relatively unformed, molecules and particles of all kinds. There are only haecceities, affects, subjectless individuations that constitute collective assemblages."[25] In this way, we might understand the relation between living human and corpse not through a divide between vitalism and mortalism but through different modes of becomings, assemblages, and speeds. Sharing the same material immanence with the living body, the corpse nevertheless has its own temporalities—the terrifying rapidity of becoming-corpse and the seemingly imperceptible slowness of decomposition—that are quite different from the speeds of human activity.

Conceptualizing the modernist corpse through its vitalism is in no way intended to elide the atrocities of the early twentieth century; on the contrary, my project regards such a redefinition of mortalism and vitalism as necessary precisely because the early twentieth century is so populated with mass corpses and mass graves. World War I carved the Earth into trench cities crowded with corpses whose individual value and loss can never be measured; we might recall *The Waste Land*'s futile attempt to "count" the endless postwar streams of death: "A crowd flowed over London Bridge, so many / I had not thought death had undone so many." Eliot depicts modernity as an "unreal" necropolis, describing an uncertain psychogeography whereby the dead overtake the living—a "death assemblage" that mortifies rather than vivifies. Deleuze and Guattari similarly characterize World War I through its production of multiplicities, titling their early-twentieth-century "plateau" from *A Thousand Plateaus* "1914: One or Several Wolves?" They locate 1914 as a critical moment when national politics irrevocably becomes global politics, when the singular body and psyche are redefined by the fate of the masses. Inhumane masses of war corpses—unburied and unmourned—imprint themselves upon witnesses, positioning the singular subject within a necropolitical continuum between living and dead. For Deleuze and Guattari the early twentieth century marks not the genesis of the Freudian subject but the schizo-logic of the multiple. Claiming that psychoanalytic models of mourning are inadequate for the losses of modernity, Deleuze and Guattari understand the corpse not as a signifier of the singular subject's death drive and traumatic losses but as a *crowd* unto itself: "Once Jung had a dream about bones and skulls. A bone or a skull is never alone. Bones are a multiplicity. But Freud wants the dream to signify the death of *someone*."[26]

Outside the immediate context of World War I, the singular corpse still embodies acts of mass destruction and production. When Gatsby's car crashes into Myrtle in *The Great Gatsby* (1925), for example, the collision between machine and human transforms Myrtle's body into an unrecognizably mechanized form, her "left breast . . . swinging loose like a flap."[27] Grotesquely inverting the good-time "flapper" of the 1920s, the strangely automated opening of the "flap" evokes the mass-production assembly line more than it does the familiar contours of the human body. While *Gatsby* culminates in the production of literal corpses, early-twentieth-century literary and cultural texts are often peopled with the metaphorically dead, walking zombies incapable of being killed despite their multiply annihilating transactions with mass culture. For this reason, Deleuze and Guattari suggest, "The only modern myth is the myth of zombies— mortified schizos, good for work, brought back to reason."[28] In *Modern Times* (1936), for example, Charlie Chaplin's character is a kind of comedic zombie repeatedly injured and consumed by the machinery of mass production, even as the conditions of such production require the ongoing sacrifice of his "life." Tim Armstrong explicitly connects such scenes of capitalist production to the annihilations of war, arguing that "the maiming of bodies in war is an intensification of a more general consumption of bodies in capitalism—signaled, for example, in narratives of cannibalism, from that in Poe's *Pym* to Upton Sinclair's depiction of severed fingers in the sausage mix at a Chicago meat works in *The Jungle* (1906)."[29]

Given this collusion between modern necropolitics and capitalism, Braidotti urges the necessity not of reiterating the subject's death-bound status but of extending the conceptual boundary separating the human from more expansive forms of posthuman "life." Against the mass corpses produced by global catastrophes, international politics, and capitalist modes of production, the corpse in modernism is often relentlessly generative, animating what has previously been presumed to be more or less dead matter or, in Frankensteinian fashion, returning from the dead to figuratively "live" in wholly unexpected ways. This vivification of the corpse and the larger ecology within which it is embedded implicitly critiques humanism's anthropocentric commitments, but such a critique does not reject the humanist aims of affirming the worth, dignity, and rights of all subjects. Rather, achieving these aims requires a redefinition of the human and its relations to the natural and the technological. Understanding the human, for example, through its separation from infrahuman animals and "dead" matter creates conceptual categories of hierarchical difference that are too readily used to subjugate racialized, gendered, and queer "others." In other words, negatively conceptualizing and treating a person as an animal, a thing, or an instrument is to some degree predicated upon understanding animals, things, and instruments as devalued, mechanistic entities whose misuse has no reciprocal impact upon the user. In this way, *The Modernist Corpse* suggests that "human rights" need to be reconceived as "posthuman rights" that would acknowledge the embedded relations between the human and its putative "others." The corpse is integral to the ethical goals of posthumanism, given that it has often been regarded with revulsion as that which must be cast aside or buried in order to live. Conceptually extending our consideration of "life" to include the unique vitality of the corpse entails an extension of what might count, in Judith Butler's terms, as a "livable" body.[30]

Critical Posthumanisms

Defining the posthuman not as a technologically determined species category that comes "after" the human but rather as an entity that emerges in the wake of the discursively defined human, *The Modernist Corpse* approaches literary and cultural texts through the lens of *critical* posthumanism. Critical posthumanism implies making critical distinctions between generative and destructive forms of posthuman life, distinguishing, for example, between productive human-machine assemblages and the technologically augmented form that is deployed only to further traditional forms of domination. As part of making such determinations, critical poshumanism necessarily has a projective and creative function; discussing Braidotti's calls for "conceptual creativity" in theorizing the posthuman, Stefan Herbrechter notes, "Only by meeting the posthuman challenge with critical creativity will the humanities have a future and be able to construct a future for humans and nonhumans."[31] Critical posthumanism also implies, however, critical self-reflexivity about the paradoxes implicit in representing the posthuman, in reading from a posthuman perspective, and in posthuman studies itself. As Herbrechter and Ivan Callus have asked, what does it mean to produce or receive texts as if one were somehow other than human? Given that writing is itself a human technology, how is it possible to engage with texts without participating in the discourses and semiotic systems that have defined the human as an exclusionary category? How is it possible to theorize the posthuman outside humanist paradigms, given that the detachment required to conceptualize the posthuman is itself one of the defining characteristics of the traditional humanist subject?[32] It is useful, then, to delineate the methodological strategies that inform my conception of posthumanism—and to consider how the corpse is implicated in these strategies—even as I acknowledge that such strategies creatively cast themselves "toward" a critical posthumanism that does not entirely escape anthropocentric ideologies.

To begin, my project treats the human not as an immutable biological category but as the product of historically situated discourses. As Herbrechter notes, critical posthumanism "understands the human species as a historical 'effect,' with humanism as its ideological 'affect.'"[33] Perhaps counterintuitively, the corpse plays an instrumental role in producing the human as a historical "effect," providing important, if typically concealed, sources of knowledge about the body. As Foucault explains in *The Birth of the Clinic*, the corpse occupies a privileged position in Enlightenment epistemology; no longer shrouded by religious and moral strictures, it has become a source of medical and anatomical knowledge:

> A fine transmutation of the corpse had taken place: gloomy respect had condemned it to putrefaction, to the dark work of destruction; in the boldness of the gesture that violated only to reveal, to bring to the light of day, the corpse became the brightest moment in the figures of truth. Knowledge spins where once larva was formed.[34]

Examination of the corpse completes the process by which the entirety of the body, and consequently the subject, is made available to view, surpassing with a penetrating gaze the limits of the bodily surface and making both internal and external operations of the body subject to analysis and categorization. But Foucault's claim also paradoxically implies an elision of the body—a transformation of viscera into knowledge, a mode of examination through which the body is, to use his metaphor, only a chrysalic pause on the way to understanding. Foucault implies an epistemology through excorporation—knowledge as that which comes out of, but also simultaneously erases, the body.

The illuminatory properties of the cadaver extend beyond the scope of the clinic, providing anatomical models that inform more general cultural perceptions of the body. The cadaver also provides a generalizable model of viewing and knowing the body, whereby knowledge is best obtained through visual invasion of a passively inert other. Karen Jacobs argues that such a disembodied viewer has occupied the center of Western culture since Descartes: "The observer's claim to a transparent body is predicated . . . on the disavowal of its own embodiment along with the production of a reviled corporeality in the Other, whose embodiment at once qualifies it as an object of knowledge and disqualifies it from epistemological possibility and subjective complexity itself."[35] Culture establishes "conventional occupants" for this "reviled corporeality," as the fictively disembodied white male viewer "purif[ies]" his gaze by casting an unwanted corporeality onto the feminized or racialized other.[36]

Although the corpse serves as the model for such "reviled corporeality," it has also paradoxically offered an Enlightenment model of objective, disembodied vision that would escape the potentially tainting influence of the other senses. Descartes proposed an experiment whereby the eye of a corpse could be used to construct a kind of corporealized camera obscura that would ensure visual objectivity:

> But you may become more certain . . . if, taking the eye of a newly dead person (or failing that, the eye of an ox or some other large animal), you carefully cut away the three surrounding membranes at the back so as to expose a large part of the humour without spilling any. Then cover the hole with some white body thin enough to let the light pass through (e.g. a piece of paper or an egg-shell), and put this eye in the hole of a specially made shutter so that its front faces a place where there are various objects lit up by the sun, and its back faces the inside of the room where you are standing.[37]

Despite its grotesqueness, Descartes's imaginary experiment describes a model of selective vision that is prevalent from the Enlightenment onward. Believing that the other senses were "deceivers, deluders, destroyers," Cartesian thought valorizes the purity and objectivity of vision separated from the other senses as an epistemological basis for understanding the world.[38] Mechanized instruments of vision such as the camera obscura—or here the eye of a corpse crafted into a makeshift camera obscura—both modeled the activity of an ideal eye and directed the enveloping power of natural light itself, allowing, in Jonathan Crary's terms, an "orderly and calculable penetration of light rays through the single opening" rather than the "potentially dangerous dazzlement of the senses by the light of the sun."[39] The corpse is thus impossibly on both sides of the equation in Enlightenment thought, providing both the ideal human object of the gaze and the model for the ideally objective gaze, but representing, in both cases, a materiality circumscribed by mortalism.

And yet for most of us, looking at the corpse is anything *but* a rational or disembodied experience. The corpse viscerally shocks us into a different state of looking. Looking becomes not the certain activity of an Enlightenment eye but an urgently embodied experience in which several senses participate: a visceral pounding of the heart, an audible pulse in the ears, tears that cloud the clarity of vision. Looking at the corpse also marks the limits of a volitional or rationally controlled gaze. I refuse to look but I cannot help but look, my gaze compelled by something other than reason. Julia Kristeva points out that the etymology of *cadaver* is *cadere*, meaning "to fall," and the processes of falling inform both the corpse and the act of looking at it.[40] I feel faint when I see the corpse: I fall and the world falls away, suddenly an unstable ground from which to construct a visual perspective. The corpse is a body that falls through the cracks of the known, an extraordinary body that fails to be recorded through quotidian modes of perception. I refuse to believe the evidence before my eyes, even as my eyes strain to record a final moment with the known person who has already passed into the realm of the unknowable. The corpse confounds epistemology.

Modernism's corpses provide a renewed encounter with the material body, complicating the analytical detachment and distanced visual perspective of the Enlightenment subject, and inviting embodied forms of perception and knowledge. The modernist text thus performs a kind of "alternative autopsy" that competes with that of traditional medicine, undoing the "brightest figure" of the medical cadaver that would suture the living body to prescribed visual models of knowledge. Offering a useful alternative to absence or disembodiment, Foucault regards death as a "teeming presence," noting that "long after the death of the individual, minuscule, partial deaths continue to dissociate the islets of life that still subsist."[41] Corpses in modernism similarly redefine corporeality through "teeming presences," molecular bodily phenomena that escape the molar individual and transgress the binaries that have typically structured the category of the human: male/female, human/animal, subject/object, natural/technological among them. Rather than the "triumphant disembodiment" of both the Enlightenment and transhumanism, my approach to modernism suggests that reconfigurations of the human urgently reconfigure phenomenological and embodied forms of knowing.[42]

A primary tactic of critical posthumanism is to shift interpretive focus away from the human and toward the perspective of the "other," considering, for example, the experience of the animal, the life of the thing, or the "artificial" intelligence of the machine. *The Modernist Corpse* similarly examines the corpse not from the human perspective of loss and mourning but rather as a site of disassemblage from the human and reassemblage with larger organic and technological networks. In this way, my discussion departs from critical studies of mourning in American modernism, such as Seth Moglen's *Mourning Modernity* and Walter Kalaidjian's *The Edge of Modernism*, both of which draw upon psychoanalytic theories of trauma, loss, and melancholy in order to discuss the acts of mourning inherent in early-twentieth-century American culture.[43] My project's posthumanist approach to the corpse also poses a counterpoint to David Sherman's recent *In a Strange Room*, which argues that tending to the dead is foundational both to ethical practice and to the category of the human: "Humans signify; humans tend to each other's corpses."[44] While this scholarship on mourning and ethical obligation is insightful and speaks in different ways to the significance of death in modernism, my project poses a different set of questions: What kind of "afterlife" does the corpse have beyond human mourning and burial rites? How might we reconceptualize the vitality of nonhuman actants, objects, and environments by adopting a necrocentric perspective rather than an anthropocentric one? In this way, my project adopts interpretive practices that, in Neil Badmington's terms, "actively oblique the order of things" so that humanism is "pushed off course, declined."[45]

The Modernist Corpse pursues posthumanism not only as it is represented through plots, characters, and themes but also through the reading practices we bring to bear upon the text. As Wolfe points out, "when we are talking about posthumanism, we are not just talking about a thematics of the decentering of the human . . . we are also talking about *how* thinking confronts that thematics, what thought has to become in the face of those challenges."[46] Decentering the human calls for new ways of thinking about literature in particular, given that written language has served as a traditional determinant of the human and its difference from both animals and "primitivized" cultures regarded as less than "fully human." In addition to its performance of linguistic "mastery," literature is also a privileged system of delivering discourses about the human; that is, literature not only *represents* the human but also plays a role in *producing* the human, modeling characterological traits, behaviors, and forms of interiority that invite readerly replication and mimesis, and, conversely, defining forms of nonhuman and infrahuman life from which the reader is distanced.[47] Adjudicating differences between the human and the nonhuman, and often reducing the material world to the subordinate role of symbolizing human life, literature functions as a "humanizing" force that indoctrinates readers into human culture, modeling a "virtual" form of the human that makes the reader "more human than human," to take a phrase from *Blade Runner*. The goal of this book is to "oblique" literature's humanizing force by considering modernist texts as having their own kind of "thing power," to use Jane Bennett's term, rather than functioning as disembodied representational fields; we might consider, for example, William Carlos Williams's "no ideas but in things," Ezra Pound's "direct treatment of the thing," and Wallace Stevens's "Not Ideas about the Thing but the Thing Itself." In this way, modernist writing foregrounds its materiality as a nonhuman technology rather than modeling forms of "humanization." Taking an interdisciplinary approach, my project also regards the experimental techniques of literary modernism as actively engaged in material assemblages with other technical media forms, such as photography, film, and sound recording. While modernism's corpses signal a crisis about the status of the human and the nonhuman in the early twentieth century, this redefinition of the human is also materially enacted through modernism's negotiation with the living-nonliving status of technical inscription.

Modernism in the Wake of the Human

One of the parodically numbered "chapters" in William Carlos Williams's *Spring and All* (1923) begins by imagining a mass human extinction, a future moment when "all human flesh has been dead upon the earth for ten million, billion years." A hybrid text composed of self-reflexive "chapters" and objectivist poems, *Spring and All* is a striking example of modernist innovation, and Williams significantly positions such experimentation in a literally *post*human space, a world that comes after the death of the species:

> Now, in the imagination, all flesh, all human flesh has been dead upon the earth for ten million, billion years. The bird has turned into a stone within whose heart an egg, unlayed, remained hidden.
>
> It is spring! but miracle of miracles a miraculous miracle has gradually taken place during these seemingly wasted eons. Through the orderly sequences of unmentionable time EVOLUTION HAS REPEATED ITSELF FROM THE BEGINNING.
>
> Good God!
>
> Every step once taken in the first advance of the human race, from the amoeba to the highest type of intelligence, has been duplicated, every step exactly paralleling the one that preceded in the dead ages gone by. A perfect plagiarism results. Everything is and is new. Only the imagination is undeceived.[48]

Williams writes "in the wake of the human," but he also refuses to imagine anything in place of the human, lingering instead upon the account of its extinction, the moment when all humanity, simultaneously and apparently without cause, becomes a collection of corpses lying "dead upon the earth," as if the human form has not decomposed but remained strangely intact for "ten million, billion years." Instead of speculating about what comes after the human, Williams describes the redundantly "miraculous miracle" whereby evolution replicates itself, "from the amoeba to the highest type of intelligence," so that the human is reproduced anew but self-identically, according to "a perfect plagiarism." The human form thus seems to be inevitable; even if extinguished, Williams suggests, the processes of life would eventually arrive yet again at the familiar human form as the pinnacle of evolution. Pointing out an uncomfortable paradox, however, one of the following chapters ("CHAPTER XIX," which nonsensically succeeds "CHAPTER 2") notes that this systematic replication of the human, which proves its inevitability, necessarily arrives again at the moment of its own extinction: "life has now arrived for the second time at that exact moment when in the ages past the destruction of the species *Homo sapiens* occured."[49] Rather than repeating this destruction, Williams introduces the first poem of *Spring and All* by abruptly pronouncing an end to such replication and making a triumphant, though unexplained, claim for "newness":

> Now at last that process of miraculous verisimilitude, that grate copying which evolution has followed, repeating move for move every move that it made in the past—is approaching the end.
>
> Suddenly it is at an end. THE WORLD IS NEW.[50]

Williams positions modernism's fixation with "newness" not in a space that comes teleologically after the human but in a much stranger space between a first destruction and a narrowly averted second. But what occurs to avert this second extinction of the human? Before abruptly pronouncing, "THE WORLD IS NEW," *Spring and All* offers a dilatory description not of the evolutionary processes by which the human once again meets its destruction but of the adjacent forms of "life" with which it coexists. Williams imagines a "majestic progress of life" that encompasses both the "huge and microscopic," and, foregrounding an animal metaphor rather than a human metaphor, he compares such "life" to "a wild horse racing in an illimitable pampa under the stars, describing immense and microscopic circles with his hoofs on the solid turf, running without a stop for the millionth part of a second until he is aged and worn to a heap of skin, bones and ragged hoofs." Rather than the corpse world with which it begins, or a repeated evolution of the human that replicates this death-bound state, *Spring and All* evokes an expansive, postanthropocentric form of life in which "men and beasts" not only coexist but become indistinguishable, "their legs advancing a millionth part of an inch every fifty thousand years." Halting the teleological evolution that culminates in the hierarchical "species *Homo sapiens*," Williams emphasizes "that progress of life which seems stillness itself in the mass of its movements." The corpse world that begins *Spring and All* thus announces the death of the traditional humanist form in favor of the human that exists along a zoological continuum with the "progress of life."[51] Opening with the unforgettable line "By the road to the contagious hospital," *Spring and All*'s first poem alludes to the hospital as the site of death, but it simultaneously emphasizes adjacency, contingency, and the viral, porous qualities of contagion rather than the singularly defined body. Locating its interests "by the road" to this Foucauldian site of biopolitical control over the body and the subject, the poem instead describes "the stark dignity of / entrance" into "life" whose limits are not circumscribed.

The opening of *Spring and All* articulates the distinction that Agamben, turning back to Greek philosophy, draws between *bios* and *zoë*, two different conceptions of "life." While *bios* describes the social and political organizations of human life, *zoë* refers to a more expansive category of biological existence shared by all living matter. When Williams proclaims that "all flesh, all human flesh has been dead upon the earth for ten million, billion years," he similarly distinguishes between the expansive "life" of *zoë*, which includes "all flesh," and the *bios* particular to "the destruction of the species *Homo sapiens*" as a taxonomic category. Attending to the zoological life of the horse, the botanical life of the pampa, the microscopic life of the amoeba, as well as more nebulous forms of "entrance" into "life," *Spring and All* repositions the human within this larger category of *zoë* and, moreover, claims that such a repositioning is necessary to achieve aesthetic newness, avoiding the "perfect plagiarism" that merely reproduces the known form of the human.

Agamben's work has been influential not because of his revival of the classical distinction between *bios* and *zoë*, however, but because of his argument about the politicization and subsequent transformation of *zoë* in modernity. Agamben argues that in modernity, *bios* is defined and maintained through its ongoing exclusion of *zoë*, which enters the political sphere not as a vital continuum but as a redefined form of "bare life," whose primary characteristic is its expendability, its ability to be killed. For Agamben, such politicized "bare life" provides the morbid foundation of modern politics, "constitut[ing] the decisive event of modernity and signal[ing] a radical transformation of the political-philosophical categories of classical thought."[52] In other words, modern political power establishes itself by selectively defining the human rights of certain subjects against those regarded as expendable forms of "bare life." Such disqualified subjects are barred from the political rights of *bios* but also from the vivifying properties of *zoë*—bare life is a form of "negative *zoë*," according to Braidotti.[53] While the person reduced to bare life can be transformed with impunity into a corpse, such a person already exists in a death-bound state, given that his or her life is outside the binary categories of both *bios* and *zoë*. For Agamben, such exclusion nevertheless plays a central role in modernity: "bare life has the peculiar privilege of being that whose exclusion founds the city of men."[54] In this way, the corpse is the paradoxical, radically uncertain foundation upon which the political and social "life" of modernity is constructed.

Braidotti's call for a vitalist reconceptualization of death reorients

Agamben's emphasis on the foundational role of "bare life," which inevitably locates the biological continuum of *zoë* "on the horizon of death, or of liminal state of non-life." While Agamben is careful not to equate *zoë* and bare life, he suggests that *zoë* is inevitably treated as bare life—as expendable and already dead—once it enters the political sphere. For Braidotti, this conception of bare life precludes other engagements with *zoë* and has generated in recent social and theoretical discourse a "forensic turn" that defines the subject solely through the "horizon of death"—through its finitude rather than its becoming.[55] Braidotti's reconceptualization of death instead theorizes the posthuman through its embedded relations with *zoë*, shifting political and cultural discourse away from an almost singular emphasis on "wound and loss."[56]

Inevitably invoking the recent atrocities of World War I, the corpse world at the beginning of *Spring and All* draws attention to the foundational "bare life" that has not so much been buried as it has been merely abandoned. When Williams refuses to repeat the processes whereby such bare life becomes a universal condition, claiming instead that "THE WORLD IS NEW," he suspends the negative horizon of death in favor of creative intensities between the human and the nonhuman. For Williams, relocating the human along a continuum of *zoë* that participates in a "majestic progress of life" is significantly involved with modernist form. When he imagines that human evolution might recapitulate itself, mimetically reproducing the human as "the highest type of intelligence," he characterizes this process as a "perfect plagiarism" and a "grate copying," claiming a parallel between hierarchical models of evolution and poetry's mimetic replication of an anthropocentric world. Rejecting familiar forms of *bios* in favor of an unknown *zoë*, he simultaneously rejects mimesis as the primary function of poetry, claiming that "only the imagination is undeceived" by such linguistic replications of life. As Agamben argues, language is the primary technology that defines and produces "man," the means by which man "separates and opposes himself to his own bare life."[57] Rather than replicating such anthropocentric linguistic practices, the objectivist poems of *Spring and All* seek materially to connect "man" with excluded forms of bare life, to "reconcile / the people and the stones."[58] "No ideas / but in things!" Williams famously proclaims, an ethos that extends beyond the direct treatment of things to include an understanding of the poem as an extensive "thing" with its own form of materiality, an opaque, and not necessarily human, corpus rather than a ghostly double. *Meataphor* rather than metaphor. *The Modernist Corpse* similarly pursues not only the thematic prominence of the modernist corpse but also modernism's famous formal "difficulty"—its aspiration toward linguistic "thingness," its nonlinearity, its antirepresentational experiments—as involved in troubling the boundary between the "life" of human and nonhuman bodies.

U.S. Postmortem

Despite *Spring and All*'s efforts to reconfigure the relations between *bios* and *zoë* and to reimagine the human as part of a "majestic progress of life," we might be skeptical about the rapidity with which Williams proclaims, "THE WORLD IS NEW." How would such a reconfiguration of *bios* and *zoë* actually be accomplished? What might be unintentionally buried in this thrust toward "newness"? And, within an American context, how does the utopian desire for such a reinvented world inevitably invoke the colonial history of the "New World" and all its attendant atrocity? Williams himself seems skeptical about the "history of the new." His own gorily romanticized approach to American history, *In the American Grain* (1925), describes the course of American colonial settlement as riddled with corpses yet to be mourned, or even properly acknowledged. The unfinished project of settler colonialism not only "haunts" the present: it persists as a living force that defines the project of modernity. Discussing Puritan New England's colonization of Native American lands and people, Williams describes the "inhuman" force of Puritanism that still animates the modern world: "It is an atrocious thing, a kind of mermaid with a corpse for a tail. Or it remains a bad breath in the room. This THING, strange, inhuman, powerful, is like a relic of some died out tribe whose practices were revolting."[59] A kind of "bad" posthuman chimera, this inhuman "THING" appears human from the waist up but trails a corpse below the surface—an apt image for forms of colonial oppression that produce a fictive image of the human by dehumanizing and conceptualizing others as bare life.

But if Williams's discussion of this inhuman "THING" draws our attention to a still-palpable history of violence that is not so easily overturned by modernism's aspirations to "make it new," his own attempts to address the corpses of the past are troubling in their own right. Mourning the Native Americans killed by European settlers, he claims a form of "authentic" identity that exists between Native American corpses and the land: "The land! don't you feel it? Doesn't it make you want to go out and lift dead Indians tenderly from their graves, to steal from them—as if it must be clinging even to their corpses—some authenticity."[60] Aside from the immediate objections we should raise to grave-robbing and "authenticity"-stealing, Jeff Webb points out that Williams's model of identity is troubling because it is achieved only through death, as Native American blood is spilled into the soil with which it then becomes united and "identical." More paradoxically, Webb argues, such identity is unattainable because it is only recognized once the "dead Indian" is lifted (however "tenderly") out of the grave, thus dislocating the corpse from the land that supposedly suffuses it with "authenticity."[61] If Williams's pronouncement that "THE WORLD IS NEW" is unconvincingly abrupt, his treatment of the past is appropriative and cursory, positing a blunt form of "identity" between human and land that precludes all the molecular, transformative processes of becoming-earth.

While my project follows Braidotti in theoretically extending the horizon of death, it simultaneously attends to a kind of "'bad' posthumanism" (to use Wolfe's term)[62] whereby the corpse is merely the dead body reanimated by ideological forces (as it is in Williams's horrific fantasy about exhuming bodies) rather than the site of vitalism and human reconfiguration. Such reanimated corpses often appear in early-twentieth-century culture as symptomatic visualizations of bare life, suggesting the extent to which adjudications of the legitimate human and the disqualified nonhuman are not only normalized but also, as Agamben argues, foundational to modern politics. Early Hollywood "zombie" films, such as *White Zombie* (1932) and *I Walked with a Zombie* (1943), for example, introduced into popular culture images of the racialized "walking dead"—a (mis)appropriated version of the Haitian *zonbi*. The Haitian tale of the *zonbi kò kadav* describes a rarely imposed social punishment whereby the soul of the accused is magically separated from the body, which is then forced into slavery on slave labor camps. As Elizabeth McAlister has argued, Americans became fascinated with the figure of the *zonbi* during the U.S. occupation of Haiti between 1915 and 1934, but rather than recognizing the continuities between Haitian and American systems of racist dehumanization, they largely regarded the *zonbi* as "the image of the Other through which barbarism comes to be the sign," such that fears of *zonbi* contagion authorized increased colonial occupation and intervention.[63] When Hollywood films adapted the *zonbi* for the screen, giving birth to a film motif that would spawn countless remakes and reanimations, they stripped away the cultural complexity and specificity of the

Haitian context. If the "zombie" is a body bereft of its soul, Hollywood replicates this "zombification" at the level of representation, extracting the "soul" of the Haitian myth and leaving only the dead image of the racialized other as walking corpse. While the *zonbi* of Haitian myth *had* a soul that still exists in a metaphysically separate sphere but with which it might eventually be reunited, the zombie of early Hollywood reifies the relation between slavery and inhumanity, constructing an imaginary binary between blackness and whiteness through a more fundamental divide between the dead and the living. Displacing the history of slavery onto a culturally flattened version of Haiti, films such as *White Zombie* and *I Walked with a Zombie* make visible the disavowed forms of bare life that seem to belong to a more "primitive" culture while simultaneously burying anxieties about the shared "life" between whites and blacks in the United States.

The promotional image from *I Walked with a Zombie* (fig. 1), for example, depicting a Haitian zombie retrieving the white zombie wife of a labor camp owner, can only imagine such shared "life" through an eroticization of the boundary between life and death. Both *I Walked with a Zombie* and *White Zombie* focus upon the white woman transformed into a zombie, suggesting that mere physical contact with the cadaverized body of the "native" zombie bears the threat of death; as Madeline's husband, Neil, claims in *White Zombie*, "Well surely you don't think she's alive, in the hands of natives! Oh no, better dead than that."[64] Being both "alive" and "in the hands of natives" apparently poses a paradox that Neil can only resolve by relegating Madeline to the category of death. While both films focus on the transformation of white women into zombies, however, this process is strangely nontransformative. "Native" zombies are identifiable by their bulging eyes, halting gaits, and overall zombie-ish aspect, but the white female zombies in both films remain function-ally similar in life and death, retaining all the gestures and conventions of white culture. One of *White Zombie*'s central scenes depicts "zombie Madeline" playing Liszt's "Liebestraum" skillfully (albeit stiffly), as if to suggest there is precious little "life" to be lost in white colonial culture. While films such as *I Walked with a Zombie* and *White Zombie* both per-petuate the semiotic association between racialization and death, they also unwittingly expose the interdependence between the putatively autonomous white humanist subject and those reduced to bare life.

The first half of *The Modernist Corpse* focuses on texts that interrogate such casual and ubiquitous associations between racialization and death

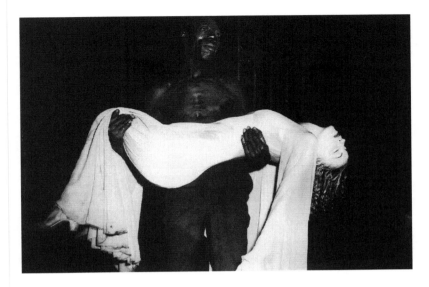

Figure 1. Darby Jones and Christine Gordon in *I Walked with a Zombie,* directed by Jacques Tourneur (RKO Pictures, 1943).

in early-twentieth-century culture. Addressing the American South's history of racial dehumanization, texts by William Faulkner, Jean Toomer, and W. E. B. Du Bois specifically critique a range of visual technologies that have traditionally been deployed to define living subjects as bare life. Seeking, instead, to vivify the corpse, these texts turn to anti-optic, auditory, and materialist modes of representation, opposing the visual techniques that subject the body to biopolitical control.

The first chapter, "Inhuman Remains," argues that two of Faulkner's most experimental novels, *As I Lay Dying* (1930) and *Absalom, Absalom!* (1936), decompose the traditional humanist figure and radically excavate the categories of the human and nonhuman upon which American slavery was predicated. *As I Lay Dying*'s central body—the corpse of Addie Bundren—is neither visually nor materially present. The emaciated "bundle of rotten sticks" she leaves behind disallows visual exploration of the body, departing from Foucault's claim that examination of the corpse completes the process by which the normative body, and consequently the normativized subject, is made available to view.[65] Faulkner's experimental "necropoetics" instead displace Addie's illness and the materiality of her corpse onto characters whose molecular decompositions redefine corporeal and subjective experience. The chapter then positions this modernist reconfiguration of the human in necessary relation with *Absalom, Absalom!* and the Civil War–era South's history of radical dehumanization. While *As I Lay Dying* disrupts visual examination of the body, *Absalom, Absalom!* dismantles the linguistic categories that have historically defined the human against dehumanized others. If language is the means through which "man," in Agamben's terms, "separates and opposes himself to his own bare life," *Absalom, Absalom!* foregrounds materialist forms of signification that have their own form of living (and thus their own form of dying): shoe polish that becomes personified ink, horny outgrowths of the body exchanged and read as signifiers, tombstone engravings that decay into illegibility, and uses of bone itself as a kind of writing material. In *Absalom, Absalom!* such material signifiers, which hover at the porous boundary between the living human and the world of putatively dead things, provide the starting-point for an expanded, materialist conception of life.

The second chapter, "Autopsy-Optics," positions Jean Toomer's *Cane* (1923) and W. E. B. Du Bois's "Georgia Negro Exhibit," an extensive collection of photographs and documents first exhibited at the 1900 Paris Exposition, within the context of early-twentieth-century lynching photographs. Drawing upon (and ultimately critiquing) Walter Benjamin's famous comparison of the photographer to the surgeon, I argue that the visual techniques of photography and autopsy provide analogous, interchangeable models for white viewers' perceptions of the often explicitly "dead" African American bodies in *Cane*. In the first section of *Cane*, set in the South, viewers selectively deploy such photographic, autoptic techniques of vision in order to discover predictable racial typologies or distant mythological "truths" that bury the history of lynching. Du Bois's "Georgia Negro Exhibit" similarly references such typologizing depictions (one of the photographic albums is explicitly titled *Types of American Negroes, Georgia, U.S.A.*), but his photographic project subverts simplistic typologies, depicting modes of visual expertise from which white viewers are excluded and representing an irrefutable African American "life" through forms of data visualization not easily reducible to a human/nonhuman binary. The second section of *Cane*, set in the North, similarly rejects such deadening photographic perspectives on the body, imagining collective, posthuman forms of embodiment that participate in decentered networks of sound technologies rather than being confined to the binaristic (and ultimately deadening) model of disembodied viewer and corporeal other.

Cane exemplifies the complexity of modernism's engagement with technical media: although Toomer critiques the photographic techniques that construct the difference between "whiteness" and "blackness" through a more fundamental divide between living spectators and dead bodies, he also embraces the sound technologies that vivify the body through human-machine assemblages. Extending this argument against the simplicity of technological determinism, my third chapter, "Sutures and Grooves," examines an array of technical media forms whose reconfiguration of the human both amplifies and disrupts hierarchical conceptions of gender. Placing literary texts by Mina Loy and Baroness Elsa von Freytag-Loringhoven in conversation with photographic and filmic work by Man Ray and James Whale, this chapter distinguishes human-machine assemblages that productively reconfigure the gendered body from those that merely augment humanist domination of the natural world. Before turning to these key modernist figures and description of the third chapter, however, I would like to briefly situate them in relation to a broader popular media context, both drawing some unexpected connections (what does Mina Loy have in common with *Krazy Kat*?) and emphasizing the spectrum of early-twentieth-century technical media forms that redefined the horizons of "life."

Early-twentieth-century media attenuated the finitude of death by reproducing images and voices of the dead; media also complicated the singularity of the event that lives and irrevocably dies in time, as viewers and listeners were able to stop, rewind, and replay recorded events. Such ability to suspend both the finality of death and the linear progression of time is clearly articulated in a 1919 *Krazy Kat* comic by George Herriman (fig. 2). Invoking the similarities between the comic strip and the sequential frames of film, the opening frame connects 1919 A.D. and 1919 B.C. through a reel of film, imagining time as a skein that can simply be rewound in order to replay a dead past. Writing in mirror-image words, "Reverse oh! Reel of time, reverse!!" (thus implying that the positions of 1919 A.D. and 1919 B.C. would need to be reversed in order to be read "correctly"), Herriman depicts film's ability to reanimate the past, but he also introduces a new kind of finitude in that the comic does not suggest the possibility of anything "new" beyond 1919 A.D. The "reel of time" significantly ends with the year of the war's conclusion, as though 1919 marks the end of time, a moment when novel events will cease to

Figure 2. In reel time. *Krazy Kat,* George Herriman, 1919. The text of the top panel is reversed and reads, "Reverse oh! Reel of time, reverse!!" The bottom panel reads, "I sure hope I'm late for that date with 'Marcatonni Mouse.'"

occur and the events of the past will be incessantly projected onto a continually spinning Earth.

Krazy Kat also suspends time through its suspension of plot, as most of the comics conclude with Ignatz Mouse lobbing a brick at the head of the hapless, yet seemingly immortal, Krazy Kat, who is repetitively revived through the weekly serialized form of the comic itself. The "Reverse oh! Reel of time, reverse!!" comic in particular gives a kind of archaeological explanation for the enmity of Ignatz toward Krazy Kat, turning back to 1919 B.C. when cat and mouse were not species enemies, but the true loves "Marcantonni Maus" and "Kleo Kat." Marcantonni Maus seeks a mode of authentic expression to convey his love, and, lamenting his own inability to write, he turns to Ptolemy Hoozis, a blacksmith who chisels a message of love into "everlasting brick," the inscription so immutable that we see the shadows of material letters flying off the anvil into the air. Marcantonni Maus directs Ptolemy Hoozis: "Make it passionate oh, Ptolemy, make it ardent I would woo her well and pay thee likewise." When Marcantonni Maus finally lobs the brick at Kleo Kat, inaugurating the form that would be repeated throughout the centuries, he does so out of a desire to impress upon her the immutable words of love; knocking Kleo Kat off her pylon is only an unfortunate consequence of passion (fig. 3). The strip suggests a continuum between 1919 B.C. and 1919 A.D. in the repetition of this gesture, but it contrasts the "heavy" brick writing of the past, which is laden with meaning, with the empty present form, repeated automatically and reflexively without any ingrained signification. Giving a pop cultural version of the death of the author, the opening panel depicts "Ptolemy Hoozis" lying next to the makeshift camera projector, literally asleep at the wheel as the projec-

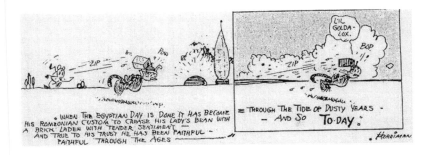

Figure 3. Archaeology of a brick. *Krazy Kat,* George Herriman, 1919.

tor carries on its automated work without the need for a human hand. In other comics, Ptolemy Hoozis the blacksmith-wordsmith becomes present-day Kolin Kelly the brickmaker—purveyor of death-dealing bricks rather than of books. Herriman inevitably implicates his own comics in this automation: plot becomes the repetition of the known, as Krazy Kat is in some sense already dead before the comic begins (getting hit with a brick is a foregone conclusion). Locating the comic in the year 1919, "After Death," Herriman situates such redundant death within the context of World War I and its immediate "aftermath," which, like the meaningless repetitions of violence in the comic world of the animal, already anticipates the coming of the next war and thus endlessly defers conclusion.

In Chaplin's *Modern Times,* scenes of redundant death similarly complicate biological birth and death as the inviolable bookends of human life. The film shows Chaplin's "Little Tramp" character impossibly surviving numerous fatal scenarios, making his body a kind of "living corpse" that repeatedly experiences death but is paradoxically incapable of being killed. In one of the film's most iconic scenes, Chaplin is consumed by the factory machine but, like Krazy Kat, is immune to physical harm, his body winding, and then rewinding, through the machine gears, which look remarkably like a film projector (fig. 4). As if to underscore film's ability to rewind and repeat events, so that death might be suspended or reenacted at will, the film later repeats this scene of machine consumption when the factory rehires Chaplin after a series of comic misfires. Chaplin is twice swallowed whole by mechanized forms of production, a seemingly dehumanizing consumption that *Modern Times* visually aligns with the medium of film, as human subjects themselves are translated into products to be reeled through a capitalist entertainment machinery.

Braidotti characterizes modernism's relationship with technology not as a posthuman interpenetration of organism and machine but as an encounter with inhuman forces whose invasive coldness paradoxically reinforces—or even produces—the "humanity" of early-twentieth-century subjects. While *Modern Times* might seem to uphold this point of view, critiquing technological modes of mass production and their complicit forms of technical media, it simultaneously endows the "living corpse" of the Little Tramp with infinitely renewable "lives" that productively extend the horizon of death. Rather than moving inexorably toward the singularity of death, the multiplicity of Chaplin's character redefines the normative human life span as punctuated with multiple moments of death so that he is repeatedly "reborn" as factory worker, protest leader, entertainer, and so forth, in response to a continually shifting environment. Engaging the "modern times" produced by technical media suggests not only the repetitively cycling end time without possibility of novelty but also the multiplicity of selves and "lives" that is not unlike the currency of contemporary gaming culture. And while *Modern Times* stages modernity's technological consumption of the human—and the analogous ability of technical media to vampirically consume the "life" of humans—the film also visually represents the reciprocity between technology and the body, as Chaplin's stylized performance of the Little Tramp admits into the body all the mechanical rhythms, automated reflexes, and angular movements that animate machines. My discussion thus deviates from Braidotti by claiming modernism's engagements with technology not as an alienating encounter between the human and the inhuman but as the site of interpenetrated assemblage that anticipates definition of the cyborg in the second half of the twentieth century.

The third chapter explores the vivifying assemblages formed between the instruments of early-twentieth-century technical media and the previously "dead" materiality of the human body—specifically the skull. I begin with Rainer Maria Rilke's essay "Primal Sound" (1919), in which Rilke fantastically imagines using the phonograph stylus to "play" the coronal suture of the skull, describing a posthuman position whereby one might use the prosthetic extension of technical media to engage in a radical auto-examination—an "auto-autopsy" that bypasses the evaluative apparatus of the Enlightenment subject and directly accesses the previously buried acoustic life of the human. While Rilke regards his

Figure 4. "The Tramp" in *Modern Times,* directed by Charlie Chaplin (United Artists, 1936).

experiment as an occult preoccupation, my chapter traces remarkably similar associations between the skull's coronal suture and technical media across a range of modernist authors and artists. In texts by Mina Loy, the Baroness, Whale, and Man Ray, sutures and grooves define new interfaces between the body and technical media as the skull is reimagined as a surface richly encoded with information, a site of technological assemblage, or a "hauntologically" uncertain material whose form is continually reinscribed. Such technological reopenings of the skull to transatlantic cable and wireless transmissions also position American modernism within a larger network of media exchanges. Although technical media allow access to the "primal sound" of the human, however, Loy and the Baroness critique uses of technical media that merely amplify gendered oppressions. Rather than turning back to a "naturalized" conception of gender, they embrace technological assemblages as a means of reconfiguring the reproductive body, anticipating not only the figure of the cyborg but also its feminist origins in Donna Haraway's "A Cyborg Manifesto."

Building upon the feminist critiques of Loy and the Baroness, the fourth chapter, "Love and Corpses," takes a posthumanist approach to gender, sexuality, and the family in Djuna Barnes's *Nightwood* (1936), asking what it would mean to love "in a posthuman way," given that love has traditionally been regarded as a humanizing force, as even the pinnacle of human experience. Providing the focal point of both male and female desire, Robin Vote's queer sexuality undoes the universalism of heterosexual reproduction, but it is also involved in the larger project of undoing the category of the human and humanist conceptions of the bi-gendered "family of man." *Nightwood* understands Robin's queer sexuality not, primarily, through the transgression of gendered norms but through her figurative and material association with the corpse and its associated domain of nonhuman "life." It is not simply the "personal" body of the beloved that one experiences through eroticism, but the body's undiscovered histories, its sedimented genealogical strands, and its mate-rial relations with animals, plants, and other nonhuman "things"—all of which undo an emphasis upon the heteronormative propagation of the human. Rather than casting her into the abject space of the social order's death drive, however, Robin's reciprocal engagements with the non-human define her as a generative source of life that flourishes where tra-ditional forms of reproduction fail in the novel.

Turning away from a potentially anthropocentric focus on the human corpse alone, the coda, "In Kind Cuts," examines the processes by which nonhuman corpses are routinely assembled with and incorporated into the living body, paradoxically regarded as sources of vitalism rather than of mortalism. Gertrude Stein's *Tender Buttons* (1914) explores the "zones of indiscernibility" (to use a Deleuzo-Guattarian term) between human matter and the putatively "dead" matter of "OBJECTS," "FOOD," and "ROOMS." In doing so, its complex verbal play explores how the reader herself manipulates, ingests, or inhabits the materiality of the text. The coda concludes the book by asking how literary texts might themselves be regarded as nonhuman corpses—an association that is etymologically invoked in referring to the body of work as a *corpus*. How might the lit-erary "corpus" exist in states of disconnection from or continuum with the living body of the reader and the author, so that the text is, in Diana Fuss's terms, both "a speaking corpse . . . detached from a living breathing body" and a nonhuman force that paradoxically "animates" the author and the reader?[66]

How Do You Make Yourself an Exquisite Corpse?

In "How Do You Make Yourself a Body without Organs?" Deleuze and Guattari describe the everyday acts of bodily disarticulation through which the singular organism opens itself to participation in larger net-works. For Deleuze and Guattari, ceasing to be a unitary organism is not a punctuated destruction that partakes in death but rather a process that occurs through artful, ongoing forms of becoming:

> What does it mean to disarticulate, to cease to be an organism? How can we convey how easy it is, and the extent to which we do it every day? . . . You don't do it with a sledgehammer, you use a very fine file. You invent self-destructions that have nothing to do with the death drive. Dismantling the organism has never meant killing yourself, but rather opening the body to connections that presuppose an entire assemblage, circuits, conjunctions, levels and thresholds, passages and distributions of intensity, and territories and deterritorializations measured with the craft of a surveyor.[67]

Such artful disarticulation of the organism and its familiar systemic organs provides a way to reconsider one of the favorite (de)compositional exercises of the surrealists, the "exquisite corpse." Surrealism is typically interpreted through the psychoanalytic lens of dreams and the unconscious, but exquisite corpse texts also actively disassemble the subject, opening the boundaries of the singular imagination and the text in ways that reveal their existence within larger productive assemblages.

Rejecting the notion of a singular productive center, exquisite corpse texts were produced through collaboration and chance formulations in which each participant contributed part of the writing or drawing. The "exquisite corpse" drawing that emerged from the collective efforts of Man Ray, Joan Miró, Yves Tanguy, and Max Morise, for example, distributes authorship among several productive origins, as each artist drew one section, then folded the paper by fourths before passing it to the next contributor (fig. 5). Authorship also involves a direct engagement with materiality, as each artist responds to the marks made by others and to the constraints posed by folds, partial images, and concealed forms. The resulting image strikingly reflects such processes of disarticulation, showing the death of "man" as a monadic entity and the production of a hybrid creature engaged in an autoerotic, auto-combative embrace. The heteronormativity of the kiss in the top fourth of the drawing—and even the possibility of a classical "androgyne"—are undone by the quadrants that follow, which redistribute human anatomy and its relation to a larger ecology of things. An eye takes the place of a nipple, a gun and its smoking chamber become prosthetic extensions of the body, reconfiguring the functions of aim, trigger, and target, and deterritorializing that weapon in turn. The second-lowest quadrant moves the body into an abstract space, suggesting an avian form on the left of the drawing,

Figure 5. "Exquisite Corpse," Man Ray, Joan Miró, Yves Tanguy, and Max Morise, 1928. Copyright 2016 Estate of Yves Tanguy/Artists Rights Society (ARS), New York. Copyright Man Ray Trust/Artists Rights Society (ARS), NY/ADAGP, Paris, 2016. Copyright Successió Miró/Artists Rights Society (ARS), New York/ADAGP, Paris 2016.

a mountain landscape on the right, and a leafy form at the center of the body—evoking the human's reciprocal exchanges with the natural world around it, which are often suppressed by a Western pictorial tradition's emphasis on the human figure. At the bottom of the drawing the vertical hierarchy of man who holds dominion over nature meets its demise— the figure is dead with eyes open, or, if living, shackled in compulsory engagement with the Earth.

The term "exquisite corpse" derived from a similar chance formulation with words, "The exquisite corpse shall drink the new wine," a phrase that uncannily expresses the animation emerging from seemingly accidental acts of authorial and figurative disarticulation. While the "exquisite corpse" is a specific exercise, it foregrounds thematic and textual practices that are central to this book's exploration of modernist texts, which similarly disarticulate the human form and trouble the linguistic conventions that enforce the unitary position of the human and its difference from nonhuman entities and things. Modernism thus invites us to read "in a posthuman way" (to quote Callus and Herbrechter's term), disarticulating the self's sense of belonging to the classificatory certainty of "species":

> To read in a posthuman way is to read against one's self, against one's own deep-seated self-understanding as a member or even representative of a certain "species." It is already to project an otherness to the human, to sympathise and empathise with a position that troubles and undoes identity while struggling to reassert what is familiar and defining.[68]

Perhaps even more than speculative fiction's *thematic* representations of the posthuman, modernism's experimental "difficulty" compels one to read "against one's self" and against one's own "species." Modernism's aspirations toward linguistic opacity, its decentering of authorship through automated processes more aligned with machinery than with the human, its fragmented, uncertain perspectives that refuse to reside securely within the normative human sensorium, its emphasis on becoming and multiperspectivalism rather than narrative teleology—all of these force the reader to encounter language anew and thus to read "against" the self who has been socially constructed by language. Modernism's experimental approaches to the corpse in particular are often anti-representational and anti-optic, requiring the reader to engage with unfamiliar forms of corporeality that require reading "against one's own deep-seated self-understanding as a member or even representative of a certain 'species.'"

Experimental modernism has sometimes been characterized as antihumanist in its aims, but my project suggests that modernism's experiments with the corpse have an inherently ethical charge, moving the reader out of her normative assumptions and into an engagement with the human in what may be its most profound form of otherness. As Bill Brown has argued, following Adorno, "accepting the otherness of things is the condition for accepting otherness as such," and this book similarly argues that accepting the otherness of the corpse is the condition for accepting an array of differences that yield a more expansive understanding of life.[69] The various—and often *exquisite,* rather than disavowed— posthuman corpses of modernism invite reconsideration of what a body can be and do. While theorizing posthumanism is in some respects a paradoxical task, and escaping an anthropocentric position in writing about the "life" of corpses and nonhuman things is perhaps an elusive goal, *The Modernist Corpse* urges the ethical imperative of attempting to do so, even if (perhaps especially if) the position from which we read is not entirely certain and the question of "what comes after the human" is not an answerable one. This book thus takes up modernism "in the wake of the human" not only in the sense of a posthumanism that comes *after* the familiar human, but also as a method of emergence and *awakening to* what the human has yet to become.

1 INHUMAN REMAINS

The Production and Decomposition of the Human in William Faulkner's South

> From the point of view of death, disease has a land, a mappable territory, a subterranean, but secure place where its kinships and its consequences are formed; local values define its forms. Paradoxically, the presence of the corpse enables us to perceive it living—living with a life that is no longer that of either old sympathies or the combinative laws of complications, but one that has its own roles and its own laws.
> **MICHEL FOUCAULT,** *THE BIRTH OF THE CLINIC*

WHAT REMAINS OF THE HUMAN once it becomes a corpse? Removed from the category of legal personhood, is the corpse also necessarily removed from the category of the human, becoming the inhuman other of life? What defines the perceptual and experiential boundary between the living and the dead, given that their forms are often mirror images of one another? Or, if we place pressure upon descriptions of death as "passing," how might we understand death not as an irrevocable boundary between the living and the dead but as a series of interconnected passages? That is, if the living pass into the realm of the dead, what might, conversely, pass from the dead into the living? Given that posthumanism seeks to redefine the human by, in Deleuzo-Guattarian terms, "opening the body to connections that presuppose an entire assemblage, circuits, conjunctions, levels and thresholds, passages and distributions of intensity,"[1] what kinds of assemblages, passages, and intensities exist between the living human and the corpse?

For Maurice Blanchot, the corpse escapes not only the categories assigned by legal and medical discourses but also ontological determinations: "What we call the mortal remains escapes common categories.

Something is there before us which is not really the living person, nor is it any reality at all. It is neither the same as the person who was alive, nor is it another person, nor is it anything else."[2] Neither the "living person" nor "any reality at all," the corpse resists binary definitions of animation and inanimation, exerting an unknowable force that circumscribes the realm in which such determinations can be made. And yet the corpse inarguably acts upon the living, momentarily hurtling us toward the condition of our own bodily mortality, allowing a premonition of what is otherwise an ultimate blind spot. Restless and nomadic, the corpse opens a road between worlds, establishing a relation, in Blanchot's terms, "between here and nowhere." If the corpse comprises the "remains" left behind by the one who has "departed," however, it also compels its own departures within the living, altering both the phenomenological experiences of those who come into contact with it and the very space it occupies. Blanchot understands the corpse not through its inert reification but through a darkly radiant power that *cadaverizes* and *corporealizes* space.

> We dress the corpse, and we bring it as close as possible to a normal appearance by effacing the hurtful marks of sickness, but we know that in its ever so peaceful and secure immobility it does not rest. The place which it occupies is drawn down by it, sinks with it, and in this dissolution attacks the possibility of a *dwelling place* even for us who remain. We know that at "a certain moment" the power of death makes it keep no longer to the handsome spot assigned it. No matter how calmly the corpse has been laid out upon its bed for final viewing, it is also everywhere in the room, all over the house.[3]

What Blanchot terms "the power of death" is a kind of "corpse-power" that re-creates the living world.

Such "corpse-power" is everywhere at work in William Faulkner's *As I Lay Dying* (1930). Addie Bundren's corpse motivates the characters, compels new modes of verbal expression, and organizes the novel's central events as the Bundren family convey her body on a protracted trip toward burial.[4] Her corpse navigates an uncertain passage between elements, as the bridge spanning the river is washed out and the very road is liberated from its quotidian fixity—"soaked free of earth and floated upward."[5] Opening a road "between here and nowhere," Addie's corpse enables phenomenological contact with material forms of otherness that remake the category of the living. Mourning Addie and physically, often agonistically involved with her corpse, the Bundren family members themselves undergo uncertain decompositions of bodily form as her corpse passes through the stages of becoming-molecular and becoming-imperceptible, to cite Deleuze and Guattari's terms. *As I Lay Dying* redefines the body not through its autonomous unity but through the volatile processes of decomposition and becoming whereby the body (whether living or dead) participates in a larger network of material assemblages.

The corpse in *As I Lay Dying* is also involved in unmaking the conceptual category of "man." Blanchot claims, "Man is made in his image: this is what the strangeness of the cadaver's resemblance teaches us. But this formula must first be understood as follows: *man is unmade according to his image.*"[6] In what way is the "strangeness of cadavers" involved in either making or unmaking an image of "man"? Our first impulse toward the corpse, Blanchot argues, is not to submit to the processes of becoming-corpse ourselves but to recuperate the corpse into the realm of everyday appearances: "we dress the corpse, and we bring it as close as possible to a normal appearance." Despite their tautological self-identity, their resistance to being understood through "any reality at all," human remains necessarily engage us in adjudications of visual resemblance and difference. Looking at the corpse, we question how "the mourned deceased begins to *resemble himself,*" or, more strangely, to supersede and amplify the life that it resembles, becoming "more beautiful, more imposing . . . so absolutely himself that it is as if he were *doubled* by himself, joined to his solemn impersonality by resemblance and by the image."[7] Here we might recall the Bundrens dressing Addie's corpse in her wedding dress, as if she could be made to *resemble herself* or to become *absolutely herself*—joined in marriage to her own "solemn impersonality," rather than becoming the body that everywhere leaks out of the garments of the known. But such resemblance or dissemblance operates only within the realm of images. Addie and the corpse she leaves behind can be identified as images in an uncanny mirror, but in no other way are they similar. Replicating that which is absent or no longer immediately living, the image, too, is the site of the departed. Given these properties of replication and departure, we can understand Blanchot's somewhat enigmatic claim that "what we learn from the strangeness of cadavers" is both that "man is made in his own image" and that *"man is unmade according to his image."* In *As I Lay Dying,* the corpse and the acts of language that mediate between the living and the nonliving similarly depart from this replicative power of the image, *unmaking* an image of "man" whose meanings have been constructed by various exteriorizing ideological gazes. As a living character, Addie has only limited forms of agency, but the body she leaves behind has its own *corpse-power*, endowed with an afterlife that unmakes exclusionary definitions of the human centered upon white patriarchal subjects.

The urgency of *As I Lay Dying*'s reconceptualization of the human becomes apparent when considered in relation to *Absalom, Absalom!* (1936), which revisits the site of Yoknapatawpha County from the perspective of the Civil War era, creating a kind of palimpsest whereby the two time periods and their respective versions of the human slide across one another like virtual overlays. While *As I Lay Dying* dismantles the figure of the patriarchal human through the decompositional powers of the corpse, *Absalom, Absalom!* describes the white supremacist lineage of this figure. *Absalom, Absalom!* critiques the culture that replicates itself through adjudications of resemblance to and difference from a white male subject, as "man" is systematically reproduced in his own image, while racialized others are systematically dehumanized. The novel's intertwined tropes of miscegenation and incest, however, threaten to collapse such adjudications, as Charles Bon is both the son who reproduces the image of the Sutpen patriarch and the multiracial "other" disqualified from full participation in the category of the human. Charles Bon induces panic about the collapsed boundaries between the human and the inhuman that can only be resolved, from the perspective of his half brother Henry, by his transformation into the corpse that resides squarely on the side of the inhuman. This murder, however, fails to maintain the boundaries of the white patriarchal human, as Bon's corpse participates in a more widespread excavation of the categories of the human and nonhuman upon which slavery and constructions of race have been predicated. Rather than replicating "man" in his own image, *Absalom, Absalom!* depicts the human through deep-time, fossilized relations with the natural world that unmake the autonomy of the white patriarchal subject. *Absalom, Absalom!* also foregrounds inscriptive modes that fail to produce mimetic images: dead letters written with shoe polish that becomes a kind of personified ink; horny outgrowths of the body exchanged and read as signifiers; tombstone inscriptions that both decay and cast themselves toward a future readership; and usages of bone itself as a kind of writing material. In *Absalom, Absalom!* such material signifiers, which have their own form of living (and thus their own form of dying), unmake the living/nonliving binary that defines race in the Civil

War–era South, providing the starting point from which to imagine less exclusionary definitions of "life."

As I Lay Dying: Decomposition

Martin Jay claims that the materializing body, that physical otherness recalcitrant to mental self-conception, threatens to reduce bodily experience to "the sameness of the cadaver."[8] The corpse at the center of *As I Lay Dying*, however, markedly refuses to function according to "sameness," attaining progressively macabre forms of animation as it decomposes during the trip toward burial. Extending beyond the borders of the singular body that can be identified as "Addie Bundren," the corpse also becomes a ubiquitous presence through a figurative corporealizing and cadaverizing of both the natural world and characters' phenomenological experience. *As I Lay Dying*'s "necropoetics," an experimental, vitalist usage of language, decomposes and remakes the body, redefining the materializing body as that which resists "sameness."

This posthuman, materialist conception of the corpse is distinct from a simplistically "naturalized" conception of the body. As poststructuralism has importantly argued, the body should be understood not as a natural, immutable entity but as a historically situated phenomenon that is produced by social power and that emerges only as the sedimented effect of performative iterations. Foucault in particular understands the body not through its material autonomy but as the unstable entity produced and destroyed through its "inscription" by discursive forms of power. He writes, famously, "The body is the inscribed surface of events (traced by language and dissolved by ideas), the locus of a dissociated self (adopting the illusion of a substantial unity), and a volume in perpetual disintegration."[9] The Foucauldian body is not only material other, an occasionally betraying strangeness failing us in moments of duress, illness, or death; it exists in states of perpetual inscription, perpetual destruction, perhaps as that which is always elusive. Foucault's reconception of the body has been widely influential, but his commentators have also discussed the ontological difficulty of the discursively inscribed body. Judith Butler in particular notes that his most pointed descriptions of bodily ontology necessarily rely upon metaphorical terms that sometimes take contradictory forms—the body understood as an inscribed "surface," for example, suggests something quite different from the body figured as a disintegrating "volume."[10] Taking a feminist perspective on

Foucault, Butler also points out that while the discursively inscribed body moves away from an older Cartesian model of mind-body dualism, it potentially introduces a new binary whereby forms of social power actively "inscribe" an *a priori* bodily materiality that is inertly passive and feminized. According to Butler, models of bodily inscription tend to imagine the human body as cadaverously passive, its "underlying" materiality merely the "blank and lifeless page" that is "always already dead."[11] Rather than imagining the prediscursive material body as "always already dead," however, *As I Lay Dying* reverses this formulation, Addie's corpse inaugurating the posthuman life of a previously unaccountable corporeality, while discursive definitions of bodily form in the novel tend to ossify and render the body dead. Where forms of social power would define the human body, through, for instance, the medical diagnosis, the anatomical model, the illustrative cadaver, or the discrete visual image, *As I Lay Dying* erodes such certainty, showing that which escapes inscription or easy metaphorization—the body's dimensionality, its densities and volumes, the "terrific hiatus[es]" (12), to use Darl's phrase, that comprise bodily existence.

While Foucault emphasizes the simultaneity of social power and the production of the body (such that the effects of power are always and only visible in their manifestation through the body), the linguistic, philosophical, and social habits of separating matter and discourse are so deeply ingrained that it is easy to conceive matter, as Butler points out, as only a kind of corpse awaiting animation by an external force. This chapter's posthumanist approach to the corpse thus seeks to develop a nuanced account of the "microphysics," to use Foucault's term, whereby the body interacts with materialized forms of discourse through the unpredictable processes of mutation. Mutation has a basis in biology and genetics, but it has also provided important concepts for posthumanism, not only in describing an overarching transformation in the species category of the human but also in escaping more traditional binaries between discourse and body, form and substance, information and matter.[12] As R. L. Rutsky argues, "Mutation names that randomness which is always already immanent in the processes by which both material bodies and cultural patterns replicate themselves."[13] Describing processes that are "ongoing and immanent" rather than externally imposed, mutation entails materially distributed and unpredictably autopoetic processes that disrupt centralized exercises of power and the self-directed autonomous subject. Mutation involves an aleatory vitality that is impossible to understand, in Rutsky's terms, through "the traditional sense that links human knowledge to human control over a 'dead' world of objects."[14]

Bodily decomposition in *As I Lay Dying* can similarly be understood through the processes and metaphorics of mutation. Rather than defining a site of medical diagnosis and visual control over the body, decomposition enacts the unpredictable processes whereby the visible unity of the body resolves into separate systemic operations. Colonies of microbial, bacterial agents populate the corpse, enacting the immanent mutations that remake the body and the environment. Far from belonging to a "'dead' world of objects," Addie's corpse can be understood through a "viral" logic whereby decomposition is replicated in the phenomenological experiences of the living characters and their uses of language. *As I Lay Dying* foregrounds materializing (and often decomposing) uses of language: heteroglossias, necroglossias, and object-oriented *res*glossias that problematize the binary between body and discourse, matter and information. Rather than understanding the corpse as a site of materiality from which consciousness is necessarily disembodied, or as a cadaverously passive site inscribed and then laid to rest by social discourses, *As I Lay Dying* uses the corpse to stage a range of interrogative representations: "What is a body?" is a question the novel continually poses through the corpse whose ontology is outside traditional conceptions of bodily life.

Beyond Visual Models of the Body

Addie's death is the inaugural event of *As I Lay Dying*, but of what does she die? Anse somewhat inexplicably claims that the *road* kills Addie, and Peabody, the doctor he belatedly summons to attend to her, offers no diagnosis but declares her "dead these ten days" upon his arrival (43). Peabody not only refrains from diagnosing; he determines her dead—and thus in some sense already a corpse—without a visual examination of her body. His visit suggests an inversion of the Foucauldian model of medical power and the subject, in that the scene depicts Peabody as the subject of *Addie's* gaze rather than the reverse:

> She looks at us. Only her eyes seem to move. It's like they touch us, not with sight or sense, but like the stream from a hose touches you, the stream at the instant of impact as dissociated from the nozzle as though it had never

been there. She does not look at Anse at all. She looks at me, then at the boy. Beneath the quilt she is no more than a bundle of rotten sticks. (44)

Peabody's description of Addie substitutes for a body that he does not directly perceive, as his sense-memory about the stream of water reveals more about his own subjectivity than Addie's physical condition. More to the point, it seems that there is no body present to examine or diagnose. Addie's body materializes through the haptic gaze that "touches" Peabody, but, like the stream that escapes from the nozzle, it is as disconnected from a physical origin "as though it had never been there." It is only after dying, in the passage between death and burial, that Addie acquires corporeal presence, becoming a substantial material burden and an invasive effluvium, defining a posthuman corporeality that also involves the bodies of those who mourn her.[15]

As Foucault argues, the corpse occupies a privileged role in Enlightenment epistemology, as medical examination of the cadaver makes the entirety of the body, and consequently the subject, available to view. The corpse that had previously been consigned to "the dark work of destruction" paradoxically becomes "the brightest moment in the figures of truth."[16] In contrast to the cadaver, whose interiority can be translated into a discourse of pathological causality, however, the emaciated "bundle of rotten sticks" Addie leaves behind disallows exploratory penetration: one can imagine that an autopsy of her body would discover not a landscape of organs ravaged by disease but only a kind of aridity. Addie's absent body functions as an epistemological aporia, a blind spot that undoes the certainty of medical diagnosis and knowledge about the body. Her corpse is known not through visual inspection but through anoptic penetration—a blind, often grotesque familiarity with an ambient corporeality, which reformulates corporeal and subjective possibilities in the novel. Through Addie's corpse, As I Lay Dying reasserts the bodily materiality that Enlightenment thought has elided, but as that which escapes the control, understanding, and visual structures of power. Although Foucault describes the centrality of the corpse to medical knowledge, he considers death itself as "power's limit, the moment that escapes it."[17] The eerie animation of Addie's corpse—which "resists, as though volitional," which "go[es] faster than a man" in water, and which speaks to Darl and Vardaman through the coffin (97, 150–51)—seems to protract or equivocate this moment of death. Death in As I Lay Dying is not so much a discernible moment as a liminal and unpredictable domain, and

Addie's corpse lives, in Foucauldian terms, with "its own roles and its own laws," marking places of escape within the gaze of power.[18]

Cora Tull, the Bundrens' officious neighbor, implies that the soul and the cadaver might be analogously explored and transformed into knowledge when she urges upon Addie a kind of autopsy model of Christian salvation. "He alone," she claims, "can see into the heart, and just because a woman's life is right in the sight of man, she cant know if there is no sin in her heart without she opens her heart to the Lord" (167). Self-knowledge, according to Cora, requires "opening" the heart to the gaze of an authority outside the self, thus illuminating the otherwise obscured recesses of the soul. But just as Addie's corpse defines a mode of bodily existence outside the visual structures of power, subjective life in *As I Lay Dying* can be neither translated into visual terms nor mapped according to the form of the normative body. There are hiatuses in mental life and its relation to the body, and consciousness often follows from the experience of localized material engagements with the environment, which are not easily reduced to ideas of personhood. *As I Lay Dying* thus decenters the panoptic perspective upon which realist representations of the subject have traditionally depended.

Abandoning this panoptic perspective requires rethinking the ways that the body and its relation to space have traditionally been mapped. Medical and discursive definitions of the body have often relied upon isolated two-dimensional representations, suppressing the body that exists "in the round" and that cannot be perceived in a single instant or image. Catherine Waldby characterizes this representational problem in the history of anatomical study as "the incommensurability between the opaque volume of the body and the flat, clean surface of the page," and she claims that a spatial conception of the body was necessary to overcome the discrepancy:

> This problem was resolved to some extent through the creation of analogies between anatomical and cartographic space, analogies evident in the fact that the book of anatomy is known as an atlas. If the interior of the body could be thought of and treated as *space*, rather than as a self-enclosed and continuous solid volume, then it could be laid out in ways which are amenable to mapping.[19]

When Anse repeatedly claims that the *road* kills Addie, he similarly spatializes her body, conceiving it as structured by the vertical and horizontal axes through which he understands the landscape.[20] He speculates, "when He aims for something to be always a-moving, He makes it long ways, like a road or a horse or a wagon, but when He aims for something to stay put, He makes it up-and-down ways, like a tree or a man" (36). Deviating from this Cartesian space in which bodies can be mapped along vertical and horizontal axes, the novel abandons the static "up-and-down ways" of "man" in favor of corporeal volumes and densities that mark the perceptual limitations of the human eye. Interrupting the Cartesian, spatialized hierarchy through which, in Jay's terms, "the spiritualizing, formalizing head" predominates over the "materializing, grotesque body," bodies in *As I Lay Dying* resist being mapped in their entirety and instead materialize in the form of molecular, mutational effects through which the human and the nonhuman enter into compositional assemblage and exchange with one another.[21] Deleuze and Guattari claim that "every great American author" inevitably "creates a cartography, even in his or her style,"[22] and *As I Lay Dying*'s representational experiments have a similarly cartographic dimension. Even as the burial trip can be tracked on the two-dimensional Yoknapatawpha map of which Faulkner named himself "sole owner and proprietor," the novel asks what a cartography of the body would be if it allowed for anoptic modes of perception—if it used the auditory, the olfactory, the haptic, as well as synesthetic mutational exchanges among the senses, to disrupt the reliable externality of the visible world.

Before Addie's death, the novel describes a boundary between external, visible form and subjective inwardness only to demonstrate its breachability; after her death, this boundary is eroded altogether. Suggesting the tenuous reversibility of interiors and exteriors, the novel opens with a series of carefully choreographed passes between Darl and Jewel, who are simultaneously passing between interior and exterior spaces. Darl initially leads Jewel as they make their way along the path from field to house; Jewel then assumes the lead after passing bodily through the windows of the cottonhouse, which Darl circumvents; Darl gains the lead on the path again when Jewel stops to take a drink. As Darl's interior monologue tracks these spatial navigations, however, it dislocates thought and observation from the physical processes of vision. Even though he is ahead of Jewel and has already turned the corner of the cottonhouse, he describes Jewel passing through the cottonhouse windows in vivid, although not entirely human, terms:

Jewel, fifteen feet behind me, looking straight ahead, steps in a single stride through the window. Still staring straight ahead, his pale eyes like wood set into his wooden face, he crosses the floor in four strides with the rigid gravity of a cigar store Indian dressed in patched overalls and endued with life from the hips down, and steps in a single stride through the opposite window. (4)

Darl further dislocates sight from his own bodily location, noting, "Although I am fifteen feet ahead of him, anyone watching us from the cottonhouse can see Jewel's frayed and broken straw hat a full head above my own" (3). Darl's remote descriptions (which culminate in his absent narration of Addie's death) and his allusion to a disembodied "anyone" watching their progress along the path conjure the specter of an absent omniscient narrator, suggesting that he has taken on this ability in the narrator's stead. But his awareness of "anyone watching" also elides the most significant act of vision at this point in the novel—Addie watching Cash build her coffin from the bedroom window. His imagined vertical perspective on the scene, which aligns him with divine or authorial panopticism and omniscience, is thus motivated by a willful act of blindness located "inside" the fictive world.

The opening of *As I Lay Dying* marks a significant departure from the visual and epistemological methods of realism, which, as Peter Brooks notes, "insistently makes the visual the master relation to the world." Brooks argues that realism is predicated upon the notion that "one cannot understand human beings outside the context of the things that surround them, and knowing those things is a matter of viewing them, detailing them, and describing the concrete milieux in which men and women enact their destinies."[23] The characters in *As I Lay Dying* do "enact their destinies" within circumscribed locations, but their milieu is not concrete, instead involving mutational exchanges between character and environment. When Jewel steps through the cottonhouse windows, for example, he transforms an aperture for vision into an uncertain material passage, transforming the human, in turn, into an uncertainly animated wooden form that is only "endued with life from the hips down." The opening of the novel thus departs from a common trope of the realist novel—the window as a figure for authorial observation in which the body remains stationary while the mind enters into visual engagement with a physically concrete world.[24] Henry James, for example, famously uses the window as a model for realist fiction, claiming, "The house of fiction has . . . not one window, but a million." Animated by visionary consciousness, such windows are "nothing without the posted presence of the watcher—without, in other words, the consciousness of the artist."[25] As Jewel's body disrupts this traditional realist frame, *As I Lay Dying* describes the death of the "posted presence of the artist" and the epistemological commitments of realism, whereby "to know . . . is to see."[26]

Jamesian novelistic perspective provides an important point of departure for N. Katherine Hayles's *How We Became Posthuman*. For Hayles, the Jamesian "house of fiction" describes a securely embodied anchor at the beginning of the twentieth century against which she discusses the "quantum leap" forward into cyberspace and technologically mediated forms of vision in later-twentieth-century science fiction, such as William Gibson's *Neuromancer*. She notes, "For James, the observer is an embodied creature, and the specificity of his or her location determines what the observer can see when looking out on a scene that itself is physically specific." Even when a seemingly disembodied, omniscient point of view is used, she argues, "the suggestion of embodiment lingers in the idea of focus," such that the "'scene' created by the eye's movement" still implies consciousness that is seated in an embodied human perspective. Hayles argues that in Gibson's fiction, and in contemporary cyberculture, consciousness is instead spirited out of the body, yoked to a point of view (pov) that is untethered by material constraints: "consciousness moves *through* the screen to become the pov, leaving behind the body as an unoccupied shell."[27] While I do not want to diminish the importance of the technological "quantum leap" that Hayles describes or the immersive experiences that are particular to cyberspace, I do want to complicate her historical account of the twentieth century as a move from embodiment to disembodiment in order to develop an understanding of posthumanism that is not technologically determined but which emerges from a range of cultural forces. If consciousness "moves *through* the screen" in contemporary cyberculture, Jewel steps *through* the epistemological frame of vision, leaving the faculties of vision and their relation to a familiar bodily form behind. Rather than moving from embodiment to disembodiment, however, Faulkner's break with Jamesian realism enacts absences from and returns to reorganized forms of matter, partial processes that never arrive at the completion of visual coherence, and fractured perceptions that are not always and only human forms of vision.

We might, moreover, regard Jamesian point of view not as securely "embodied" but as merely tethered to a kind of imaginary or "virtual" body achieved through the repression of other sensory experiences. As Cary Wolfe notes in his discussion of the need for an embodied post-humanism, Freud's *Civilization and Its Discontents* locates the production of the human species in the "organic repression" whereby the human rejects not only nonvisual senses but also the phenomenological sensations and material engagements afforded by those senses.[28] Freud distinguishes the upright human and its distancing acts of vision from other forms of animal life whose olfactory, auditory, and tactile senses are more closely embedded in the materiality of the natural world. Wolfe argues that posthumanism provides the occasion to reconfigure the sensorium in order to unseat vision as "the master relation to the world." In this way, we can understand experimental modernism not as part of an overarching twentieth-century progression from embodiment to technologically determined disembodiment, but as participating in a material reorganization of the human sensorium that *has yet to become* embodied.

Necroglossias

As I Lay Dying begins by tracking bodies through a Cartesian space that can be visually mapped according to horizontal and vertical axes, but Darl's concluding onomatopoeia marks a representative mode that operates not through visual description but through sound, as he is no longer followed by Jewel but by the ambient "Chuck.   Chuck.   Chuck." of Cash's adze (5). The onomatopoeia achieves its sonic effect by emphasizing the visual spacing of the words on the page, transgressing the "invisibility" of the printed word through which fictive worlds are created.[29] Even as the inclusion of space draws attention to the visual aspects of the text, however, it also returns us to the fictive, interior world of *As I Lay Dying*, as the rhythmic spacing of the "Chuck.   Chuck.   Chuck." links the time of our reading to the experiential time of character. This linkage between reader and character depends upon certain "bodily" aspects of the text—the auditory aspects of rhythm and onomatopoeia—but bypasses the visual externality of bodily description. This positing of, and subsequent withdrawal from, the visible world structures many of the early sections of the novel. Before Addie's death, most of the sections begin with visual description or references to seeing but end with speech, sounds, or echoing quotations of what someone "says." The certainty of the visible scene erodes, and consciousness recedes from watching a scene perceived as external to the more internal, embodied experience of audition. Characters are often perceived by others through the echo of their voices—acousmatic separations of voice from body, received in the absence of visual context. Despite Addie's status as just "a bundle of rotten sticks," for example, her voice remains "harsh and strong" the moment before her death. Like the mythological Echo, Addie is also a voice without a body, as her self-echoing call of "Cash . . . you, Cash!" follows Peabody outside her bedroom (46). Abandoning the visual techniques of realism, *As I Lay Dying* relies upon auditory perceptions of bodies unmoored in space, perceptions that, in Darl's terms, "sound as though they were speaking out of the air about your head" (20).

More importantly, *As I Lay Dying* decenters the human voice as the singular organizing principle in the novel, placing human speech alongside the sounds and "speech" of nonhuman actants. When Darl's stream of consciousness is interrupted by the "Chuck. Chuck. Chuck." of Cash's adze, Faulkner suggests the rhythmic resonance between thought and matter, describing the sonic assemblages between the human and the nonhuman. Both natural and technological worlds vibrate with sound in *As I Lay Dying*: "the fans go whish. whish. whish" (87); "the wheels murmur alive in the water" (144); the saw "sounds like snoring" (9); the river "goes with a plaintive sound, a musing sound" (142); the mule makes "a sound almost human" (149); and Cash closes the novel by referencing his "talking machine" (190), emphasizing not the technological replay of the human voice but the animated properties of the machine itself.[30] Addie's death effects both the death of the human as a perceptual, vocal center and the subsequent sonification of the material world. Her death is an optical death, her eyes described as "two flames [that] glare up steady for an instant" before being extinguished, but her vitality immediately translates into the material world, as the bed is jarred into "a chattering sibilance of mattress shucks"—an inhuman but nonetheless animated testament to death (49). Addie's corpse itself becomes a sonifying presence that "talks in little trickling bursts of secret and murmurous bubbling" (212), providing a way to hear not only the speech of the dead but also the decompositional processes of becoming-earth, becoming-water, becoming-air—and finally the becoming-imperceptible processes of "ravel[ing] out into the no-wind, no-sound" (207), which escape the human perceptual apparatus altogether. Such "corpse-language" is a medium that connects the living with the particular sonic vitality of the putatively "dead" world.

Bakhtin's conception of heteroglossia is useful in understanding language as a vitalist medium in *As I Lay Dying*.[31] For Bakhtin, language is not a system of abstracted signifiers related to the material world by arbitrary association but a materially instantiated phenomenon; in this way, language functions only insofar as it vibrates on the tongue, circulates from speaker to speaker, materializes in print, hangs in the air with its own forms of sonic decay, or is illuminated, pixelated—here—on my screen. Created anew with each citational usage, language is (to cite Bakhtin's own terms) "a living, socio-ideological concrete thing" that "lies on the borderline between oneself and the other," mediating relations between living things.[32] The novel in particular functions as a heteroglossic field in which multiple languages and citational acts intersect, struggle against one another, and "live a real life."[33] While Bakhtin understands novelistic heteroglossia as a human phenomenon, claiming, "the human being in the novel is first, foremost and always a speaking human being"[34] who populates the text with citations of what "people say" or "everyone says," such citational speech acts also problematize the autonomy of the humanist subject, as speech and language acts are never one's own but are always and only the speech of another—quoted, remade, and assimilated into "the ideological becoming of a human being."[35] *As I Lay Dying* foregrounds such citational becomings, as speech is often a direct quotation of what "folks says" or sometimes, self-reflexively, what "I says." Aside from such direct quotations, speech in *As I Lay Dying* is never unitary, but transitions among various living and socially inflected registers: even Darl's announcement that *"Addie Bundren is dead"* (52), for example, evokes an "Addie Bundren" who exists within a larger social context, rather than Addie Bundren, his mother.[36]

In addition to considering language as a heteroglossic medium that "live(s) a real life," however, we might expand Bakhtin's notion of heteroglossia in order to consider both the "necroglossias" of Addie's "secret and murmurous bubbling" and an object-oriented *res*glossia that "lies on the borderline" between the human and the nonhuman. Giving voice to the "Chuck. Chuck. Chuck." of the adze and the "whish. whish. whish." of the fan, language in *As I Lay Dying* has a kind of "thing-power" that mediates relations between the human senses and nonhuman matter. These necroglossias and *res*glossias deemphasize the role of sight in favor of sound, voice, and audition; but just as sound vibrations are experienced by the body as a whole, rather than being confined to the ear, this emphasis on sound is involved in larger reconfigurations of the human sensorium. The section immediately following Addie's death, for example, is Vardaman's first in the novel, offering a childish or "new" perspective that describes not a passage from the visual to the auditory, as previous sections do, but a reconfiguration of bodily form altogether, as his body is uncertainly involved with that of Peabody's horse.

> I can hear wood, silence: I know them. But not living sounds, not even him. It is as though the dark were resolving him out of his integrity, into an unrelated scattering of components—snuffings and stampings; smells of cooling flesh and ammoniac hair; an illusion of a coordinated whole of splotched hide and strong bones within which, detached and secret and familiar, an *is* different from my *is*. I see him dissolve—legs, a rolling eye, a gaudy splotching like cold flames—and float upon the dark in fading solution; all one yet neither; all either yet none. I can see hearing coil toward him, caressing, shaping his hard shape—fetlock, hip, shoulder and head; smell and sound. (56–57)

Vardaman's "perceptual mourning" of Addie begins by tuning his ear to the inaudible—first to "wood," then to "silence." But the passage progresses so that Vardaman is not only hearing an acoustic world that is typically silenced but also experiencing a synesthetic confusion so that he can "see hearing" and then "see hearing . . . caressing." Rather than being revealed in its totality through the illumination of vision, the horse is decomposed as a molar entity and remade through a mutational sensory exchange between the human and the nonhuman. Vardaman posits a difference between himself and the horse—"an *is* different from my *is*"—but, far from establishing an ontological distinction, this "difference" is simultaneously "detached and secret and familiar," emerging from the immanent sensory differences between them, rather than an externally imposed taxonomic difference. Vardaman's sense of "difference" also depends upon the performative, italicized use of *is* being able to signify differently each time he uses it: "an *is* different from my *is*," whereby the meaning of *is* mutates each time he uses it.

Vision plays a limited, physically circumscribed role in this reconfigured sensorium. When characters describe other bodies in visual terms, their descriptions emphasize the visual and corporeal limits of both gazer and other, often focusing on those aspects of bodily life that resist self-perception. The novel contains numerous, idiosyncratically specific descriptions of Anse's hump and the backs of bodies and necks; Darl, for example, fixates on Jewel's neck, which is "trimmed close, with a white line between hair and sunburn like a joint of white bone" (39). Unlike the fictive bodies of the realist novel, freely available to the untrammeled vision of a panoptic narrator, images of blind backsides in *As I Lay Dying* emphasize not only the impenetrable corporeality of the one gazed upon but also the limited, embodied, and necessarily subjective perspectives of observers, each of whom operates from a position of partial blindness.[37] Even the experience of "embodiment," then, implies a kind of dislocation, given that parts of the body always escape self-conception. Characters are often depicted looking over one shoulder, turning to look backward, emphasizing the positional limits of the visual field and the body's orientation in space. Rather than yielding to the epistemological powers of the observer, the body of the other becomes an obdurate surface, such that Anse's eyes, "like pieces of burnt-out cinder," and his brogans, "hacked with a blunt axe out of pig-iron," are equal in their reified enervation, both inhuman objects that bar discovery (32, 11).

The reification of these blind backsides suggests that a cadaverous materiality overtakes many of the bodies in the novel, rather than being confined just to Addie. But while the corpse defines an inert corporeality that fails to yield knowledge through visual examination, it also generates a vivified, anoptic corporeality. Addie dies somewhat anticlimactically early in the novel, but she has a strange afterlife, reappearing in other characters' phenomenological experience and acts of perception. Darl's complex figurative description of Dewey Dell's face, for example, departs from the certainty of vision, developing new forms of perception, consciousness, and bodily experience that are uncertainly involved with Addie's corpse:

> Her face is calm and sullen, her eyes brooding and alert; within them I can see Peabody's back like two round peas in two thimbles: perhaps in Peabody's back two of those worms which work surreptitious and steady through you and out the other side and you waking suddenly from sleep or from waking, with on your face an expression sudden, intent, and concerned. (103)

Darl's description of worms boring through Peabody's back suggests visual penetration of the body to understand character, but it occurs here within the convex mirrors of Dewey Dell's eyes, emphasizing embodied, binocular vision, rather than the transcendent vision of an ideally positioned, omniscient viewer. The ocular reflection of "two round peas" makes of the doctor a kind of literal "peabody," implying the inextricability of body and language, imagining a body that fulfills the meaning of its name, or a name become flesh.[38] The passage between the body and language, however, is not easy or mutually reinforcing, but produces the experience of shock or astonishment—a subject momentarily awakened through awareness of being seen, although not, in this case, by an outsider. From what position *could* Darl see Peabody reflected in Dewey Dell's eyes? Such a reflection could only be seen in intimate proximity and would thus reflect himself, rather than Peabody. Vacillating between the convex distortions of the physical eye and the equally distorting realm of his imagination, Darl's trope of penetrative vision performs a displaced enactment of Peabody's failed examination of Addie, and the scene *decomposes* as the image of a body riddled with worms intrudes into his field of vision. The mutational properties of Addie's corpse are thus displaced onto characters who become sites of decomposition, involving not only the decomposition of the body but also the production of an excess awareness through the decomposition of body, vision, and the fictive frame that would contain them.

In this way, *As I Lay Dying* deviates from the notion of a virtual "homunculus" inside the mind—a mental model of an intact bodily figure according to which perception of the outside world is structured. Nor is the body easily demarcated from the stuff of the world. The novel describes a perpetual, labored dislocation of the body onto its surrounds as well as a distorting reconstruction of the outer world through perception. Several critics have remarked upon the relation between reified bodies and personified objects in the novel, such that Jewel, for example, is frequently "woodenbacked," while the thwarting river log *"surged up out of the water and stood for an instant upright"* (148).[39] There is an excess in these displacements between animate and inanimate, an ambient corporeal remainder that resists definite form. Darl's description of the river, for example, conjures the diseased corporeality that Addie herself never experiences. He remarks upon its "yellow surface dimpled monstrously," as though with fatty excess, and describes it as "skummed with flotsam and with thick soiled gouts of foam as though it had sweat" (141). Darl's allusions to "gouts," sluggish circulation, and sweating struggle displace onto the landscape all the fleshy corporeality and diseased travail that Addie, in her emaciated, quiet extinction, escapes. The thickly "skummed" surface of the river cannot be visually penetrated but "talks up to us in a murmur" like a person; Addie's corpse, conversely, with its "little trickling bursts of secret and murmurous bubbling," sounds like a river (141, 212). Neither speech is decipherable; both emit textured sounds, grained and tautological. Foucault claims that death provides a conclusive point at which the diseased body can be translated into a discourse of causality, but here no such interpretive discourse exists.

As I Lay Dying's necroglossia culminates in Addie's startling narrative. Literature is full of ghosts who speak to humans from beyond the grave, but Addie is no ghost and she has no message for the living. More unsettlingly, Addie's language conveys the phenomenological experience of decomposition, as her opening memories of being a teacher resolve into the more physically immediate sensations of "the quiet smelling of damp and rotting leaves and new earth." If "language lies on the borderline between oneself and the other," Addie's corpse-language lies dying on the borderline between her own decomposing body and the humus produced by decaying organic matter. Her narrative replicates in concentrated form the linguistic negotiations of the novel as a whole, which move from heteroglossic exchanges between humans to object-oriented acts of necroglossia. Addie first reflects upon her death by citing the speech of her father—"my father used to say that the reason for living was to get ready to stay dead a long time" (169)—but she quickly divests herself of such patriarchal discourse, most notably through her evacuation of the name "Anse." Immediately after quoting Anse, at his tender best, urging her to increase the family—"you and me aint nigh done chapping yet, with just two"—Addie drains his name of signifying power by "seeing" it as a materialized form capable of being emptied:

> He did not know that he was dead, then. Sometimes I would lie by him in the dark, hearing the land that was now of my blood and flesh, and I would think: Anse. Why Anse. Why are you Anse. I would think about his name until after a while I could see the word as a shape, a vessel, and I would watch him liquify and flow into it like cold molasses flowing out of the darkness into the vessel, until the jar stood full and motionless: a significant shape profoundly without life like an empty door frame; and then I would find that I had forgotten the name of the jar. (173)

Addie's sensory manipulation of Anse's name enervates him to such an extent that he becomes merely the "dead" form she lies beside, but this shift from patriarchal signification to materiality also attunes her to the vivified materiality of her own "dead" state, enabling audition of "the dark land talking the voiceless speech" (175). While Addie's narrative takes the form of distanced, past-tense reflection upon her life, it simultaneously provides an immediate, present-tense account of her own corpse, giving expression to the decompositional, mutational processes of becoming-earth as she "hear[s] the land that was now of my flesh and blood" (173). We can thus understand her narrative as not only a heteroglossic, but also a necroglossic interaction of different materialities, affects, voices, and speeds—the temporalities of human memory colliding with the corporeal speeds of becoming-earth. Reflecting upon her affair with Whitfield and her betrayal of Anse (who is hard to betray, given his "dead" status), Addie notes: "But for me it was not over. I mean, over in the sense of beginning and ending, because to me there was no beginning nor ending to anything then" (175). This circularity applies just as readily to her own physical becoming through death. Vitally engaged with "the land that was now of my flesh," Addie's corpse refuses to "stay dead a long time."

Becoming-Corpse

It is worth asking what it means to think about posthumanism within the southern, rural context of *As I Lay Dying*, which is seemingly so far removed from the technological determinism and futurism often associated with the posthuman. At the most fundamental level, however, the burial trip is enabled only by the close cooperative assemblage of human, animal, and technological elements. For Deleuze and Guattari, the "man-horse-bow"[40] assemblage is the basic unit of the war machine, and in *As I Lay Dying* the "human-animal-wagon" assemblage is the basic unit of the Bundren machine, the materiality of each element so closely intertwined and interactive that "[the wagon] and Jewel and the horse was all mixed up together" (154). The burial trip from farm to town can be understood as describing a temporal progression from an American agrarian past toward a more technologically determined modernity, but *As I Lay Dying* also defines posthumanist assemblages that occur outside teleological understandings of the human's technological "progress." Posthumanism in *As I Lay Dying* involves a retrospective "ravel[ing] out" (207) of the historical figure of the human, to use Darl's term, leaving the characters in states of "terrific hiatus" (12) that are severed from the past.

Jani Scandura and Michael Thurston argue that the corpse is significant in modernism because it symbolically "encrypts" the past through a kind of willed forgetfulness:

The modern does not so much imply an erasure of the past . . . as an encryptment of certain uncomfortable narratives. Indeed, the suggestion that progressive modernity throws itself to the future is itself a denial of the obsessive attention that modern cultures paid to "looking back" to Darwinian origins, nostalgic folk histories, and the childhood wounds of oedipal dramas. Still, modernist nostalgia was not marked so much by a longing for a past, as by a desire for not having had one.[41]

Different acts of retrospection and retrogradation similarly constitute Addie's corpse. Her inverted placement in a "clock-shape[d]" coffin to accommodate her wedding dress is a spatial inversion that also implies a temporal return to her wedding day, and her burial entails the retrograde motion toward Jefferson, which signifies both personal and national origins (88). But this journey, which Darl describes as "so dreamlike as to be uninferant of progress," becomes an alienating odyssey rather than a return "home" (108), and, from a narrative perspective, the novel never reaches this origin, as Addie's burial in Jefferson is never directly narrated, and Cash's proleptic description of their life with the new Mrs. Bundren seems to erase the "original" Mrs. Bundren. Her death, then, involves both a retrograde return and a proleptic forgetting. Anse seems to recognize both the relevance and the impossibility of retrogression, claiming, with his characteristic homespun philosophy, "It aint no luck in turning back" (140). Wandering for most of the novel between Addie's origins in "Jefferson" and the modernity promised by "New Hope," the characters are suspended between past definitions of the human and the realization of a modernity that would come "after" the human.

The novel nevertheless depicts this suspense between the past and the future not as a state of death but as the site of a nascent, posthuman experience that escapes Darwinian and familial "origins" of the human. Dewey Dell's conflation of the past and the future during the burial trip, for example, is resolved through a fantasy about her own death and the murder of Darl, which allows her imaginatively to re-create bodily form outside the biological inheritance of family and its definitions of gender. She fixedly anticipates the future during the approach to New Hope ("New Hope. 3 mi. it will say. New Hope. 3 mi. New Hope. 3 mi."), even as she turns back in this section toward the past, conflating childhood experience and phantasmic memories with their present task: "That was when I died that time. *Suppose I do. We'll go to New Hope. We wont have to go to town.* I rose and took the knife from the streaming fish still hissing and I killed Darl" (120, 121). Dewey Dell's claim that she "died that time" suggests not that she "identifies" with Addie's corpse but that her grieving contact with the corpse allows an escape from the hierarchical family roles that dictate gendered phenomenological experience. Her allusion to the fish recalls Vardaman's own substitution of a nonhuman form for Addie, and she completes the impulse to sever the exigencies of biological relationship by "killing Darl" with the knife drawn from the "fish still hissing." She immediately "encrypts" this violent fantasy of having killed Darl within her own uncertain bodily experience, an encryptment that accomplishes his death all the more thoroughly, as though she never had a family at all:

> *I had a nightmare once I thought I was awake but I couldn't see and couldn't feel I couldn't feel the bed under me and I couldn't think what I was I couldn't think of my name I couldn't even think I am a girl I couldn't even think I nor even think I want to wake up nor remember what was opposite to awake so I could do that I knew that something was passing but I couldn't even think of time then all of a sudden I knew that something was it was wind blowing over me it was like the wind came and blew me back from where it was I was not blowing the room and Vardaman asleep and all of them back under me again and going on like a piece of cool silk dragging across my naked legs.* (121–22)

No longer a daughter or sister who sees her features mirrored back to her in the familiar face of a mother or a brother, Dewey Dell *"couldn't even think I am a girl,"* and instead experiences her body in a negatively creative space. It is not merely that her consciousness "bleeds" outward from bodily form; there is no prior body here whose bounds could be transgressed. Destabilizing the notion of a somatic base from which consciousness extends, her liminal corporeality suggests that the interruption of the mind's attachment to the body is not solely the domain of death but also that there are death-like breaches within bodily life and the skein of awareness. Bodily form requires the work of language to delineate its borders, becoming tenuously articulated only with the simile of the wind passing over her *"like a piece of cool silk."* The simile gestures toward a phenomenological aporia, in that her body is not naturally possessed but brought into understanding through a claim of what it is "like." The novel not only claims moments of sensory mortification; it makes the more radical suggestion that the body is phenomenologically constructed from prior absences.

Anse (whose mourning of Addie is not particularly profound) is an exception to bodily experience in the novel. Unlike the other Bundrens, who suffer physical trauma and attrition, Anse experiences a bodily increase, his new teeth making him "look a foot taller" by the novel's conclusion (260). Anse exerts control over his family's fate so that their conditions are all worsened because of his actions; despite this control, however, the novel's reconfigurations of the body continually elude his grasp and indeed the very notion of personhood that his control suggests. Anse's repeated references to the horizontal/vertical axes that structure the body are continually undone, and the novel poses this patriarchal model of control as a foil against which it reconfigures the posthuman body.

When Anse uses upright images to depict the human, he claims its absolute orientation in space as dictated by an outside perspective and authority. He imagines Addie suffering a kind of dying fall: she is upright and "well and hale" until she takes to her bed, her prone form then making her as good as dead (37). Deleuze similarly uses a vertical bodily image to describe a dominant, and limited, mode of cognition: "the image of a naturally upright thought, which knows what it means to think."[42] Deleuze describes the tyranny of this form of cognition, the way in which iteration of this *a priori* bodily image substitutes for the more violent "encounter" that defines the actual process and event of thought. Anse's static, upright body functions in the same way as a foregone substitute for actual thought, leading him to such inept conclusions as, "Because if He'd a aimed for man to be always a-moving and going somewheres else, wouldn't He a put him longways on his belly, like a snake?" He further casts thought into upright bodily form, noting, "It *stands* to reason He would" (emphasis mine) (36).

Despite the many images of inversion and retrogradation that constitute Addie's body, the corpse enacts its resistance not just through a simple inversion of the "naturally upright" image of the human figure in relation to the world, or the world turned upside down, but by giving rise to a radical reconfiguration of human form. We can see such a reconfiguration in the Deleuzian "violent encounter" between Jewel and his horse, which offers a protracted, uncertain response to Anse's deceptively simple question, "Where's Jewel?" (10).

When Jewel can almost touch him, the horse stands on his hind legs and slashes down at Jewel. Then Jewel is enclosed by a glittering maze of hooves as by an illusion of wings; among them, beneath the upreared chest, he moves with the flashing limberness of a snake. For an instant before the jerk comes onto his arms he sees his whole body earth-free, horizontal, whipping snake-limber, until he finds the horse's nostrils and touches earth again. (12)[43]

In characterizing the image of upright thought as "know[ing] what it means to think," Deleuze claims the complacency of an easy analogy between thought and predetermined bodily form; Darl's description, in contrast, uproots both the body and consciousness from the certainty of the image. The rapid violence of the encounter would seem to disallow physical sight, but sight occurs here within the uncertain bodily geography of singular moments rather than participating in a socially constructed tradition of vision. That Jewel "sees his whole body"—a perspectival impossibility—suggests the coincidence of becoming and awareness of becoming, a radical positionality through which control and the certainty of bodily location are suspended. And Darl, although ostensibly an outside observer, is also reformed, momentarily "earth-free" through the precarious regress of "seeing" Jewel "see his whole body." Bodily location and visual perception are mobile and interleaved with the figural: in the fleet serpent and "glittering maze" of hooves and wings, Darl conjures the figures of a caduceus or a Pegasus, but they never coalesce into final form. His description "turns back" toward classicism even as this meeting of the perceptual and the figural evokes something unrecognizably new.

Posing a question that could aptly refer to Jewel's encounter with the horse, Deleuze and Guattari ask, "Who has not known the violence of these animal sequences, which uproot one from humanity, if only for an instant . . . ?" They describe the process of becoming-animal by which the subject does not simply mimic or exist in analogical relation with an animal but instead experiences a "block" of animality "in the interstices of [the] disrupted self."[44] For Deleuze and Guattari, these moments of animality do not "represent" atavism or some way to locate the human on a scale of evolution or devolution; becoming-animal, they claim, is a real, and not necessarily uncommon, experience that escapes traditional articulations of the human. Citing a study of "wolf-children" conducted by René Schérer and Guy Hocquenghem, Deleuze and Guattari write that these children

> appeal to an objective zone of indetermination or uncertainty, "something shared or indiscernible," a proximity "that makes it impossible to say where the boundary between the human and animal lies," not only in the case of

autistic children, but for all children; it is as though, independent of the evolution carrying them toward adulthood, there were room in the child for other becomings, "other contemporaneous possibilities," that are not regressions but creative involutions bearing witness to *"an inhumanity immediately experienced in the body as such,"* unnatural nuptials "outside the programmed body." There is a reality of becoming-animal, even though one does not in reality become animal.[45]

Darl's metaphors not only describe Jewel as *like* a serpent, or the horse as *like* a winged creature; they provide a language for the invisible reality of the inhuman within the body, a reality that occurs outside "programmed" conceptions of the body. Simultaneously ophidian, equestrian, avian, and human, the becoming-animal of Jewel and horse challenges normative taxonomies, performing the "unnatural nuptials" that exist outside, or alongside, traditional classificatory models and that problematize diachronic conceptions of evolution. The novel's posthuman bodies escape modernism's fixation on primitivism and progress, allowing for "other contemporaneous possibilities" beyond such linear exigencies. Jewel's relation with the horse is thus not merely a substitute for Addie; the intercorporeality through which Jewel, horse, and, arguably, Darl are momentarily inseparable exceeds the logic of substitution. Even as Darl's repeated claims that "Jewel's mother is a horse" homonymously, insultingly recall Addie's infidelity and Jewel's "bastardy," the tropological confusion of Jewel, horse, and viewer defines a competing notion of generation that shuttles across a species divide, challenging the paradigm of the family and its rules of legitimacy and illegitimacy.

Deleuze and Guattari include authorship in the processes of becoming-animal, noting, "If the writer is a sorcerer, it is because writing is a becoming, writing is traversed by strange becomings that are not becomings-writer, but becomings-rat, becomings-insect, becomings-wolf, etc."[46] Granting and withholding life where we least expect, *As I Lay Dying* may well be animated by a kind of sorcery, and we can consider a textual awareness not merely as contained within or expressed through identifiable characterological bodies but also as traversing a range of family resemblances among the Bundren "pack." Eric Sundquist argues that the novel's individual sections, which, like Addie, fail to cohere as a unified body, paradoxically point us toward the author: "the authorial 'I' . . . is dead as a single identity but still alive in the episodes that continue to refer themselves to that identity and continue to constitute it even more emphatically in our desire to locate Faulkner's own 'language,' his own 'story,' in the voices of his characters."[47] I think it is not drawing too fine a distinction, however, to suggest that the absent author "outside" the text is not just analogically "like" the corpse but also that the writing is possessed by something of a becoming-corpse, which can be understood neither as an absence nor as a predictable decomposition. A textual awareness obtains that does not just refer to the absent author but, "like" Addie, has a particular kind of animation that resists discursive definition. The corpse thus provides for Faulkner what the animal provides for Deleuze and Guattari: both serve as sites of transformation and becoming, redefining the human outside traditional notions of "personology."

The becoming-corpse of the novel outlives the moment of death, acting not just through the discernible figures of Addie's corpse or characterological bodies but through, in Foucault's term, "teeming presence[s]," molecular and partial bodily phenomena that escape the individual.[48] Deleuze and Guattari, using terms similar to Foucault's, argue that becoming occurs through localized microprocesses that reform the body and its perceptual apparatuses, noting, "the affects of a becoming-dog . . . are succeeded by those of a becoming-molecular, microperceptions of water, air, etc."[49] Rippling outward from Addie's death, such microperceptions reformulate the body in relation to a natural world that is sporadically vivified into "islets of life."[50] Darl's description of drinking from a water bucket, for instance, mingles the properties of water and air, uncertainly casting them into the form of a spectral body: "It would be black, the shelf black, the still surface of the water a round orifice in nothingness, where before I stirred it awake with the dipper I could see maybe a star or two in the bucket, and maybe in the dipper a star or two before I drank" (11). He relocates the sky in miniature within the dipper, his "dipper" a punning reference to the constellation such that it is both an instrument of reflection and reflected image, and Darl the viewer is uncertainly located between sky and water. His comparison of the water's surface to an "orifice in nothingness" conjures a body, but it is a negative body, vertiginously dependent upon the mutational tracings of language, reproducing in spectral form the irredeemable body whose transformation has imparted a corporeal resonance to the natural world.

Faulkner juxtaposes this spectral corporeality, which temporarily escapes the restraint of any force that would shape it, with the bluntly material body that so emphatically bears the imprint of economic necessity. Darl's reverie immediately precedes a flatly prosaic description of Anse's feet as "badly splayed, his toes cramped and bent and warped, with no toenail at all on his little toes, from working so hard in the wet in home-made shoes when he was a boy" (11). Anse's body in this passage is more corpse-like than anything we can associate with Addie herself. *As I Lay Dying*'s posthuman bodies thus offer alternatives to the body formed by the economic and social pressures of the early-twentieth-century South, describing bodily, subjective possibilities not available to characters within the plot. The novel shuttles between two distinct bodily modes: the molar, characterological human rooted within its social context, and the molecular corporeality unleashed from such constraints. Citing Nathalie Sarraute's discussion of literary modernism, Deleuze and Guattari claim that the modern novel is characterized by two distinct "planes of writing":

> a transcendent plan(e) that organizes and develops forms (genres, themes, motifs) and assigns and develops subjects (personages, characters, feel-ings); and an altogether different plane that liberates the particles of an anonymous matter, allowing them to communicate through the "envelope" of forms and subjects, retaining between them only relations of movement and rest, speed and slowness, floating affects.[51]

As I Lay Dying similarly passes between two different "planes." The novel is "about" economic and social deprivation—Addie's death is only the most pronounced symptom of an economically induced ailment from which all the Bundrens suffer—but this death simultaneously gives rise to a liberating reorganization of matter and subjectivities. This is not to diminish the novel's investment in representing a specific social milieu; character and setting are "envelopes" to which the novel repeatedly returns, but its experimental bodies reorganize the "anonymous mat-ter" of a corporeality that escapes this milieu, marking the death of the completed form of the human in favor of an ambient corporeality, or, in Deleuzo-Guattarian terms, the death of molarity in favor of molecularity. Against the entropy of the plot—the sense that all possibilities of redemp-tion for the Bundrens have been foreclosed by the novel's end—the novel poses the liberations of becoming. If the corpse typically suggests bodily form at its most objective, finite, and available to view, *As I Lay Dying*'s necropoetics paradoxically announce the death of such bodily finality. Far from being merely morbid or negating processes, the corpse and the material mutations it compels erode the human body traditionally con-stituted through the certainty of the image, claiming instead an emergent ontology of the human, continually reiterated and reformed.

Absalom, Absalom! The Corpse of the South

While critical discussions of *As I Lay Dying* often regard the novel as an isolated experiment in modernist form, its decomposition of the autonomous human subject acquires an ethical and political urgency when placed in conversation with *Absalom, Absalom!* In his epic account of the Civil War–era South, narrated from the perspective of the early twentieth century, Faulkner depicts an ideology of the white supremacist human produced through the systemic enslavement of persons regarded as instrumentalized things or evolutionarily inferior "beasts." In *As I Lay Dying*, a vitalized environment "speaks" alongside the human, but in *Absalom, Absalom!* the radical dehumanization of persons is complicit with the exploitation of the material environment, its vitality so extracted that the South is a kind of corpse-world. In drawing these two texts together, however, my intention is not to suggest a model of linear progression from the antebellum South to the early-twentieth-century South such that *As I Lay Dying*'s posthumanism is simply the teleological successor or revision of an ideologically mystified human in *Absalom, Absalom!* In *As I Lay Dying*, Faulkner resists linear narratives provided by Darwinian and oedipal origin stories; in *Absalom, Absalom!* he similarly complicates contemporary narratives about the human by taking archaeological, deep-time perspectives that show the human's embeddedness with a biological world that predates human history. Both texts develop modes of becoming that are positioned alongside, but deliberately severed from, historical narratives about the human.

Given its setting during the Civil War, *Absalom, Absalom!* is notable for an absence of corpses. Rather than depicting the war and slavery through a body count, Faulkner interrogates the South's systemic dehumanization through the corpse of Charles Bon, the multiracial, and thus disavowed, son of the white southern patriarch Thomas Sutpen. Bon is introduced early in the novel not by name and not as a living character but merely as the "bloody corpse" that his half brother Henry "practically fling[s]" at the hem of their mutual sister's wedding gown.[52] While the corpse in *As I Lay Dying* attenuates the boundary between life and death, the corpse in *Absalom, Absalom!* reinforces this boundary in order to instantiate socially constructed, externally imposed forms of racial "identity." Such racial "identity" in *Absalom, Absalom!* follows the logic of "self-identity," whereby bodily existence is tautologically made to cohere with categorial signifiers of race, precluding the vitalist becomings described in *As I Lay*

Dying. This tautological "self-identity" is achieved in *Absalom, Absalom!* only by reducing Charles Bon to an inert corpse, suggesting that definitions of the human predicated upon exclusionary identitarian categories of race are unlivable.

The "Self-Made Man"

Thomas Sutpen—who is born into poverty in West Virginia, becomes overseer of a sugar "plantation," or, to describe it more accurately, a slave labor camp in Haiti, and then founds his own labor camp in Mississippi—seems to exemplify the "self-made man" who is such an enduring fixture of American mythology.[53] *Absalom, Absalom!* deconstructs this myth of the self-made subject, however, by depicting the design and construction of Sutpen's Hundred—and, by extension, the design and construction of the South itself—as emerging unpredictably from nonhuman bodily states rather than from the agency, volition, or reason of rationalist subjects. *Absalom, Absalom!* often avoids referring to Sutpen in "human" terms, describing him instead as a skeletal, archaeologically incomplete "frame" around which flesh variably accrues and erodes and over which his eyes hold only a detached vigilance (24). In opposition to this sketchy incompletion, he is also an excessive chimera, the "man-horse-demon" who does not have a stable narrative origin but instead "abrupt[s]" into the novel "out of a quiet thunderclap" (4).[54] Sutpen slides across the evolutionary scale, both the "beast" who regularly wrestles his slaves ("as if their skins should not only have been the same color but should have been covered with fur, too" [20–21])[55] and the automaton whose impersonal "electricity" is subject to periods of alternating "life" and stasis ("as if . . . someone had come along and removed, dismantled the wiring or the dynamo" [31–32]). Animal and mechanical, Sutpen avoids the position of the human altogether, but unlike the generative assemblages in *As I Lay Dying*, he represents a kind of "bad" posthumanism that exploits and disavows its relationships of assemblage in order to achieve a hierarchal position of white supremacy.

Reversing the truism about the self-made man, *Absalom, Absalom!* suggests that ideologies of the human are only belatedly produced from prior material assemblages of human and nonhuman forces. Forming an assemblage between the laboring body and the physical materials that constitute Sutpen's Hundred, Sutpen constructs a kiln to make bricks and works alongside his slaves to extract the house brick by brick from the clay material of the surrounding swamps. Coated with the very clay that later forms the house, as though the house itself is only the formal exfoliation of bodily labor, Sutpen and the slaves are "distinguishable one from another by his beard and eyes alone and only the architect resembling a human creature" (28). These mud-plastered "creatures" suggest a devolutionary regression back to the Edenic creation story in which man is created from earth, as though their construction of the South has less to do with modernization and progress than it does a retrograde negotiation of the basic components of the human figure. The clay coating also obscures the visible markers of race that would distinguish slave from enslaver. The material methods of constructing Sutpen's Hundred thus belie the fiction of racial difference upon which the South depends. Rather than acknowledging their material interconnection, however, Sutpen treats both his slaves and the earth as "dead" materials to be exploited, an assemblage necessary only to achieve certain ends; his own gaunt flesh is a "dead impervious surface as of glazed clay" (24), and when he "tore violently a plantation" (5), to use Rosa's phrase, he tears it from the swamps, from the Native Americans who formerly owned the land, and, most viscerally, from the bodies of the slaves who labor on the land. This violent "tearing" of the "plantation" from a human-nonhuman assemblage also produces racialized discourses about the human. Faulkner describes the unnatural process whereby white "human life" is imposed upon the house: Sutpen's "presence alone compelled that house to accept and retain human life; as though houses actually possess a sentience, a personality and character acquired not from the people who breathe or have breathed in them so much as rather inherent in the wood and brick" (67). *Absalom, Absalom!* thus distinguishes between the "human life" that is tenuously "accepted" and "retained" by the house and the *a priori* "life" of the house itself, vibrant with its own inherent materiality and the activity of those who produced it. In other words, the "product" of this assemblage of laboring body and earthen material is not just a working labor camp and its output of goods and crops but an ideology of the white supremacist human.

Compelling the house to "retain human life" implies the presence of a family, but Sutpen produces a family not through the transmission of anything that can be regarded as a living essence, a coherent genealogical lineage, or a set of recognizably human traits but, more strangely, through the transmission of his skeleton and what the novel repeatedly calls the "Sutpen skull." Sutpen's white, and thus "legitimate," daughter Judith is the unfortunate inheritor of this ossified form, her "Sutpen skull" overpowering the fleshier biological inheritance from her mother's side so that "the skull show[s] through the worn, the Coldfield flesh." The novel also depicts Judith and Sutpen as aging in the same way:

> not as the weak grow old, either enclosed in a static ballooning of already lifeless flesh or through a series of stages of gradual collapsing whose particles adhere not to some iron and still impervious framework but to one another as though in some communal and oblivious and mindless life of their own like a colony of maggots, but . . . with a kind of condensation, an anguished emergence of the primary indomitable ossification which the soft color and texture, the light electric aura of youth, had merely temporarily assuaged but never concealed. (151)

Absalom, Absalom! sorts the characters not through visible forms or humanist traits but through a more primordial distinction between those associated with the mineralized structure of the body and those associated with its soft tissues. While this distinction would still seem to valorize the vitality of the individual and its "iron" will over and against the supposed morbidity of those who communally cling to one another *"like a colony of maggots,"* even this individualism operates through a form of *"oblivious and mindless life."* While the construction of Sutpen's Hundred and the creation of the Sutpen family can be attributed to this *"primary indomitable ossification,"* it would be generous to call Sutpen's activity an intentional, self-directed "design," as he repeatedly does. The "design" produces Sutpen's Hundred and the Sutpen family, but it is described in its most fundamental form as simply "getting richer and richer" (209), a mindlessly incremental accretion of the stolen "Spanish coin" (26) with which he begins, rather than anything that can be attributed to reason or stratagem.[56] *Absalom, Absalom!* thus depicts the family not as a humanizing force but as the transmission of inhuman biological forces that problematize the autonomous, liberal subject.

Manuel De Landa usefully defamiliarizes the "humanness" of the human skeletal form by extracting it from its anatomical context and considering its affinities with mineralized geological forms. While we tend to regard human mobility as directed by reason and emerging from the human as an organic whole, De Landa points out that from an evolutionary point of view it is mineralization in particular that enables the mobility and activity we commonly associate with the human:

In the organic world . . . soft tissue (gels and aerosols, muscles and nerve) reigned supreme until 500 million years ago. At that point, some of the conglomerations of fleshy matter-energy that made up life underwent a sudden *mineralization,* and a new material for constructing living creatures emerged: bone. It is almost as if the mineral world that had served as a substratum for the emergence of biological creatures was reasserting itself, confirming that geology, far from having been left behind as a primitive stage of the earth's evolution, fully coexisted with the soft, gelatinous newcomers. Primitive bone, a stiff, calcified central rod that would later become the vertebral column, made new forms of movement control possible among animals, freeing them from many constraints and literally setting them into motion to conquer every available niche in the air, in water, and on land. And yet, while bone allowed the complexification of the animal phylum to which we, as vertebrates, belong, it never forgot its mineral origins: it is the living material that most easily petrifies, that most readily crosses the threshold back into the world of rocks. For that reason, much of the geological record is written with fossil bone.[57]

Commenting on this passage, Jane Bennett reverses the truism whereby the living agency of the rationalist subject directs the more or less dead matter of the skeleton, arguing that human agency is instead a kind of belated effect of mineral matter itself: "In the long and slow time of evolution, then, mineral material appears as the mover and shaker, the active power, and human beings, with their much-lauded capacity for self-directed action, appear as *its* product."[58] In this way, Faulkner's emphasis on Sutpen's *"primary indomitable ossification"* invites us to decouple the activity of his "design" from traditional understandings of human agency; Sutpen is not so much a "self-made" man as he is an autocombative entity placing "his own fallible judgment and mortal clay against not only human but natural forces" (41).

Understanding the body from a deep-time perspective, as having its own archaeological substrata, such that the soft tissues of muscle and nerves evolutionarily predate the hard, spiny structures of bones, *Absalom, Absalom!* does not, however, "naturalize" Sutpen's racialized domination of other humans. On the contrary, such deep-time perspectives on the body destabilize the Darwinian narratives about race that circulate within the social world of the novel, such as the characterization of Sutpen's slaves as "beasts half-tamed to walk upright like men" (4). While such discourses simultaneously dehumanize racialized others and position the white, "upright" man as the culmination of evolution, the mineralized "mortal clay" of Sutpen's body precedes such racialized binaries. Emphasizing the skeletal structure of the body also belies Civil War–era discourses that evaluate race through the visible legibility of skin or the fetishized "purity" of white blood, according to which "one eighth of a specified kind of blood shall outweigh seven eighths of another" (91). Sutpen's "primary indomitable ossification" also transgresses the categories of legitimate kinship upon which the South is predicated. Judith inherits the "Sutpen skull," but so does Clytie, Sutpen's disavowed, multiracial daughter. In Rosa's narrative of the climactic scene in which Henry "flings" Bon's corpse onto the hem of Judith's wedding dress, Rosa has her own confrontation with Clytie, whose "sphinx face" (109) is a "replica of his own which he had created and decreed to preside upon his absence" (110). In this way, Rosa perceives Clytie not through contemporary discourses about race but from an archaeological perspective, describing her face as "rocklike and firm and antedating time and house and doom and all" (109). When Clytie touches Rosa's arm, the *"eggshell shibboleth of caste and color too"* fall away, and Clytie and Rosa are instead joined *"like a fierce rigid umbilical cord, twin sistered to the fell darkness which had produced her"* (112). The novel's deep-time perspectives on the body thus erode contemporary fictions of racialized difference, uniting Rosa and Clytie—at least momentarily—through a more immediately embodied connection.

This moment of physical, "umbilical" connection between Clytie and Rosa opens the possibility for a *post*humanity that would exceed the novel's exclusionary, racialized definitions of the human, but Rosa fails to realize the potential of this union. She misrecognizes the temporarily fractured *"eggshell shibboleth of caste and color"* as applying only to Clytie rather than to the "whiteness" that constitutes her own claim to humanity. Her narrative thus involves an unexamined paradox, combining the symmetry of "twin sisters" with the asymmetry of an "umbilical" feeding, unwittingly calling into question the physical dependences by which her own "life" is maintained. In spite of her poverty, Rosa imperiously commands any nonwhite person to do her bidding, "as though she were living on the actual blood itself like a vampire . . . to keep the crass foodbearing corpuscles sufficiently numerous and healthy in the stream" (68). Faulkner insists upon the "actual blood itself," emphasizing vampirism not as a figurative embellishment that might have its place in

Rosa's own poetry but as an "actual" feeding, a dependent intermateriality through which Rosa consumes the products of others' energy and labor, and thus their very bodies. Failing to recognize the dependency through which her life is constituted, Rosa retreats to a dead space, or as she explicitly claims: "Then she touched me, and then I did stop dead" (111). Further disavowing the vampiric, "umbilical" feeding that maintains her life, Rosa reconstructs the fractured "shibboleth" of racial difference through a more fundamental claim about their "species" difference. Despite living in close relation with Clytie during the war, she describes her as

> so foreign to me and to all that I was that we might have been not only of different races (which we were), not only of different sexes (which we were not), but of different species, speaking no language which the other understood, the very simple words with which we were forced to adjust our days to one another being even less inferential of thought or intention than the sounds which a beast and a bird might make to each other. (123–24)

In this reconceptualization of race through the taxonomic division of species, Rosa does not, as we might expect, position herself as human and Clytie as the inhuman other. Evacuating the position of the human, both she and Clytie are "beast and bird" dispossessed of traditional forms of language, reduced to making inchoate sounds at one another. While linguistic mastery has traditionally been an exclusionary technology used to circumscribe the borders of the human, Rosa unwittingly suggests that speaking across a fictionalized racial "species" divide dehumanizes speakers and auditors alike rather than securing the boundaries of the human.

Written with Bones

Negotiating the status of the human and the nonhuman produces a narrative condition in which the most significant exchanges among the characters occur through the mediation of material objects, through materializing forms of inscription, and through the body itself. De Landa points out that "much of the geological record is written with fossil bone," and the characters in *Absalom, Absalom!* similarly favor forms of inscription related to mineralization and ossification—the hard, seemingly immutable materials of the body rather than its soft tissues. During the war, for example, the definitive act Sutpen performs is ordering and inscribing "the best" (153) Italian marble to use as gravestones in the family cemetery, as though such inscription is itself a battle, the stakes of which are life and death.[59] During the war, Sutpen's own blank stone leans against the walls of Sutpen's Hundred, "as though it were his portrait" (154) and the skeletal form of activity that animates him could cross back into the world of rocks and clay. Sutpen seeks to construct an irrefutable family history written in bone and minerals, as though the lasting form that he is creating is not a family or even Sutpen's Hundred but rather a monument to be read in the future. Not just a site of memory, the Sutpen cemetery is a site of writing, a scripted model of the white family that would definitively unwrite the biological relationship of multiracial family members such as Clytie and Charles Bon. Such geological, skeletal inscriptions are far from fixed, however, casting themselves toward future readers—a human not-yet-arrived who would read these grave inscriptions according to different understandings of race and personhood.

Once Sutpen's body is interred, the Sutpen gravesite assumes its function as a site of reading. Bon's "octoroon mistress" (whose name, as Faulkner notes in the genealogy, is "not recorded") and his son Charles Etienne de Saint Valery Bon gather there to read the marble tombstones cryptically inscribed with only names and dates, as do, at a later date, Quentin Compson and his father. Even at the most material level, however, these gravesite inscriptions prove not to be as ossified and immutable as Sutpen would have liked. Judith's eventual burial of both Bon and his son marks the material return of those disavowed family members, collocating their bones with those of the Sutpens and corporeally enfolding them into the family.[60] This burial and the engraving of their names on the same stone that Sutpen uses are acts of deep inscription that surpass both paternal authority and the legal discourses that would discount Bon and his son as not only outside the family but outside the realm of full personhood. Judith's inscriptions also provide a way to speak what would otherwise be an impossible utterance within the context of the novel—namely, that Charles Bon is both multiracial and her brother.

These grave inscriptions provide a way to think more generally about modernism's emphasis on the materiality of the sign, which, as Walter Benn Michaels has influentially argued, is critical to questions of identity. The materiality of the sign, for Michaels, implies not only its physical properties but also its singularity: identical only to itself rather than to the material world it represents, the material sign is involved in early-twentieth-century conceptions of self-identity. As an example, Michaels cites Quentin Compson's performative claim in *The Sound and the Fury,* *"I have committed incest I said,"* arguing that, for Quentin, saying that one has slept with one's sister is tantamount to actually having slept with one's sister. Using this example as a point of departure, Michaels argues that modernism uses the materiality of the sign to engage with social debates about identity, the family, and the family's role in the nativist project of protecting the "purity" of American blood. He articulates the coupling of formal and social concerns in modernism as

> the relation between a certain fantasy about the sign—that it might function, in effect, onomatopoetically, without reliance upon a system of syntactic and semantic conventions—and a certain fantasy about the family—that it might maintain itself incestuously, without reliance upon the legal conventions that turn otherwise unrelated persons into husband and wife.[61]

In his modernist depiction of the Civil War–era South, however, Faulkner combines in the figure of Bon two seemingly competing tropes— miscegenation, which would admit "outside" blood into the putatively "pure" white blood of the family line, and incest, which would ostensibly guard the family from such outside invasion.[62] The possibility of Bon's incestuous relationship with Judith thus functions quite differently than Quentin's fantasy of incest with Caddie. When Judith writes Bon into the family through burial and gravestone inscription, performing her own enactment of the sign's materiality, her inscription does not affirm the autonomy of the family but instead radically reinscribes its meanings, recognizing the family in the American South as a site racial hybridity, rather than sameness. What Judith memorializes is not a tragically incestuous desire for her half brother but rather the notion that the family and the family name can function as bearers of identity. Judith's material inscriptions also complicate notions of the "self-identical" and autonomous individual more generally. While Michaels attributes the power of the material sign to its independence from the signified world, Judith's material inscription achieves its power precisely through its communication with other inscriptions of the Sutpen name and its gesture toward the physical communication of Bon's bones with Sutpen's. Here is not a fantasy of material autonomy but the interdependence of the material sign and organic life.

In *Absalom, Absalom!* the materiality of the sign is important, then, not because its uniqueness implies self-identity but because its materiality is necessarily involved with the material grounds upon which persons are admitted or disqualified from full participation in the category of the human. When Bon writes Judith during the war, for example, the letter tautologically emphasizes the dehumanizing conditions that inform and produce the letter, conveying the story of how his battalion, "an assortment of homogeneous scarecrows," captures the stove polish with which he writes the letter.

> *Because what* WAS *is one thing, and now it is not because it is dead, it died in 1861, and therefore what* IS . . . *is something else again because it was not even alive then. And since because within this sheet of paper you now hold the best of the old South which is dead, and the words you read were written upon it with the best (each box said, the very best) of the new North which has conquered and which therefore, whether it likes it or not, will have to survive, I now believe that you and I are, strangely enough, included among those who are doomed to live.* (104)

Absalom, Absalom! characterizes the war through a "curious lack of economy between cause and effect which is always a characteristic of fate when reduced to using human beings for tools, material" (94), and Bon's letter performatively demonstrates this interchangeability between humans and tools, allowing the "voice" of the improvised ink to convey the dehumanized position of soldiering. In Bon's letter it is not so much the "soul" of the writer that is expressed but ink itself, ink acquiring a tongue to speak about the war machine and its destructive assemblage of humans, tools, and materials. When ink speaks, it describes war as an adjudication of the human enacted through the body, a force that phenomenologically dehumanizes and imposes the desire for *"something between the sole of the foot and the earth to distinguish it from the foot of a beast"* (103). The materiality of the sign is also subject to its own processes of material deterioration and its own forms of mortality that call into question the boundaries of "life." Judith values Bon's letter (which enacts their engagement without its being directly signified) not because of its content but because the act of giving the letter to Quentin's grandmother is an embodied act subject to the mortality of physical bodies, "mak[ing] a mark on something that *was* once for the reason that it can die someday" (101).[63]

    Absalom, Absalom! thus interrogates not only the materiality of the sign but also the signifying properties of matter itself. Bon, for example, imagines Sutpen sending him a material extension of his body, which would convey their biological relationship more immediately than an authored message would. He wishes first for a "bare-bones" letter that would say only *"'I am your father. Burn this.'"*; then for *"a scrap of paper with the one word 'Charles' in his hand"*; and then for only *"a lock of his hair or a paring from his finger nail"*—not an inscribed message at all but a sign that performatively joins genetic material with a message about genetic relationship (261). In Bon's fantasy, the living-nonliving, personal-impersonal properties of these materials make them most suited to affirm his own personhood, transgressing the legal discourses that make it impossible for him to be both multiracial and the acknowledged son of a white enslaver. His fantasy extends the scope of what can be regarded as "writing"—that privileged medium of human communication—suggesting that even a lock of hair or a fingernail can be regarded as inscription once it is recontextualized and reframed as a message.

As these somewhat pathetically inadequate signs of familial relation suggest, however, "identity" is a form of mortality when it functions as the "self-identity" detached from other material engagements, other intersectional identities. After a protracted internal debate about whether the "sin" of miscegenation between Bon and Judith trumps that of incest, Henry locates his negotiation of Bon's racial/familial identity at the boundary of the human and the nonhuman, as that which can only be resolved through the production of a corpse. His strange proclamation to Judith—*"Now you cant marry him ... Because he's dead"*—circumvents the intersectional nature of racial and kinship identities, forcing Bon to assume the morbid self-identity of the corpse, bypassing what would be, for Henry, a paradoxical utterance: Now you can't marry Bon because he's our brother *and* he's multiracial (139). When Henry "flings" the bloody corpse at the hem of Judith's wedding dress,[64] his gesture functions not so much as an act of retribution or as the vengeful defense of family honor but as the tautological embodiment, performance, and proof of his claim, *"Now you cant marry him. ... Because he's dead."* Henry's murder extracts Bon from the realm of marriageable persons—and, indeed, from personhood—and Bon's dead body, spilling its blood onto Judith's wedding dress through a kind of "corpse-writing," communicates to her the "truth" of his identity, even as it conveys the impossibility of marriage to such a nonperson.

That Judith writes Bon into the family plot signals her awareness of a future when the meanings of "blood," familial relationship, and personhood might be adjudicated quite differently. *Absalom, Absalom!* models this future perspective (even if it is a somewhat shallow future, only a couple of generations after the war) when Mr. Compson and Quentin visit the Sutpen gravesite to read the tombs cryptically inscribed with only names and dates. Mr. Compson dismisses Judith's act as a sentimental ritual, one of "the little puny affirmations of spurious immortality" (156) that women perform, but Quentin is unconcerned with immortality, turning his attention to the material decomposition of the interred remains and pragmatically noting, "there could have been nothing to eat in the grave for a long time" (153). While Mr. Compson disparages the "beautiful lives" of women and strangely frames his narrative of Bon's "octoroon mistress" and son visiting Bon's grave by comparing it to a "garden scene by the Irish poet, Wilde," Quentin reflects upon the material processes of becoming-earth and, quite literally, becoming-animal through which the body escapes such gendered and racialized narratives of personhood (157). Quentin's readership of these stone inscriptions decenters and defamiliarizes the human perspective from which language is produced and received; as he physically "brush[es] away some of the cedar needles to read the next one," one of his dogs "thrust[s] its head in to see what he was looking at like a human being would, as if from association with human beings it had acquired the quality of curiosity which is an attribute only of men and apes." Quentin's readership is also embodied readership, as he "smooth[s] with his hand into legibility the faint lettering," as though this mineralized inscription requires an act of the body in order to be properly read (155). In this way, readership involves not only the transparent production and reception of discourse but also an awareness of how embodiment informs the position from which we read; in Quentin's case, his privileged position as a white male in the early-twentieth-century South necessarily constructs his access to and interpretation of the buried bodies of the past.

Absalom, Absalom!'s complex narrative frames raise the question of how one can narrate the human without replicating the exclusionary discourses that have thus far defined it, how one can read backward into human history without redeeming the rough materials of the past into the smoothness of discourse. The novel concludes uncertainly by refusing a predictable narrative position. Quentin's account of his own visit to Sutpen's Hundred foregrounds the voice of Bon's grandson, Jim, "howling with human reason" (300)—a critique of the reason that supposedly guides human speech—while Rosa is carried away in an ambulance, "foaming a little at the mouth" (301), as though the tale she has just told Quentin cannot be contained in language and spills over in a rabid froth, leaving her in a position that is not quite human in the way she was before. Quentin's own transmission of Rosa's narrative to Shreve in their Harvard dorm room leaves him in a similar position, "panting in the cold air, the iron New England dark" (304). While Faulkner emphasizes the privilege and cold remove from which Quentin narrates the South, his "panting," like Jim's "howling" and Rosa's "foaming," also suggests the physically labored, and not entirely human, residue of speech. Quentin also emphatically refuses his own tale. When Shreve asks him, at the end of the novel, "Why do you hate the South?" (303) he replies in exclamatory, rather than narrative mode: *"I dont. I dont! I dont hate it! I dont hate it!"* (304). Shreve's question is somewhat illogical, given that Quentin's narrative is rife with acts of murder, enslavement, exploitation, abuse, and dehumanization—all of which amply explain why he would hate the South. Quentin's emphatic *"I dont. I dont!"* can thus be read not only as a reply to Shreve and a refusal of his own narrative but also, perhaps, as a larger refusal of his own familial ties to the South, an inversion of J. L. Austin's exemplary performative, "I do," whereby kinship unions are formed. In this way, Quentin rejects his own performative claim, *"I have committed incest I said,"* through which, as Michaels argues, Quentin fantasizes about incestuously preserving the "whiteness" of his own family from the invasion of outside "blood" in *The Sound and the Fury*.[65] Quentin's *"I dont"* thus acknowledges his own complicity in the tale he has just narrated, even as it creates a negative space of refusal.

From the perspective of Faulkner's own literary "corpus," however, Quentin is already dead when he narrates *Absalom, Absalom!* Quentin's narrative in the Harvard dorm room precedes (and perhaps precipitates) his suicide in *The Sound and the Fury*, published seven years before *Absalom, Absalom!* His suicide represents a symbolic refusal to return to the South and assume the patriarchal position that is expected of him, as well as a refusal of the humanist tradition of a Harvard education: in Quentin's view, Harvard is a site of enervation rather than growth, a place "where the best of thought Father said clings like dead ivy vines upon old dead brick."[66] Placing his epic tale of the South in the mouth of a dead narrator, Faulkner recognizes the inherent problem of narrating the dehumanization of the South from the perspective of one of its elite. Even before Quentin begins to speak, however, Faulkner characterizes his narrative as "the long silence of notpeople in notlanguage" (5), the ghostly tale of one "who was still too young to deserve yet to be a ghost but nevertheless having to be one for all that, since he was born and bred in the deep South" (4). Unlike the vivified speech of Addie's corpse, Quentin's narrative is a tale told by a ghost, full of the South's inhuman remains.

2   AUTOPSY-OPTICS

Jean Toomer's Cane through the Photographic Lens

ON SEPTEMBER 28, 1919, a white mob lynched William Brown in Omaha, Nebraska, part of a series of race riots that occurred across the United States in what James Weldon Johnson termed the "Red Summer." A photograph of the lynching was taken, grotesquely capturing the burning of Brown's already desecrated body and the white mob semi-circling his corpse, as though posing alongside a trophy. Both the photograph and its subsequent descriptions emphasize the superfluity of death, the apparent need not just to murder Brown but to murder him repetitively, as though the mob were systematically rehearsing a catalog of ways in which a body can die. In *Without Sanctuary: Lynching Photography in America,* for example, James Allen writes that Brown was first "hung from a lamppost," his corpse then "mutilated" and "riddled with bullets," and the remains of his body then burned.[1] The photograph bears evidence of this ritualized repetition of murder. Brown's head falls backward from his body, engulfed in a corona of flames so that the features are illegible; his limbs have been severed from his body so that only the torso remains; and the skin of his torso has been flayed and burned so that the entrails of his body are horrifically visible. Not merely capturing the dead body, the photograph has qualities of an autopsy, actively exposing its interior in an absolute evisceration of personhood. Brown was accused of raping a white woman, and the task the lynch mob seemed to set for itself was the excavation of a body imagined to contain, by virtue of its blackness, a subterranean sexual threat. The purpose of lynching here is not killing a living person but redundantly killing a corpse—killing what has already been disqualified from life.

Despite this excess of death, the photograph depicts the white male mob through a visual rhetoric that distributes culpability. No one is actively engaged with Brown's body, and no one holds a weapon that could have accomplished his death. In opposition to the repetitive stripping of Brown's body, so that first his clothes and then even his skin are removed, the mob is dressed in almost identically interchangeable clothing, forming a kind of human phalanx protecting an invisible white femininity, which is "sanctified" and protected because it is invisible. The mob's presence as a unanimously complicit body seems to provide its own kind of justification—or obviates the need for justification altogether. With the exception of a few spectators craning to look at Brown's body, the men look directly at the camera, self-conscious, and in some cases even apparently triumphant, about being photographed. Their unabashed manner belies the radical dehumanization that they have performed—precisely because lynching is regarded as killing that which is already less than human.[2]

The photograph of Brown's corpse was subsequently deployed in ways that both deviate from and reinforce this visual rhetoric. Addressing an international audience, the NAACP published the image in a 1920 brochure titled "An Appeal to the Conscience of the Civilized World."[3] The brochure included only a pared-down list of lynching statistics and images, allowing the atrocity of Brown's lynching to speak for itself. Silencing the testimonial power of Brown's body, the *Chicago Tribune* published a cropped version of the photograph that showed only the white lynch mob and removed Brown's body, which was deemed "too revolting for publication."[4] The photograph of Brown's corpse was also sold as a disturbing "souvenir" of the Omaha riots, a circulation that ramified Brown's murder at the level of representation, as the "right" to kill what has already died is replicated through the "right" to reproduce an image of what was already regarded as less than fully human. As many theorists have posited, such "souvenir" circulation of lynching images not only reinforces the fiction of white supremacy but also produces an ideology of whiteness itself.[5] Shawn Michelle Smith, for example, argues of lynching images such as Brown's: "The black corpse remains bound and circumscribed by white supremacy in these images; displayed front and center, the corpse functions as the negated other that frames, supports, and *defines* a white supremacist community."[6] Lynching photographs represent but, more importantly, *construct* racialized modes of viewership that, in turn, construct lived relationships.

Lynching photographs produce these ideologies of racial difference, however, through the more trenchant production of ideologies of the human. Literalizing both the division between white and black bodies and the division between living and nonliving bodies, lynching photography inexorably associates whiteness with life and blackness with death. In the case of William Brown, this division between the living and the nonliving is insidiously demonstrated through the repetitive assault on his body, as though the goal of lynching is not the extinction of life but the extinction of evidence that such life ever qualified as human. The "souvenir" circulation of such images provides an ideological lens that trains white viewers not to regard such photographs as circumscribed images that can be multiply deployed and interpreted, but rather to see the association between blackness and the inhuman as "naturalized" and to produce repetitively the "proof" of such inhumanity through continued violence.

Published in 1923, a few years following the events of the Red Summer, Jean Toomer's *Cane* similarly depicts lynching through a formalized divide between a living white body and a black corpse.[7] Emblematizing many of *Cane*'s representational concerns, "Portrait in Georgia" performs a macabre parody of a blazon, first detailing the parts of a white woman's face and body, then depicting the lynching that her body seems to evoke.

Hair—braided chestnut,
    coiled like a lyncher's rope,
Eyes—fagots,
Lips—old scars, or the first red blisters,
Breath—the last sweet scent of cane,
And her slim body, white as the ash
    of black flesh after flame.[8]

Toomer's "portrait" moves between two different representational modes, such that the body anatomized at the beginning of each line occupies a unified temporality, while the lynching unfolds in stages, moving from the proleptic threat of the lyncher's rope to the retrospective image of a cremated corpse. Each living part of the white woman's body—hair, eyes, lips, breath (and, finally, the totality of "her slim body")—is defined by a lynching instrument or a repetitively injured black body, such that "old scars" are reopened as "first red blisters." The black body is not simply dehumanized or deprived of a once-human status; it emerges only as the belated evidence of its destruction—the "ash / of black flesh after flame." Walter Benn Michaels argues, as Smith does of lynching photography more generally, that the lynched body in "Portrait in Georgia" produces "whiteness": "black flesh is burned in order to make a white body."[9] The "making" of whiteness is thus inextricably bound with the status of the living and the nonliving. Hanging like a noose at the end of the poem, the epigrammatic final lines define the supplement of "whiteness" as emerging in living, if illusory, unity only as the sexual threat implied by the black body is simultaneously "proven" and erased through death.

The paradox of such "life," of course, is that it emerges as that which is already unlivable, dependent upon the death of the other, and itself radically death-bound. And while this ideology of the human depends upon the specularity of both seeing the dead body and seeing "into" this body, "Portrait in Georgia" also describes a series of impossible viewerships. Who is looking at "her slim body" or at "black flesh after flame" in Toomer's poem? If vision is the domain of the woman, whose face seems to either occasion or preside over the lynching, this vision is ultimately self-reflexive, seeing the body of the other only insofar as seeing constitutes the outlines of the self. If the poem depicts the perspective of a male viewer, such viewership places him in the impossible position of seeing his own corpse, as his gaze moves outward to seek the parts of the woman's face, only to return to him his own body in ruin. The poem gives an anatomy of gazes and, more specifically, an anatomy of the impossible viewerships that define looking at "race." What do viewers "see" when they see "whiteness" or "blackness," given that such binary categories are co-defined through ideologies of the human and the nonhuman?

This chapter argues that ideologies of the human and the nonhuman are most effectively deployed in *Cane* through two of the most privileged social gazes—the photographic gaze and the clinical gaze. Although nowhere explicitly referenced, the techniques of film and autopsy provide analogous, mutually reinforcing models for understanding visual constructions of both the black and the white body; their explicit absence from *Cane* only reinforces the extent to which individual viewers have seamlessly incorporated these gazes. Autopsy and film have both served as important, if concealed, origins of knowledge about the body, providing anatomical models and images that inform cultural perceptions. Autopsy and film have also provided more general epistemological models predicated upon the disembodied examiner who discovers his own disavowed corporeality in the body of the other.[10] Viewers in *Cane*—both white and African American—attempt to align themselves with this tradition of disembodied viewership and knowledge by visually examining the other whose materiality borders on the cadaverous or who is described, in several instances, as explicitly "dead."[11] The specter of lynching informs visual constructions of the black body even in its absence, often appearing out of context to mortify what was once living; attempting to escape this specter of violence, viewers in the first section of *Cane*, set in Georgia, selectively deploy photographic, physically penetrative techniques of vision in order to discover predictable racial typologies or more distant mythological "truths" that conceal and bury more immediate truths—namely, the history of lynching.

In order to make these implicitly photographic, autoptic techniques of vision more "visible," my discussion connects *Cane* with W. E. B. Du Bois's "Georgia Negro Exhibit," an extensive collection of photographs, graphs, charts, and legal documents first exhibited at the 1900 Paris Exposition. Demonstrating an acute awareness of the importance of photographic representation, Du Bois's exhibit included 363 photographs of African Americans living in Georgia, which were organized into two albums titled *Negro Life in Georgia, U.S.A.* and *Types of American Negroes, Georgia, U.S.A.*[12] Much like Du Bois's photographic albums, *Cane* comprises a collection of verbal "portraits" of both African American "life" and various "types" of African Americans: in character sketches such as "Karintha," "Fern," "Becky," and "Esther," characters seem to recur not so much as autonomous figures but as variations on themes. As this chapter argues, however, both Du Bois's "Georgia Negro Exhibit" and *Cane* turn the ideological apparati of white culture back onto itself, subverting photographic depictions that would typologize African Americans or construct race through a binaristic division between the living human viewer and the corpse.

My discussion of the autoptic gaze in *Cane* represents a culturally and technologically expanded form of the clinical gaze I discussed in the first chapter, drawing upon social science studies of autopsy, ethnographic approaches to film and photography, and the history of lynching to show the permeation and subsequent naturalization of a penetrative, autoptic gaze throughout a range of social contexts. Approaching technical media through a discussion of race in these first two chapters is critical to my project's understanding of posthumanism. When posthuman studies claims technology as a determinant force that categorically and equally reformulates "man," it often implicitly replicates the centrism of the white humanist subject by either presuming the white cultural ownership of technology or failing to consider technology's role in producing a spectrum of ideological constructions of race and gender. Far from categorially reconfiguring the human, human-technological assemblages often reinforce the fiction of a white supremacist human whose vitalism is understood in binary opposition to the mortalism of racialized others. *Cane* suggests engagements between the organic eye and the camera eye that are so interpenetrated as to be cybernetic, but these "naturalized" incorporations of technology are deployed to inscribe the boundaries of a white supremacist human. Against this dehumanizing use of technology, however, the "Georgia Negro Exhibit" and *Cane* also depict irrefutable forms of African American life through alternative uses of technology. Alongside its archive of photographic portraits, the exhibit includes forms of data visualization not easily reducible to binary understandings of "life." The second section of *Cane*, set in the North, deploys sound technologies through which the body participates in a decentered, wired network rather than being confined to the model of disembodied, living viewer and corpse-like embodied other.[13] Returning to the South in its final section, *Cane* proposes the "completely artificial man," a collective, posthuman figure that consciously admits the technological apparati of vision into the body, reshaping those technologies in turn.

"It Is from the Height of Death That One Can See"

The corpse is paradoxically central to living epistemologies, given that examination of the cadaver provides the origin of much anatomical and medical knowledge. As Foucault has argued, however, autopsy is best understood not as a material encounter but through processes of illumination, focal clarity, distanced observation, and domination over life:

> It is from the height of death that one can see and analyze organic dependences and pathological sequences. Instead of being what it had so long been, the night in which life disappeared, in which even the disease becomes blurred, it is now endowed with that great power of elucidation that dominates and reveals both the space of the organism and the time of the disease.[14]

Where the obfuscation of death had previously "blurred" the operations of the body, autopsy places the viewer in a position of telescopic "height" and visual mastery. The effect of a new scientific materialism's exploration of the corpse is not to recuperate bodily materiality but to translate the body into a domain of knowledge ruled by a transcendent clinical gaze.

The very methods of autopsy belie the notion of a direct, unmediated encounter with the body. Describing his experience as a medical examiner and pathologist, Eugene Arnold points out that although autopsy claims the primacy of vision and first-hand investigation, it views the corpse through the lens of long-established knowledge. He notes: "The word *autopsy* comes from the Greek *autoa* (self) and *opsis* (to see), which is usually rendered as 'to see with one's own eyes.' This is a limited translation, since the autopsy is really informed observation with deductions based upon the accumulated knowledge of our antecedents."[15] Variations among individual bodies are seen only as contributing to this accumulated knowledge or deviating from preestablished pathological and anatomical types. Arnold notes that "within that dead husk there are answers," as if the corpse itself were only a material shell housing an interior store of truths.[16] Autopsies, he claims, are also retrospective processes, "intellectual exercises in reverse problem solving," providing an endpoint from which to construct the temporal sequence of a physical and pathological narrative.[17] And while autopsy promises access to the body in its totality, the viewing is a temporal practice that unfolds in stages. Stefan Hirschauer describes surgery as a "sequence of looking and cutting" in which "one must *see* to cut, and one cuts to see *more*." Seeing in autopsy is not simply attaining the interior of the body all at once, but a visual penetration through descending layers of bodily surfaces. The medical cadaver must be "manufactured" from the garden-variety corpse, whose corporeality is made to correspond with established anatomical models. Hirschauer notes: "Another film seems to be spread out on the patient-body like an overlay: the anatomic film."[18]

Hirschauer concludes his study of the body in surgery by drawing an analogy between surgical and ethnographic methods, both of which depend upon an objectifying invasion of the person:

> Apparently it is a basic feature of sciences whose objects are human beings that the object always has to be conquered against the specific resistance of living and sense-making individuals. Ethnographic science studies, too, try to gain access to a foreign territory. It is not the bodies or souls of individuals, but a web of symbols, practices and interaction that constitutes social fields. They are entered for a limited period, and the fleeting perceptions are captured in language by painstaking descriptive work.[19]

Similarly comparing the role of the ethnographer to the physician, or even the pathologist conducting an autopsy, Fatimah Tobing Rony notes that one of the earliest anthropological organizations, La Société d'anthropologie de Paris, was largely composed of physicians and that there was thus "an intimate connection between the object of the physician's scrutiny—the pathological—and the object of the anthropologist's scrutiny—race."[20] She notes that Félix-Louis Regnault, who produced time-motion studies of West African performers for the 1895 Ethnographic Exposition in Paris, explicitly compared his proto-filmic study of the body with the study of the cadaver. Regnault suggested that the new technology of film picks up where autopsy leaves off, allowing the viewer untrammeled study of the body in motion: "Surely it is true that the artistic anatomy, the dissection of the cadaver, is not a sufficient reproduction, since it is necessary to see again the tendons and the muscles, flaccid when studied under the scalpel, flexing and releasing through action."[21] Regnault specifies that autopsy is not a direct seeing of the body but a "reproduction," and he suggests that the supplement of film provides a way to "see again" that which the autoptic reproduction misses. There is thus an elision, both historically and in practice, between the methods of autopsy and the ethnographic film: both rely upon an optimized viewership that produces an image of the body by suppressing the other's subjectivity. The surgical gaze is also aided by a range of mechanical devices such as "reflecting instruments, pairs of magnifying glasses, microscopes, forehead mirrors and lamps."[22] In the most literal sense, then, the autoptic gaze does not "see with its own eyes" but, like the filmic gaze, employs a panoply of optical devices in its production, or reproduction, of bodily form. Walter Benjamin makes the analogy explicit, famously comparing the photographer to a surgeon who "penetrates deeply" into the patient's body. Film does not merely train its eye upon the bodily surface; overcoming a "natural distance" from the body, film, in Benjamin's terms, "penetrates" its human subjects while nevertheless abstaining from a "man to man" encounter.[23]

Such autoptic, filmic modes of vision inform depictions of the body in *Cane*'s first section, set in Georgia. Narrators access the body in the manner of film—through lingering close-ups, floating panning shots, and perspectives that impossibly combine distance and proximity. These implicitly filmic depictions of the body function like a penetrative autopsy, as viewers visually penetrate the "dead husk" of the other in order to "discover" ethnographic typologies and more generalized "truths" about the South. Hirschauer provocatively compares the surgeon's headlamp to that of the miner, and in *Cane*, penetrating the bodily surface is often equivalent to a subterranean excavation of the South's hidden meanings. The body of the other is often so many "layers of skin and tissue" obstructing the view of a mythologized South, or a remotely "primitive" Africa.[24] Like the retrospective work of autopsy, viewing the body in *Cane* has a temporal dimension, as viewers look backward from the present, inert body to reach a more primitive imaginary past, eliding the present violence that constructs racial relations in the United States.

The formal experiments of literary modernism, which *Cane* itself helped to inaugurate, might seem opposed to this emphasis on viewership. That is, even as *Cane*'s narrators are centrally occupied with viewing and describing the body, its fragmentary form and experimental bodily representations would seem to disrupt the visual power of these narrators. The "old scars . . . first red blisters" in "Portrait in Georgia," for instance, suggest a wound that refuses to cicatrize and, more generally, a body whose incoherence would prove to be an unruly object for either autopsy or photography.[25] Bodily tropes often recur in different sections of *Cane*, seeming to belong to more than one character and disrupting the fiction of the narrator's objectifying visual control. A hybrid text composed of poems, lyric fragments, character sketches, short stories, a closet drama, as well as the graphic arcing lines separating each of its three sections, *Cane* offers a catalog of bodily fragments, enacting an uncertain relation between the singular character in its fictive context and transpersonal histories of race. *Cane* would thus seem to escape the scene of photographic, autoptic viewership I have been describing.

Jonathan Crary points out that "we are often left with a confusing, bifurcated model of vision" in modernity: whereas film and photography might be regarded as the culmination of a realist tradition that continues unbroken from the Renaissance and its interest in perspectival space, experimental modernism breaks with this realist tradition, offering radically new modes of vision and signification.[26] Karen Jacobs resolves this apparent contradiction by claiming an affinity between literary modernism and the optical devices that give rise to visual culture, arguing that modernism's fixation on *interiority* is linked to the "proliferation of technologies intended to bring more and more of the body into view."[27] Film and photography proliferate images of the bodily surface, but they also allow, as Benjamin suggests, a proximity suggestive of penetration, and they are linked, both technologically and in the cultural imagination, with more literally penetrative technologies such as the X-ray. If the fractured surfaces of the modernist text discourage direct translation of physical sight into knowledge, modernism nevertheless claims access to "more hidden zones of visibility," reinforcing more trenchant forms of vision as a source of knowledge. Discussing *The Waste Land* in particular, Jacobs argues, "social science discourses and practices are relevant to modernism, not only in the sense in which T. S. Eliot adapted Frazer's *The Golden Bough,* that is, as sources of anthropological and mythological detail that lent allusive richness to modernist texts, but in a more primary way, as a method of knowledge."[28]

Building upon Jacobs's claim, I would venture that the perspective of white literary modernists is often that of the autopsy, penetrating through the "remains" of culture in order to recover—or invent—more distant cultural truths. "The Love Song of J. Alfred Prufrock," for instance, begins with the image of the "patient etherised upon a table"—suggesting the inert status of the modernist subject—but it imaginatively resurrects this body as "Lazarus, come from the dead," and concludes with the claim of transcendent vision, of having "seen [the mermaids] riding seaward on the waves." While the speaker is excluded from its promise, such "vision" still exists within the poem as a valuable, if inaccessible, repository of knowledge. In this way we can see the various kinds of authority that accrue around the autoptic gaze. While Faulkner's anoptic modernism rejects the panoptic authority of realism as well as the metaphysical gaze that, in Cora Tull's terms, "see[s] into the heart," Eliot's fragmentary modernist technique still claims a form of "vision" that operates "from the height of death." Toomer noted in a letter to Horace Liveright, who had published *The Waste Land* the year before *Cane,* that he was "glad to be in the fold" with Eliot, but *Cane* sharply cuts away from Eliot's metaphysical fold.[29] Systematically critiquing the social and technological gazes that penetrate through the "dead husk" of the other's body in order to establish self-reflexively the viewer's claim to knowledge, *Cane* also implicitly critiques the ways in which the "vision" of modernism is often both complicit with, and an extension of, a penetrative, ethnographic, and ultimately deadening gaze.

Portraits of Georgia

Cane's three sections do not describe a simple progression from South to North and back. The first section describes not the South itself but the way in which ethnographic modes of viewership construct perspectives on the South, even those of African American viewers. The narrator of "Fern," for example, an African American from the North visiting "the soil of [his] ancestors" (25), turns upon Fern a culturally inflected mode of vision through which he himself has been objectified. Through his visit to the South he conducts a kind of anthropological "field work," as his implicitly filmic perspective allows him visual proximity to Fern while still affording him the distance to establish Fern as a predictable type or specimen, a metonymic stand-in for the whole of the South.

Viewing Fern through the train window or walking up the "Dixie Pike," the narrator's vision suggests the mobility of the cinematic camera, while Fern remains the still focus of his gaze:

> Anyone, of course, could see her, could see her eyes. If you walked up the Dixie Pike most any time of day, you'd be most like to see her resting listless-like on the railing of her porch, back propped against a post, head tilted a little forward because there was a nail in the porch post just where her head came which for some reason or other she never took the trouble to pull out. (22)

The description suggests viewership through an optical device rather than the unaided eye, in that the close-up implied by seeing her eyes coexists with the distance implied by walking up the Dixie Pike—we see the detail of the post nail even as we can take in the sweep of the landscape. Framed by the horizontal railing and the vertical post, Fern is an aestheticized object, and the descriptions of her face evoke the cinematic close-up, such that the narrator is privy to "the soft suggestion of down slightly darkened" on her upper lip before having interacted with her at all. Fern's magnified face elicits a powerful emotional response; the narrator notes, "If you have heard a Jewish cantor sing, you will know my feeling when I follow the curves of her profile" (21). The narrator's descriptions of Fern's face not only evoke the conventions of filmic viewership but seem to supply their own sound track as well.

Almost in the manner of shot/reverse shot, the narrator then gives us a panoramic view of the landscape, supposedly capturing Fern's perspective. Her slow gaze, "idly" panning the horizon, however, is directed by the narrator himself, who notes that "maybe [her eyes] gazed at the gray cabin," and "perhaps they followed a cow," and "like as not they'd settle on some vague spot above the horizon" (23). Combining the "fantasy of dominance" with "the self-effaced, noninterventionist eye," the narrator establishes his visual dominance over the scene through his imagined direction of Fern's gaze, but his visual exploration of Georgia never leads him into this landscape.[30] When he turns his gaze back upon

Fern, it instead penetrates the surface of her face in order to discover the previously inaccessible "life" of the South: "Like her face, the whole countryside seemed to flow into her eyes. Flowed into them with the soft listless cadence of Georgia's South" (23). Fern's face passively engulfs the landscape, and her "unusually weird and open" eyes provide a suggestive bodily aperture or cavity that invites the narrator's penetration. Fern herself is secondary to this bodily opening; less important than the aesthetic qualities of her face or the psychological interiority it might reveal is the mythological essence of the South that seems to unfold through the act of visual penetration. As the narrator returns North, his gaze lingering longer on Fern's face than the departing train would seem to allow, he discovers "the countryside and something that I call God" flowing into her eyes (26). The narrator's ostensibly exterior perspective erodes, and the infallible metaphysical eye he posits in its place accomplishes a reorganization of the scene such that he himself is a bodily absence.

Rather than seeing "with his own eyes," the narrator turns upon Fern a technologically and ideologically produced gaze that positions him on the side of rationalist observation and analysis. Although Fern's vegetative somnolence never seems to rise to the level of activity, he includes her in an ethnographic typology of hypersexualized behavior from which he excludes himself: "That the sexes were made to mate is the practice of the South. Particularly, black folks were made to mate. And it is black folks whom I have been talking about thus far. What white men thought of Fern I can arrive at only by analogy." He notes several times that "Men were everlastingly bringing her their bodies" (22), as though men are seeking not only sexual experience with Fern but also a way to disavow their own unwanted corporeality. Although the narrator distances himself from the sexual mores of the South, his narrative achieves the same bodily disavowal, aligning him with the disembodied ethnographer or cinematographer such that his own corporeality "flows" into the passive chasms of Fern's eyes. That Fern never quite materializes as a body, never presents the viewer or reader with this image of repressed corporeality, suggests a double disavowal. The narrator is not just discovering the "mating practices" of the South by visually penetrating the binaristic other; he is engaged in a kind of metaphysical autopsy, becoming the visionary who sees through this primitivized sexuality in order to discover "something that I call God."

Jacobs points out that while photography and film seem to re-create the world mimetically, they simultaneously interrogate the objectivity of such images and often foreground perspectives that are frankly subjective. "Fern" similarly problematizes vision as a basis of objective knowledge, showing the narrator's implicitly filmic vision elide into subjective experience. Modernism responds to the "tensions between the documentary and visionary" modes of photography through what Jacobs terms a particular kind of "interior gaze":

> Inherited from the social sciences, this "interior gaze" is a form of disavowal of the subjective character of gaze and image which relocates visual truths to an "interior"—literal or conceptual—where they can be recovered only by a properly expert vision. The interior gaze thus preserves . . . a positivist fantasy of the availability of visual truths by strategically conceding their difficulty of access.[31]

In the same way, the narrator, whose typology of African Americans in the South serves as the basis for mystical experience, stages his sole physical interaction with Fern through an interiorized space that is unavailable to the reader. When he invites Fern for a walk, the one moment of mobility she is afforded, his vision of her deviates from previous perceptions: "Something told me that men before me had said just that as a prelude to the offering of their bodies. I tried to tell her with my eyes. I think she understood. The thing from her that made my throat catch, vanished. Its passing left her visible in a way I'd thought but never seen" (25). The narrator does not translate this new mode of visibility, which establishes him as an expert viewer distinct from the men who are merely "bringing her their bodies." He instead assumes the role of the visionary who can guide the reader not only to the South's regional characters but also to the mystical truths that reside within. Dusk settles immediately after this shift in vision, obscuring the story's prior exteriorizing perspectives, and the narrator claims: "I felt that things unseen to men were tangibly immediate. It would not have surprised me had I had vision. . . . When one is on the soil of one's ancestors, most anything can come to one." In the midst of this visionary mode, he takes Fern into his arms and confusedly notes, "I must have done something—what, I dont know." The narrator remains physically detached, but the implicit sexuality of his gesture threatens to destroy Fern: "Her body was tortured with something it could not let out. Like boiling sap it flooded her arms and fingers till she shook them as if they burned her" (25–26). The imagery of burning and boiling sap directly recalls the lynching imagery of "Portrait in Georgia," but here the narrator disturbingly recasts the tropes of lynching as mystical vision.

The physical threat is cast entirely onto Fern, while the narrator occupies the role of detached seer. Fern only materializes, acquiring "arms and fingers," through this recapitulation of violence; her body thus obtains only to entomb the history of lynching that threatens his own suppressed corporeality. Seeking to see through the body of the other in order to discover a more distant mythological truth, the narrator bypasses the historical and present violence that saturate the South. He thus combines the perspective of the worldly ethnographer and traveler with that of the mystical seer in order to construct a complex but ideologically mystified subject position.

While "Fern" depicts the perspective of an African American character who adopts the visual mode of white culture, "Esther" directly depicts this mortifying gaze. Beginning with a description of the multiracial Esther's "dead" face, the story quickly shifts to the scene of Barlo's public bodily mortification, as he inexplicably falls to his knees in a trance state around a public spittoon. Barlo, who is described as a "clean-muscled, magnificent, black-skinned Negro" (29), seems qualified for such a role through his corporeality, and the surrounding white men cover his face with expelled tobacco juice. Barlo becomes a tragically literalized receptacle of disavowed corporeality, and his mortified body becomes a spectacle as the townspeople gather to watch. Recalling Kristeva's claim that bodily excretions such as the expelled tobacco juice must be cast aside in order to maintain the illusion of subjective coherence ("I expel *myself*, I spit *myself* out, I abject *myself* within the same motion through which 'I' claim to establish *myself*"), the white spectators expel and abject their unwanted corporeality onto Barlo in order to achieve their own spectatorial coherence. Kristeva claims the corpse is the absolute of "improper" corporeality, calling it "the utmost of abjection"; corpses do not just "signify" death, she claims, but "as in true theater . . . corpses *show me* what I permanently thrust aside in order to live."[32] In the same way, Barlo *shows* the white spectators, who tellingly use a "coffin-box" to obtain a better view, the bodily "stuff" that they must thrust aside in order live.

As in "Fern," the power of this disembodied gaze is affirmed not only by projecting disavowed corporeality onto the dehumanized other but also by making the other's body yield to the interiority of mystical vision. Dusk falls, as it does in "Fern," obscuring physical sight and inaugurating visionary sight: "Barlo rises to his full height. He is immense. To the people he assumes the outlines of his visioned Africa." Resurrecting the mortified state of Barlo's tobacco-doused body into the metaphysical form of a "visioned Africa," the town's vision of Barlo only describes another mode of autopsy, in which the disembodied viewer peers through the material body in order to examine the "outlines" of the ancestral dead. Toomer's own anatomizing examination of this white gaze, however, reveals its instability, as the position of the disembodied viewer depends upon the ongoing mortification of the bodily other. This binary between the living and the dead falters, as the town, perhaps unable to take in the "immense" vision of Barlo, is thrown into a bodily confusion that transgresses racialized boundaries: "old Limp Underwood, who hated niggers" is reported to have awoken the following morning "to find that he held a black man in his arms" (31). Rather than transforming the racial dynamics of the town or leaving any real bodily "remains," however, this fantasy of physical union only provides a temporary dissolution of boundaries out of which the perimeters of the white social body are paradoxically reestablished.

Such ideologically constructed modes of vision predominate in *Cane*'s South, but before they concretize, *Cane* opens with a character sketch, "Karintha," that resists these visual regimes. Karintha is described as occupying a blind spot, evoking the apparatus of the camera itself rather than the object upon which it is focused. She is "a wild flash," "a bit of vivid color . . . that flashes in light," and thus resists capture. The opening lyric compares Karintha's skin to "dusk," asking, "O cant you see it, O cant you see it" (3). In the character sketches that follow, dusk signals the transition from documentary mode to visionary mode, a recession from the inert shell of the body to its interior repository of mythological meanings, but here Karintha's flashing mobility refuses to provide a point upon which vision can be focused. Her bodily surface is that which cannot be seen, that which refuses to reify into an inert corpse.

Karintha only materializes through a traumatic childbirth, as the story abruptly fixes her flashing mobility and orients her in narrative time, claiming that "Karintha is a woman, and she has had a child." The child's fate is an uncertain elision, but the story suggests that it has been either stillborn or aborted:

A child fell out of her womb onto a bed of pine-needles in the forest. Pine-needles are smooth and sweet. They are elastic to the feet of rabbits . . . A sawmill was nearby. Its pyramidal sawdust pile smouldered. It is a year before one completely burns. Meanwhile, the smoke curls up and hangs in odd wraiths about the trees, curls up, and spreads itself over the valley . . .

Weeks after Karintha returned home the smoke was so heavy you tasted it in water. (4-5; ellipses in original)

The passage withholds the story of the child through ellipses, through shifts between the past tense of narration and the present tense of description, and through the seeming irrelevance of the pine-needles, the rabbit, and the sawmill. Moving from the moment of the child's fall (a moment made temporally uncertain through the proleptic designation of a "child" rather than an infant) to the time of the burning pile of sawdust, to Karintha's return home, the story suggests that the child, whether still-born or aborted, has been left unmourned. The ellipses performatively enact the town's perhaps willed ignorance of this child, but the child never-theless has an uncertain afterlife, returning as the smoky "wraith" that haunts the scene and poisons the town's water supply. The child indi-rectly enters the bodies of the townspeople, collapsing the boundary between the living and the dead, and reorganizing bodily relations in the text, even though the surface narration is free of visible bodily form. The passage suggests an invisible transfer of corporeality that would elude penetrative models of vision, a liquid continuum among bodies rather than the polarized separation of spectator and object; the smoke sug-gestively "curls up" in fetal shapes, but remains diffuse and envelop-ing. "Karintha" thus describes a contagious or infectious corporeality—precisely that against which white supremacist culture would shield itself through the imposition of a lens.

Despite viewers' efforts to project a mortified corporeality onto the other who is regarded not merely as subhuman or infrahuman but as explicitly "dead," the very landscape in "Karintha" and *Cane* as a whole is haunted by a shadowy corporeal violence that is palpable, if not pre-cisely visible. The incompletion of Karintha's story encourages us to seek its conclusion in "Reapers," the poem that immediately follows; its agri-cultural setting invites comparison with Karintha, who is herself repeat-edly called a "growing thing ripened too soon."

Black horses drive a mower through the weeds,
And there, a field rat, startled, squealing bleeds.
His belly close to ground. I see the blade,
Blood-stained, continue cutting weeds and shade. (6)

The "belly" of the field rat evokes the pregnant Karintha, who is poten-tially a victim of the r(e)apers, and the final line, "cutting weeds and

Figure 6. "Two African American men standing next to a tree in Georgia," W. E. B. Du Bois, African American Photographs Assembled for 1900 Paris Exhibition, Prints and Photographs Division, Library of Congress.

shade," suggests both the material world and a shadowy double that conjures her wraith-like child in attenuated form. But rather than the illuminating surgical incision that would unfold the body's interiority, the poem concludes with the more obscure image of "cutting" only "shade." Perhaps a way of throwing shade over the epistemological certainty of Enlightenment forms of vision, the poem evacuates the human figure from the Georgia landscape, but nevertheless evokes, through the imagery of the horse, the field rat, and the stained blade, a submerged history of lynching that suffuses the visible world.

One of the photographs from Du Bois's "Georgia Negro Exhibit" similarly conjures the threat of death that permeates the Georgia landscape. Included among a series of photographs depicting African American–owned businesses, educational institutions, neighborhoods, and churches, all of which depict rich and varied scenes of African American lives, the photograph of two men next to a tree (fig. 6) evokes in shadowy form the death-haunted status of the landscape. The men, the tree, the coincidentally descendent tree limbs, and the cruciform telephone poles indirectly comprise a scene of lynching. Far from a neutral, technological reproduction of the natural world, the photograph describes a morbid ecology whereby trees look like instruments of death, shadowy lines look like nooses, and humans, at first glance, look like corpses. Abel Meeropol's anti-lynching protest song, "Strange Fruit," popularized by Billie Holiday, similarly evokes the morbid southern ecologies whereby "Southern trees bear strange fruit / Blood on the leaves and blood at the root." Lynching transforms the living body into the "strange fruit" comprising a "strange and bitter crop," which, like the corporeal transfers in "Karintha," mortifies the whole of the natural world—crows, rains, winds, trees, and humans alike.[33] Toomer claimed that he was composing *Cane* as an elegy to a dying southern way of life, and both Toomer and Du Bois depict Georgia as a domain of death, saturated with violence despite its placid appearance.

The Corpse's Gaze

Posing a striking contrast to the distanced perspective of this tree photograph, the "Georgia Negro Exhibit" also contains hundreds of photographic portraits of African American faces. Du Bois explicitly—but, I would suggest, strategically—claimed that the presentation of "Negro Life" to an international audience was motivated by the humanist goals of showing "the human face of blackness" that has traditionally been concealed by "representations of blackness as absence, as nothingness, as deformity and depravity."[34] This humanism entails vivifying, at the level of representation, what has been a kind of mortifying "nothingness" and substituting African American "presence" for "absence," but it also necessarily involves trading in "types": the exhibit presents photographs of what Du Bois terms "typical Negro faces, which hardly square with conventional American ideas,"[35] thus offering a corrective to more historically visible photographic depictions of African Americans, such as the lynching photograph, the ethnographic photograph, and the mug shot.[36] Smith has insightfully discussed the way in which the exhibit self-consciously adopts methods of white portraiture and thus "signifies" upon a history of deadening photographic representation. Du Bois's photographs also resist a historical association between blackness and the body, showing faces that directly meet the gaze of the observer and that challenge an easy identification of race. The photographs show a spectrum of skin colors and deploy a visual rhetoric that invites mirroring identification from white viewers, rather than presenting African Americans as the inert object of the gaze.

Du Bois, however, is not simply working toward the universal humanism implied by "showing the human face of blackness." His "Negro Exhibit" instead interrogates the criteria by which the exclusionary category of the human has traditionally been constructed. Du Bois's essay "The Souls of White Folks" turns an eviscerating gaze onto white culture, uncovering the historically constructed category of the human as "ugly":

> Of them I am singularly clairvoyant. I see in and through them. I view them from unusual points of vantage. . . . I see these souls undressed and from the back and side. I see the working of their entrails. I know their thoughts and they know that I know. . . . And yet as they preach and strut and shout and threaten, crouching as they clutch at rags of facts and fancies to hide their nakedness, they go, twisting, flying by my tired eyes and I see them ever stripped,—ugly, human.[37]

Du Bois's description of visual "clairvoyance" is akin to an autopsy, claiming a vantage point that is able to penetrate into the "entrails" of the white human. Reprinted the year following the events of the Red Summer, Du Bois's essay recalls the atrocities visited upon bodies such as William Brown's and the souvenir photographs that turned corpses into visual spectacle. While the "Georgia Negro Exhibit" predates this essay, his photographic albums are arguably motivated not by the simplistic goal of inviting white viewers to identify with the previously undiscovered "human face" of blackness but by the more radical goal of turning the ideological apparati of white visual culture back onto itself.

The "Negro Exhibit" depicts African Americans who not only return the gaze of white viewers, but also possess their own forms of visual expertise from which white viewers are excluded. The photograph of a young girl (fig. 7), apparently pausing in contemplation of her own set of photographs, creates a set of interior images legible only by the girl herself. It is not only that the appearance and mien of the girl "hardly square with conventional American ideas" about race, but that these interior images themselves literally refuse to "square" with viewers' sight. They are invitingly poised so that viewers can see the images, but they are set at an oblique angle that prohibits reading them. The visual rhetoric of the girl's image also breaks the geographic and ideological frame of what white viewers might expect from *Negro Life in Georgia, U.S.A.* Dressed in

Figure 7. "African American girl, half-length portrait, with right hand to cheek, with illustrated book on table," Thomas Askew, African American Photographs Assembled for 1900 Paris Exhibition, Prints and Photographs Division, Library of Congress.

nautical garments, surrounded by objects imported from international contexts, she looks off-frame at something viewers cannot see, as though pausing for a moment before setting off on her next conquest. Her affect is every inch *Le Penseur*, but her body is covered, her limbs rearranged so that she literally points to the activity of an apparently capacious mind— even as she seems utterly self-conscious of cutting a figure for the viewer. The photograph provides a powerful demonstration of Du Bois's theory of double consciousness (first articulated a few years before the Paris Exposition), whereby the African American is "always looking at one's self through the eyes of others" but also "gifted with second sight in this American world," such that the African American "sees" her own double-ness and the particular ideological blindness that structures normatively white forms of vision.[38]

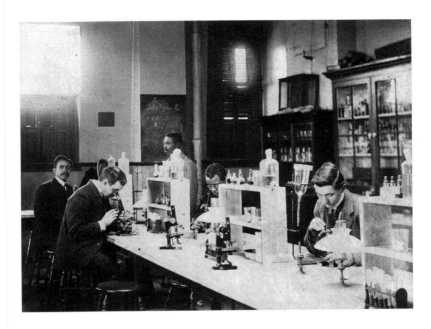

Figure 8. "Howard University, Washington, D.C., ca. 1900—class in bacteriology laboratory," W. E. B. Du Bois, African American Photographs Assembled for 1900 Paris Exhibition, Prints and Photographs Division, Library of Congress.

The "Georgia Negro Exhibit" thus suggests ways in which being the traditional object of photographic and clinical forms of vision might be aligned with double consciousness and the difficult "gift" of second sight. A photograph from Howard University (fig. 8), for example, depicts a group of African American scientists, one of whom looks directly at the camera while the others are absorbed by the scene concealed beneath their microscopic lenses. The microscopic lens through which the scientists look inevitably conjures the photographic lens through which viewers look, drawing attention to "the thoroughgoing permeation of reality with mechanical equipment," to cite Benjamin's terms.[39] The image makes the photographic lens "visible," referring to the role of authorship through the implied presence of the African American photographer who frames the scene.[40] More complicated than just depicting the black viewer who takes up the technical instruments of a normatively white culture, or who returns the white gaze, is the way the photograph challenges such binaristic categorization altogether, asking viewers to look at African American viewers who use instruments privileged by white culture to look at something microscopically concealed. The image defines a series of blind spots for white viewers and gestures toward a penetrative form of viewership that is not binaristic but through which "life" resolves into granular components.

The second section of *Cane,* set in the North, similarly makes visible the photographic lens that is so thoroughly permeated with seemingly "natural" forms of vision as to be invisible.[41] Unlike the anesthetized bodies in the South, somnolent objects awaiting visual penetration, the bodies in the North break away from photographic models, often taking fantastic forms. The second section thus reverses the model of the "interior gaze": rather than penetrating the inert surface of the body in order to discover the remote mythological truths residing within, this section turns the body inside out, describing models of vision and knowledge that emerge from the body itself.

"Seventh Street," the prose poem that opens the second section, for example, is set in Washington, D.C., one of the cities in which the racial violence of the "Red Summer" occurred; it thus evokes the violent spilling of African American blood, but it constructs this violence through representational modes very different than those informing the photograph of Brown's lynched body. The images of blood in "Seventh Street" represent the body through an unrestrained flow that escapes the inscribable boundary of the skin—a fluid corporeality that pulses through the prose poem and resists the familiar spectator-spectacle binaries that undergird discourses of race. While the penetrative investigation of autopsy requires the still pooling of the blood, here the dizzying circulation, "Flowing down the smooth asphalt," "Eddying on the corners," and "Swirling like a blood-red smoke," makes autoptic vision impossible, emphasizing the present-tense vitality of the body, rather than corporeality that yields to an interiorized vision of the past. "Seventh Street" also refuses to regard the spilling of blood as productive of "whiteness." Its blood currents portend violence capable of being channeled in multiple directions, both fluid for the vampiric "Blood suckers of the War" and a coagulant "wedge" that "thrust[s] unconscious rhythms" into the structure of Washington and "split[s]" open its "stale soggy wood" (53). Blood functions here through collective movement, circulating through a network of bodies and emphasizing the body itself as a network rather than a singular entity. "Seventh Street" imagines a circulatory network of bodies overlaid upon the urban circulatory systems of the North, such that we can understand the Great Migration as the interpenetration of networked systems that effects the deterritorialization of both.

In "Box Seat," for example, Dan visits Muriel at her boardinghouse in a white neighborhood, unsettling its modes of dehumanizing viewership and turning its primitivizing conceptions of African Americans back onto white culture. Anticipating the tropes of theatrical viewership with which "Box Seat" ends, Dan scripts his own street theater that translates a previously disavowed corporeality onto white authority figures, described as "mighty, juicy, meat-hook men":

> Dan: Break in. Get an ax and smash in. Smash in their faces. I'll show em. Break into an engine-house, steal a thousand horse-power fire truck. Smash in with the truck. I'll show em. Grab an ax and brain em. Cut em up. Jack the Ripper. Baboon from the zoo. And then the cops come. "No, I aint a baboon. I aint Jack the Ripper. I'm a poor man out of work. Take your hands off me, you bull-necked bears. Look into my eyes. . . . Dont laugh, you mighty, juicy, meat-hook men."

Toomer recapitulates the power relations that inform the mortification of Barlo in the South, but here, Dan rehearses a psychic defense against the immediately palpable (and tragically still familiar) dangers posed by police to young African American men in urban settings. Enacting a form of double consciousness, Dan imagines that the police see him as the inhuman "baboon from the zoo," and he attempts to defuse the violence inherent in such dehumanization by inviting the police to instead "look into my eyes." Toomer suggests that such psychic rehearsals of the status of the human and the inhuman construct Dan's interiority, but this interiority also allows for the critical distance of irony, as the passage concludes with Dan's shift to a placidly contained tone: "Some one might think he is trying to break in. He'd better knock" (77). As "Box Seat" progresses, however, Toomer dismantles the interrelated binaries by which human/inhuman and interior/exterior are constructed through one another, disrupting the penetrative gaze through which the humanist subject has traditionally defined itself.

Inside the boardinghouse, whose bourgeois respectability is fiercely guarded by Mrs. Pribby, Toomer describes a series of internecine gazes that destabilize the relation between viewer and object. Suggesting that Mrs. Pribby's position in the North is a function of fortification and watchful defense, Toomer describes her "retreat" to the rear of the house after Dan's violent entry: "There is a sharp click as she fits into her chair and draws it to the table. The click is metallic like the sound of a bolt being shot into place" (78). Commenting upon the visual technologies that construct modern living spaces, Tom Gunning argues that the living room is "not only the protective shell one fashions for oneself but also the locus of optical devices . . . that seem to open the viewer's gaze onto a different world."[42] Suturing her vision to a normative white gaze, Mrs. Pribby's ubiquitous newspapers similarly provide her a set of watchful eyes with which to gaze upon the outside world, as well as a defensive counterattack against Dan. Newspaper reading has made her eyes "weak," but despite their weakness, the "blue . . . steel" of her eyes "gimlets" Dan in the manner of a surgical instrument (77). Given these reversing interplays of defense and attack, the interior of the boardinghouse resists what Jacobs calls the "positivist fantasy" of an unraided interior. Benjamin writes that the new interior is a "box in the theater of the world,"[43] and in *Cane*'s "Box Seat" the interior similarly gazes upon, and even contains, the exterior.

The carefully choreographed scene between Dan and Muriel, which borders on both dance and pugilism, and which presages the actual theatrical performance later in the story, similarly resists penetrative viewing. Mrs. Pribby attempts to disrupt Dan and Muriel's physical engagement, using her newspaper as a kind of weapon: "A sharp rap on the newspaper in the rear room cuts between them. The rap is like cool thick glass between them. Dan is hot on one side. Muriel, hot on the other. They straighten. Gaze fearfully at one another" (82). The documentary mode of the newspaper here materializes as optical device, as the "cool thick glass" of her rap evokes the disembodied lens of photojournalism. The "sharp" rap "cuts" between Dan and Muriel, recalling Benjamin's image of the camera lens as a surgical device, but here, the lens fails to divide disembodied subject from bodily other. The "cool" detachment of the lens only contrasts with the reciprocity of their gazes and the equanimity of the bodily "heat" from which these gazes emanate. Earlier in the scene, Dan's violent entry similarly evokes the image of a lens, as the "raw bone" of his knuckles threatens to break the "thick glass door" of the boardinghouse (77). In keeping with Benjamin's metaphor, Dan's entry uncannily suggests the "raw bone" of the surgically splayed body rapping back on the photographic lens. But although his physical force "rattles" the glass, "Box Seat" does not simply substitute the life of the body for that of the disembodied mind. Even as Dan's perceptions of Muriel suggest a corporeality that borders upon animality, what Dan terms the "crude absurdity" of physical desire coexists with his philosophically elegant advice: "Life bends joy and pain, beauty and ugliness, in such a way that no one may isolate them. . . . Perfect joy, or perfect pain, with no contrasting element to define them, would mean a monotony of consciousness, would mean death" (82, 81).

Exploiting the differences between live theater and film, the theatrical scene that concludes "Box Seat" further disrupts the demarcated spaces of the spectator and spectacle. The story presents the position of the spectator through overtly corporeal imagery: Dan "shrivels close beside a portly Negress whose huge rolls of flesh meet about the bones of seat-arms" (85). Rather than reinforcing the disembodiment of the viewer, theatrical viewership has been relocated within the body—the physical space of the theatre is imagined as an artificial skeleton over which the flesh is draped. Muriel is positioned midway between audience and stage so that when she turns toward her friend, "the audience is square upon her" (84). In this way, Muriel is as much the performative focal point of the audience's gaze as she is the spectator of a circumscribed performance. Discussing "Box Seat," Susan Edmunds argues that the performative self-consciousness of the black audience suggests mimicry of middle-class white culture, particularly since theaters were historically white venues that initially only allowed African Americans limited access as audience members. This trope of mimicry erodes, however, as the space between audience and stage collapses so that the dwarves boxing onstage and the audience are united in a common bodily action: "[The dwarfs] pound each other furiously. Muriel pounds. The house pounds. Cut lips. Bloody noses" (88). The anonymous "lips" and "noses" imply a bodily confusion, suggesting that the onstage wounds might be transferred onto the audience. The "dwarfs" have "foreheads bulging like boxing gloves," but their "wrists are necks for the tight-faced gloves" (87). While the somnolent, anesthetized faces of the South are depicted through lingering close-ups, the glove-like heads and head-like gloves in this live performance offer a pugilistic defense against a penetrative gaze. Deviating from the smooth completion of the filmic close-up, Muriel's own face suggests a teeming corporeality, operating through the independence and particularity of its parts: "Muriel's mouth works in and out. Her eyes flash and waggle. . . . Her face . . . is hot and blue and moist" (82). With its mobile mouth and its strangely "waggling" eyes, Muriel's face is more akin to the Bakhtinian grotesque body, defined by animated offshoots and protuberances, than to the catatonic faces in *Cane*'s first section.[44] As though to further ward off or destabilize a penetrative gaze, the fight scene unexpectedly transforms into a musical performance as the champion serenades Muriel. He offers her a white rose whose petals are stained from his still-bleeding nose, and he holds a mirror, positioning it so that it "flashes in the face of each one he sings to," mirroring the gaze of the audience back upon itself (89). Through its reversals of the categories of the performative and the spectatorial, "Box Seat" suggests not just mimicry of white culture but a reconfiguration of the modes of viewership through which white culture has defined itself.

The staging of the body in "Theater" seeks to relocate spectatorship entirely within the body. As John initially watches Dorris dance, the pair simultaneously rehearse the social differences that act as barriers to their relationship. John reflects that she is "Dictie, educated, stuck-up," and Dorris, even as she is supposedly absorbed in her performance, thinks, "Aint I as good as him? Couldnt I have got an education if I'd wanted one?" (69). The distance of specularity is then overcome, so that Dorris and John are united in an uncertain corporeal space: "They are in a room. John knows nothing of it. Only, that the flesh and blood of Dorris are its walls." Here, John reflects, "Dorris, who has no eyes, has eyes to understand him." "Theater" suggests a chiasmus such that it is not the theater that houses or contains the body; the body itself becomes anoptic theater, a corporotopia that eludes the earlier spectatorial definitions of race and bodily form in *Cane*. The story imagines not just a light source trained on a body but vision illuminated through flesh—the theater lights in John's fantasy are "soft, as if they shine through clear pink fingers." Although the fantasy of this embodied vision is not available to the characters—the story concludes in their separation as Dorris finds John's face "dead"—the fantasy of corporeal vision is a significant construction of a new kind of "interior gaze" (72). John is not just visually penetrating an inert body in the mode of an autopsy; his fantasy suggests a gaze that originates within the "flesh and blood" walls of the body. Here, the corpse looks back.

While *Cane* exposes the technological apparati that have constructed the body, it does not, however, merely revert to a naturalized understanding of the body. *Cane* imagines the body in technological assemblages that are not just the camera-eye assemblage that Benjamin describes but a more thoroughly imbricated relationship. "Her Lips Are Copper Wire," for example, offers a direct response to "Portrait in Georgia." The title announces the mode of the blazon, but rather than fixing a penetrating gaze upon inert bodily fragments, the poem describes the concurrence of technical media with an atmospheric circulation of the body. The female figure evoked in the title is not just a body constructed or instrumentalized by technology; the copper wire of technical media materializes through her speech, and her words obtain through the technological infrastructure of the city:

> whisper of yellow globes
> gleaming on lamp-posts that sway
> like bootleg licker drinkers in the fog
>
> and let your breath be moist against me
> like bright beads on yellow globes
>
> telephone the power-house
> that the main wires are insulate
>
> (her words play softly up and down
> dewy corridors of billboards)
>
> then with your tongue remove the tape
> and press your lips to mine
> till they are incandescent (73)

Opening the lips' muted seal, the final stanza suggests a resignifying repair of the "old scars . . . first red blisters" in "Portrait in Georgia." The regenerative bodily contact of the kiss contrasts with the imperiled viewership of "Portrait," in which desire bears the threat of death and the speaker's body is returned to him in fragments. The final image of incandescence concludes the poem with a flare of light that would blind the anatomizing gaze of the autopsy. While the techniques and apparati of film and photography inform depictions of the body in the first section of *Cane*, even if photography is not explicitly mentioned, "Her Lips Are Copper Wire" explicitly references technologies of communication precisely because this electrically charged reconfiguration of the body is such a marked departure from the text's visual modes. Rather than capturing, freezing, or incising the body, technology here endows the body with mobility and ubiquity.

"As a Completely Artificial Man Would"

Cane's movements from South to North only to return South again in "Kabnis" raise several questions about how to read its representations of vision and bodily form. First, while the section set in the North figuratively vivifies the corpses of the South, it would be simplistic to imagine that a move northward, while potentially improving social conditions for African Americans, escapes the ideological constructions of bodily form that Toomer describes in the first section. Second, if the corpse, as I have suggested, "looks back" in the second section of *Cane*, rather than being the passive object of various ideological gazes, what kind of body is it that looks? The second section's attempts to invest the body with vision often take fantastic or grotesque forms—faces like boxing gloves, eyeless bodies, and corpses that gaze. I would suggest that this resignifying repair performed by the second section is more interested in making visible the covert visual techniques of the first section than in describing "livable" bodies. In some sense, we only "see" the camera eye as it falters in this second section, materializing in the discordant image of the body rapping against the cool thick lens. Third, while the second section offers a powerful corrective to the deadening ethnographizing gazes described in the South, it paradoxically does so by composing a collection of bodies and personae that must be categorized according to similarity and difference: Fern, Karintha, Barlo, and Esther in South; Dan and Muriel, John and Dorris in the North—they come to us as recurring "types" rather than distinct characters. How does *Cane* avoid re-creating the distanced gaze necessitated by the anthropological archive and its collection of specimens and "types"?

Cane's final section, "Kabnis," turns away from a totalizing gaze, frustrating the tendency to compose the text into a linear form. It rejects the model of autoptic, filmic vision, both as a formal strategy and a characterological practice, describing a character who attempts to see the body not with his "own" naturalized eyes, but with a gaze that actively interrogates its own technological and ideological construction. While the second section offers *images* of embodied vision that often take fantastic form, "Kabnis" describes the sustained development of a single character whose embodied experience is painfully sutured and unsutured from normative white gazes. Returning to the South, *Cane* also asks the reader not only to "see" the South again but also to "see" the South as an embodied, *felt* experience, disrupting its prior logics of vision and disavowed forms of bodily experience.

Like the narrator of "Fern," Kabnis is an African American from the North who is visiting the South, but he is not just performing a kind of anthropological study of its characters; an aspiring writer, Kabnis initially seeks to become the expressive "face of the South," perhaps bypassing a traumatic American history of the body altogether.[45] He reflects, "my songs would be the lips of its soul," suggesting that the "soul" of the South might be seamlessly, incorporeally expressed through writing. Unlike the narrator of "Fern," however, who translates Fern's corporeality and the South's history of lynching into metaphysical "vision," Kabnis quickly recognizes that bodily experience is not so easily elided. The opening of "Kabnis" abruptly shifts from Kabnis's romantic yearning, expressed through images of the face, to his unexpectedly violent decapitation of a chicken, which leaves only the "hopping body, warm, sticky." After this figurative descent into the body, Kabnis physically drops to his knees, abandoning his vision of the South's "radiant beauty" for a more careful observation of "Hog pens and chicken yards. Dirty red mud. . . . Lynchers and business men." When Kabnis rises, he does so in a new bodily form: "He totters as a man would who for the first time uses artificial limbs. As a completely artificial man would" (114). The passage describes a progression such that Kabnis is first only "using artificial limbs" but then is entirely remade, a "completely artificial man."

The notion of the "completely artificial man" makes overt, amid the rural setting of the South, the technologies of vision that take the body as their focal point in the early twentieth century. After rising in his "completely artificial" form, Kabnis moves into the interior of Fred Halsey's home and self-consciously reflects upon the collection of family portraits displayed upon the wall. The portraits trace Fred's family back to an English great-grandfather and a multiracial great-grandmother, but they impose upon all the family members—both multiracial and white, contemporary and ancestral—the same visual codes of European portraiture that originate with the great-grandfather. *Cane* demonstrates the mystification of Fred's identification with such visual modes when Kabnis turns his attention away from the portraits and toward Fred himself. When Fred and Layman enter the living room, they immediately mention the violence that enforces the fiction of binaristic racial difference. Kabnis objects that "they wouldn't touch a gentleman—fellows, men like us three here," invoking an imagined identification with the "English gentleman" depicted in Fred's ancestral portraits, but Layman corrects him:

"Nigger's a nigger down this away, Professor. An only two dividins: good an bad. An even they aint permanent categories. They sometimes mixes um up when it comes t lynchin" (120). Layman then recounts the lynching of a pregnant Mame Lamkins, an atrocity that involves the double murder of both Mame and her unborn child: "She was in th family-way, Mame Lamkins was. They killed her in th street, an some white man seein th risin in her stomach as she lay there soppy in her blood like any cow, took an ripped her belly open, an th kid fell out. It was living; but a nigger baby aint supposed t live. So he jabbed his knife in it an stuck it t a tree. An then they all went away" (124). The lynching of Mame Lamkins retells the historical lynching of Mary Turner in Valdosta, Georgia, in 1918. Mary Turner's lynching, like that of William Brown, emphasizes an excess of death, the need not only to kill but to kill redundantly the person who has already been deprived life. Mary Turner was hung upside down by her bound ankles, doused with gasoline and set on fire, and then slit open with a knife. After her eight-month-old child was killed, her body was then riddled with bullets. In both Mary Turner's lynching and Toomer's representation of it through Mame Lamkins, lynching accomplishes not only double murder but the symbolic extinction of the African American body's ability to either house or produce "life." Layman explicitly conveys that African Americans are disqualified from the category of the living when he says "a nigger baby aint supposed t live."

Immediately after Layman relates the story of lynching, a rock bearing a threatening message to Kabnis "crashes through the window" of Fred's living room, shattering the visual techniques and framing devices through which Fred claimed family identification with the perceived "humanity" of white culture. Through this rupture, Kabnis actively unsutures his gaze from such constructions of vision, uncovering the encrypted racial violence that has traditionally been disavowed or visually projected onto the other. The terrifying violence of Mame Lamkin's lynching is immediately transposed onto Kabnis, admitted into his phenomenological experience, as his bodily form seems to replicate her pregnant condition: "Fear flows inside him. It fills him up. He bloats" (124). Kabnis then appears in the next scene in a disjointed bodily form that reiterates the notion of the "completely artificial" man: "A splotchy figure drives forward along the cane- and corn-stalk hemmed-in road. A scarecrow replica of Kabnis, awkwardly animate. Fantastically plastered with red Georgia mud" (125). In this "scarecrow replica of Kabnis," Toomer describes a "replication" process whereby Kabnis is no longer a singular subject but an embodied collective. Just as Kabnis embodies the violence done to the fictional Mame Lamkins and the historical Mary Turner, this "replica" figure, "fantastically" stained with blood-red Georgia mud, embodies a larger history of violence. Rather than "encrypting" that violence within disavowed, inert forms of corporeality, however, this replicated figure "animates" that violence and thus "reanimates" it into the possibility of new life. As this composite body "drives" along the road lined with cane, Toomer also invites us to consider the titular significance of *Cane* and the history of morbid ecologies whereby African American blood, labor, and life are lost in order to raise "cane," a product that is "refined" and "whitened" into the form of sugar, consumed and taken into the body as a luxury good. Toomer reverses the trajectory of this ecology, reanimating the collective history of disavowed bloodshed into a posthuman bodily "replica" of Kabnis, who is "half numb with the immediate threat" of violence but also "half defiant," implying a difficult form of collective, *impersonal* "agency" in constructing bodily form.

"Kabnis" also reconstructs the visual fields in which this collective, artificial body exists, calling for forms of vision that would "see" the human embedded within larger ecological and social networks rather as an autonomous image. Toomer describes uncertainly dislocated and "felt" forms of vision so that seeing resolves into bodily sensation: "He sees himself yanked beneath that tower. He sees white minds" (115); "After me. On me. All along the road I saw their eyes flaring from the cane" (125). Kabnis occupies the impossible position of seeing his own corpse "yanked beneath that tower," seeing the threat to his personhood that has previously been invisible, but like the "unusual points of vantage" Du Bois describes, he also transparently sees "in and through" the environment in order to "see white minds." Describing "eyes flaring from the cane," Toomer dislocates the white gaze from any individual viewer and relocates it within the ecological environment, discovering the ideologically constructed gazes that are so seamlessly permeated with "reality" as to be invisible. Uncovering these ideological gazes, *Cane* disrupts the literary representational practices that, in Peter Brooks's terms, "insistently make the visual the master relation to the world."[46] The separations among character, reader, and environment falter, inviting the reader to position herself not as someone with visual "mastery" but as a participant in the construction of a "completely artificial" human—and all its attendant possibilities.

If autopsy is a retrospective act, an "exercise in reverse problem-solving,"

Cane invites a more complex form of retrospection that is not oriented toward "problem-solving." In its progression from South to North to South, *Cane* asks us to look back, to question how its fragmentary tales and poems cohere as a unified body and to examine the patterns that exist among its various characters. At the same time, the radically different representation of the South in "Kabnis" undercuts the first section, making phantasmic any narrative of bodily coherence we might be tempted to construct. Kabnis's abandoned authorship also contributes to this undercutting, such that the previous sections acquire a spectral quality, things that Kabnis might have written in a different context. Toomer himself, however, claimed that *Cane* could be organized in ways such that it does not conclude with "Kabnis," writing that "from the point of view of the spiritual entity behind the work," the text concludes in the North.[47] How might we graph the circling returns, nodal leaps, or lines of flight through which *Cane* concludes in the North? And what might it mean for there to be a "spiritual entity"—neither human nor shade—behind the work?

Both *Cane* and Du Bois's "Georgia Negro Exhibit" take a distanced view of African American "life" that includes modes of visual representation not attached to the visual representation of persons. Such visualizations of "life," gesturing toward an unknown potentiality, are *post*human in the sense that they escape the human/nonhuman binaries that have traditionally produced the white human subject. Du Bois's "Georgia Negro Exhibit" depicts forms of "life" not only through the singularity and visual legibility of the human figure but also through forms of data visualization that demand different kinds of visual interpretation. Du Bois claimed that such statistical representations of life were meant to be transparently legible: "At a glance one can see the successive steps by which the 220,000 Negroes of 1750 had increased to 7,500,000 in 1890; their distribution throughout the different States; a comparison of the size of the Negro population with European countries bringing out the striking fact that there are nearly half as many Negroes in the United States as Spaniards in Spain."[48] Meticulously hand-drawn and hand-lettered, however, these data visualizations bear a corporeal imprint in excess of what can be taken in "at a glance," depicting the body through the trace of the living hand, rather than the image. The charts and graphs also entail a surplus signification in excess of the data they represent. The "City and Rural Population" graph (fig. 9), for example, tracks a movement from rural to urban areas, but the enigmatic sign, combining a spiral and a

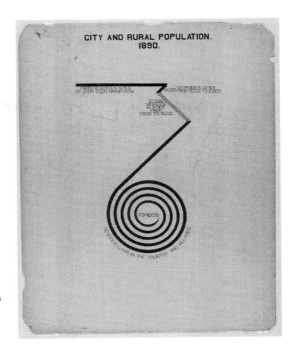

Figure 9. "City and rural population, 1890," W. E. B. Du Bois, African American Photographs Assembled for 1900 Paris Exhibition, Prints and Photographs Division, Library of Congress.

jagged line, vibrates with its own semiotics. The spiral designating rural populations captures the eye, perhaps suggesting the increasing insularity of rural life in Georgia, or a recursively circling dialectical passage outward toward urban or northern spaces. The line designating urban life ends abruptly at the left-hand margin of the page, the place where reading typically begins. The sign is laden with excess signification, *almost* like a musical clef uncoiling to trace a fugitive line that moves outward onto an unmarked plane, probing a nonvisual sonic space, *almost* like an ampersand refusing to enfold upon itself, refusing to become simply an additive "and others" attached to the recognizably human social forms that already exist.

The graphic arcing lines that introduce each of the three sections of *Cane* similarly entail surplus forms of signification, both marking the page and defining aporias that resist any linear model of "progress" or construction of the text into fixed signifying patterns. If *Cane* is motivated by what Toomer terms a "spiritual entity," we only access its promise by remaining with the surface of the text, by regarding its fragmentary pieces as implicated in a reconfiguration of the past and future of the human, rather than gesturing toward a lost store of mythic truths residing within the culturally etherized other. Toomer's experimental modernist form is thus distinct from other modernisms, such as Eliot's, whose distanced treatment of the etherized body in "Prufrock" manages to discover the mermaid singing within the corpse. *Cane* departs from an autoptic strain of modernism, which paradoxically uses fragmentary form as the basis for metaphysical vision—and, indeed, it resists the "autopsy" that my own reading has performed. Encouraging multiple constructions, *Cane* remains startlingly alive.

∃ SUTURES AND GROOVES

*Mina Loy, Baroness Elsa, and the Corpus
of Early-Twentieth-Century Media*

Have a gramophone in every grave or keep it in the house. After
dinner on a Sunday. Put on poor old greatgrandfather. Kraahraark!
Hellohellohello amawfullyglad kraark awfullygladaseeragain hellohello
amarawf kopthsth.
JAMES JOYCE, *ULYSSES*

There's nothing to fear. Look. No blood, no decay. Just a few stitches.
FRANKENSTEIN (1931)

ON DECEMBER 12, 1901, AT 12:30 P.M., Guglielmo Marconi claimed to
have received the first transatlantic radio signal. Sent from Cornwall,
England, and received in St. John's, Newfoundland, the transmission con-
sisted of the three audible clicks designating the letter "S" in Morse Code:

$$\bullet \quad \bullet \quad \bullet$$

Transmitted without reliance upon undersea telegraph cables, the signal
marked an important moment in the development of wireless technology. The signal also seems to escape the embodied nature of enunciation,
as the phonetic properties of "S," the sibilant hissings onomatopoetically
embedded in the letter, are first reduced to the on/off binary switch of
the dot and the dash, then translated into the radio wave patterns that
invisibly, sinuously cross the Atlantic. Even Marconi's choice of a transmission time—midway through the twelfth hour of the twelfth day of the
twelfth month—signals an interest in the sparseness of code rather than
the linguistic conventions that typically record historical events. And
while the "S" was chosen for its telegraphic simplicity, as the three dots

allowed for the reduction of noise in favor of signal, the punctuated clicks also seem, cannily, to take the form of an ellipsis, an incomplete trailing off acknowledging that this first message will be followed by many other disembodied sounds, voices, and images that cross oceans, reanimations of bodily and sensory forms that are no longer present or, in some cases, literally dead.

An inaugural event at the beginning of the twentieth century, Marconi's wireless transmission might be regarded as an important part of the story of how, to cite N. Katherine Hayles, *"information lost its body"* in the twentieth century, as technology seemingly enables the separation of information and matter.[1] According to a transhumanist view, such separation culminates in the eventual transcendence of bodily form altogether. Hans Moravec, for example, predicts that the body and the senses will become obsolete as technologically enhanced prosthetic senses, cognitive-technological interfaces, and virtual forms of sensory experience gain ascendency.[2] Enabling sounds and voices to be broadcast from one shore and received almost immediately on another, Marconi's transmission offers such prosthetic sensory extension and accelerates information so that it overcomes the limits posed by material distances, seeming to uphold Moravec's claim that "beings will cease to be defined by their physical geographic boundaries."[3] In Moravec's view, once information is technologically freed from the restraints of materiality, "technical evolution will go into overdrive" and intelligent machines will overtake the cognitive processes of humans, who either "becom(e) robots themselves . . . or retire into obscurity."[4] These intelligent machines, according to Moravec, will then undergo their own processes of dematerialization, rearranging "space time and energy into forms best for computation"; such "coarse physical transformation" will then be "overtaken by a faster wave of cyberspace conversion, the whole becoming finally a bubble of Mind expanding at near light speed."[5]

This chapter seeks to counter this transhumanist narrative about technology and disembodiment. While Moravec trains his eye on a remote future, his "visions" of transhuman disembodiment represent an extension of the humanist gazes I discussed in the first two chapters, whereby the disavowed body is viewed, in Foucault's terms, "from the height of death." Moravec's transhuman "bubble of Mind" similarly establishes itself in the wake of bodily matter, which is regarded as "mere jelly." Rather than positioning wireless telegraphy as a seminal event in a narrative of linear evolution and technological postevolution toward Moravec's emptied "bubble of Mind," my discussion offers a nonlinear narrative about the mutational interactions between bodily materiality and an array of early-twentieth-century technical media, which, far from spiriting information out of the body, provide new understandings of language, semiotics, and code as embodied phenomena. I examine literary, artistic, and cultural texts that understand technical media not through its disembodied reproduction of that which is absent or dead but rather through its engagement with the materiality of the corpse—and, more specifically, the human skull.

The skull signifies the human in perhaps its most *telegraphic* form: a white expanse, three distributed cavities, and a grinning line of teeth—a Morse code of the human form. For early-twentieth-century artists, however, the skull often functions not as a semaphore or an emblem of mortal limits but as a site of assemblage with technical media, which provides new access to the encoded materiality of the body. But even Marconi's wireless signal was not without new forms of embodiment and sensory engagement. Although the 1901 transmission has performative power as the first transatlantic wireless signal, there were contemporary disputes about whether Marconi "misled himself and the world into believing that electrostatic atmospheric noise crackling was in fact the Morse code letter 'S.'"[6] Marconi's own version of the 1901 transmission foregrounds the need for acute listening to separate signal from noise, and if the familiar sibilant hissings of the "S" were silenced they were replaced by a technologically produced soundscape that included atmospheric crackling as one of its new textures. If the skull, for modernists, is a site of material assemblage with technical media rather than a disembodied semaphore, how might the skull, too, produce new sensory affects, new material sutures and sensory grooves?

In both the alphabetic form of the "S" and the coded form of the three Morse dots, Marconi's inaugurative transatlantic transmission also signifies the possibilities of the multiple, as wireless technology crosses geographic boundaries, multiplying and translating nonlocal sounds into new territories. While the first two chapters focused on Faulkner's Mississippi, Toomer's depiction of movements between the North and South, and Du Bois's publication of "Negro Life in Georgia" for an international audience, this chapter pursues an American modernism responsive to transatlantic currents, focusing on modernists whose artistic identities were characterized by geographic mobility: Mina Loy (née Mina Gertrude Lowy), the British-born poet and visual artist dubbed the epitomic "modern woman" upon her arrival in New York; Boris Karloff (né William Henry Pratt), the British-born actor whose performance in Hollywood's *Frankenstein* (1931) gave us perhaps the most iconic posthuman figure of the twentieth century; Man Ray (né Emmanuel Radnitzky), the American-born photographer whose work in Paris explored new human-machine intersections; and Baroness Elsa von Freytag-Loringhoven (née Else Hildegard Plötz), the German-born artist whose poetry and improvised street performances in New York were an influential force in American futurism and dadaism. Contributing to an American modernism open to nonlocal transmissions, their work often deployed technical media to produce sounds and images interpretable without reference to specific linguistic traditions. Disrupting geographic boundaries, such artistic engagements with technical media neverthe-less compel a reengagement between the senses and material phenom-ena rather than suggesting disembodiment or sensory obsolescence.

My discussion thus begins not in the United States but in Europe, stitching an unlikely connection in the otherwise divergent early careers of Mina Loy, the modernist, and Rainer Maria Rilke, the romanticist. Rilke and Loy both studied anatomy for artists at L'École des Beaux-Arts in Paris at nearly the same time—Rilke at the end of 1902 and Loy in 1903.[7] In these artistic anatomy classes, Rilke and Loy both had early encounters with the corpse, which was used to demonstrate the artic-ulation of the human form. And both artists wrote narrative accounts of their impressions: Rilke speculated about the former identity of the corpse before it unwittingly became an artist's model, and Loy, initially mistaking the corpse for a wax model, described its uncannily lifelike pose—"hung from an iron hook fixed in its cranium to a seated posture on a rickety chair."[8] For both Rilke and Loy, however, the corpse provides the occasion to speculate not only about human mortality and anatomy but also—and more surprisingly—about technical media and its atten-dant reformulation of the human.

Rilke's 1919 essay "Primal Sound," which provides the basis for Friedrich A. Kittler's influential discussion of sound recording, recounts a childhood school exercise in which he constructed a phonograph from everyday objects; the essay then skips ahead fifteen years to his anatomy studies at L'École des Beaux-Arts, describing his perplexed fascination with the human skull, a fascination that "reached such a pitch finally, that I procured a skull in order to spend many hours of the night with it."[9] After many such nights Rilke realizes, in an epiphanic moment, that the coronal suture in particular fascinates him because it bears a striking resemblance to "one of those unforgotten grooves" of the homemade wax cylinder. Rilke then fantastically imagines using the phonograph needle to "play" the coronal suture, liberating from within the human skull a previously unheard range of "sounds, music, [and] feelings."[10] In a remarkable affinity with Rilke, Loy's essay "Incident" also locates the skull's coronal suture as the site of critical engagement with technical media. "Incident" recounts a surreal episode in which she "all at once . . . actually became a corpse."[11] Narrating from the impossible position of death, Loy describes her coronal suture reopening in order to admit a phenomenologically electrified, "reanimated" bodily form (38). "Primal Sound" and "Incident" both claim a posthuman positionality whereby the prosthetic extension of the senses enables radical forms of auto-examination—an "auto-autopsy" that bypasses the evaluative apparatus of the Enlightenment subject, directly accessing the previously buried acoustic life of the body or allowing sensation of technological "reanimation."

While Rilke regards his obsession with "playing" the coronal suture as an occult preoccupation, and Loy relegates her narrative to the category of an idiosyncratic "incident," this chapter tracks an uncanny line of associations between the coronal suture and technical media across a range of modernist texts. Like Loy's "reanimated" corpse, the creature in James Whales's *Frankenstein* is also a dead body reanimated into new life through technology. The stitched seams and scars of his skull exteriorize and redraw the lines of the cranial suture, tracing a posthuman form that is no longer biologically inherent but dependent upon external technological forces. The creature's seams and scars also invoke the formal cuts and sutures that constitute film itself, describing both the fragmented, recombinant body on the screen and the perceptual processes of the filmic viewer who interfaces with technology. More etherealized than the iconic skull-face of *Frankenstein,* Man Ray's "rayographs" produce images of distorted human skulls by suturing together everyday objects. Depicting the human and the nonhuman as embedded within one another, "hauntologically" uncertain images of the skull emerge as the objects are exposed to the transformative action of light and chemically treated paper. In each of these texts, sutures and grooves define new interfaces among the body, nonhuman matter, and technical media, as the skull is reimagined as a surface richly encoded with information, a malleable substance that can be opened and closed, an exoteric form sutured to technical media, or an image produced through mutational chemical reaction. The skull also serves as a site to reconceptualize literary and artistic production. Rather than housing the mind whose imagination, memory, and creativity are "expressed" through the work of art, the skull signifies a mode of posthuman artistic production that emerges from the material assemblages of the body and technical media and that intersects with more widespread modernist practices, such as collage techniques, which sutured together objects in unexpected, sometimes jarring combinations.

Such assemblages between the skull and technical media resist the technologically enhanced "autoptic" gaze I discuss in *Cane*: reopening the cranial suture, treating it as a sound source, and blurring its contours, the texts I examine position the skull as an unruly object for the autoptic gaze and its attendant tradition of epistemological mastery. But this chapter also explores something like an *acoustic autopsy* which similarly deploys technology to penetrate the surface of matter, accessing the previously unheard sounds of the body and matter in order to exercise new forms of hierarchical humanism. Rilke's fantasy about playing the skull's groove performs such an acoustic penetration, but it is also more generally aligned with the goals of dadaist sound poets and futurist noise artists, who similarly aspired to bypass the limits of language in order to access the sound embedded within materiality or to "speak" in ways that were consonant with new technological noise. Discussing the onomatopoetic emphasis in his sound poetry, for example, F. T. Marinetti argues that futurism's "growing love for material things" is compelled by "the will to penetrate them and recognize their vibrations," conceiving matter as the passive substance to be manipulated by a disembodied "will."[12] This chapter thus analyzes forms of "primal sound" that are not an augur of the posthuman but only a familiar humanist expression. Loy's work in particular critiques technological recordings of the voice that amplify an already culturally dominant masculinist voice rather than exploring the human-nonhuman assemblages made possible by technical media. In this way, I am not simply positioning sound and sound technology as inherently antidotal to autoptic forms of vision. If Toomer's turn to sound technology in "Her Lips Are Copper Wire," for example, represents a strategic rejection of the visual technologies that construct race in *Cane*, it is not because sound itself is redemptive but because Toomer understands sound technology as a reciprocal force that reconfigures the human and the nonhuman as well as "the speaker's" sensory and affective experiences.

Emphasizing technical media as a form of embodiment rather than a bloodless escape from materiality, the chapter concludes by considering Baroness von Freytag-Loringhoven's street performances and sound poetry as a living enactment of the posthuman sutures and grooves between the human and the nonhuman. Walking the streets with her head shaved and painted blood-red, or with technological objects such as an airplane propeller affixed to her skull, the Baroness provided with her body a living testament to the ways in which early-twentieth-century technological "evolution" was embedded in the often regressive and destructive contexts of the recent war. The Baroness's sound poetry also transformed the body itself into a sonic medium that broadcast the "primal sound" of war and hierarchical domination, suggesting that technologies such as Marconi's wireless telegraphy are not simply part of an euphoric evolution toward disembodiment but are instead involved in the production of emphatically material corpses.

Primal Sound

Rilke's imaginary placement of the phonograph stylus in the coronal suture creates an assemblage that exemplifies the unity between vitalism and mechanism. Grafting together the instruments of technical media and the organic material of the skull allows access to the acoustic data encoded within the body, as the ridges of an ossified groove are translated into sound. "Primal Sound" also emphasizes the organic properties of technical media itself—media as the rearrangement of natural objects rather than technological other. Rilke's fascination with the childhood phonograph experiment arises from the realization that everyday objects can be reassembled in order to make a "mysterious machine." He writes:

> Nothing more was needed than a piece of pliable cardboard bent to the shape of a funnel, on the narrower round orifice of which was stuck a piece of impermeable paper of the kind used to bottle fruit. This provided a vibrating membrane, in the middle of which we stuck a bristle from a coarse clothes brush at right angles to its surface. With these few things one part of the mysterious machine was made, receiver and reproducer were complete. It now only remained to construct the receiving cylinder, which could be moved close to the needle marking the sounds by means of a small rotating handle. I do not now remember what we made it of; there was some kind of cylinder which we covered with a thin coating of candle wax to the best of our ability.[13]

Pliable cardboard, impermeable paper, boar's bristle, and candle wax: the experimental phonograph is a product of malleable, organic materials, revealing that the "mysterious" properties of sound recording had been contained within natural objects all along and only required invention of the phonograph to show us how to assemble them in new ways.

"Primal Sound" also characterizes the playback of the recorded voice not as an alienating encounter with machinery but as the production of "infinitely soft" sound. This "soft" sound is neither human nor mechanical, but instead makes audible "a new and infinitely delicate point in the texture of reality":

> When someone spoke or sang into the funnel . . . the sound which had been ours came back to us tremblingly, haltingly from the paper funnel, uncertain, infinitely soft and hesitating and fading out altogether in places. . . . The phenomenon, on every repetition of it, remained astonishing, indeed positively staggering. We were confronting, as it were, a new and infinitely delicate point in the texture of reality, from which something far greater than ourselves, yet indescribably immature, seemed to be appealing to us as if seeking help.[14]

But what do Rilke and his classmates hear when listening to this "positively staggering" playback? What is the ontological status of this sound, which is not properly a "voice" but a "phenomenon"? And what kind of "appeal" for "help" is embedded within it? Here it is not a question of fidelity between the recorded voice and the "live" voice; the students hear a sound that is mediated "tremblingly, haltingly" through the cardboard, paper, boar's bristle, and wax—an uncertain, hybrid sound that both speaks through and gives voice to previously silent organic materials. "Far greater than ourselves, yet indescribably immature," the sound is an embryonic echo of a posthumanist future, "appealing to us as if seeking help" in order to be brought into existence. The auditory prescience of this future form nevertheless immediately reformulates their relation with materiality, introducing "a new and infinitely delicate point in the texture of reality" that ramifies outward from the boar's bristle pressed into the soft wax.

When "Primal Sound" skips ahead to Rilke's anatomical study at L'École des Beaux-Arts and his acquisition of the skull, Rilke characterizes skeletal form not through its mortality or fixity but through its vitality and malleability. He comments upon the "energy and elasticity" of the skeleton, calling the skull in particular an "ambiguous object" and "the utmost achievement . . . of which this chalky element was capable," as though its "chalkiness" contains the power of inscription. Rilke accordingly rewrites the skull into the form of a new machine, noting, "By candlelight—which is often so peculiarly alive and challenging—the coronal suture had become strikingly visible, and I knew at once what it reminded me of: one of those unforgotten grooves, which had been scratched in a little wax cylinder by the point of a bristle!"[15] Describing his subsequent obsession with using the phonograph stylus to "play" the skull, he bypasses the discursive structures that have historically produced the human, directly accessing the preverbal, and previously inaccessible, material sounds of the human. He creates a collage of human and nonhuman materials, suturing together materials that have not yet been combined, imagining the moment when the negative gap of the fissure becomes a seam encoded with information—the moment, that is, when the body becomes data.

"Primal Sound" inverts expectations about material container and spiritual contents, emphasizing not the singular mind or psyche but the impersonality and ingrained complexity of the skull's material surface. In addition to mining the audible grooves of this surface, the experiment inscribes the human in more abstract ways, complicating traditional understandings of memory, reason, and agency. Rilke regards the analogy between wax cylinder and coronal suture with "unrelenting mistrust," claiming that it is only the "most definite impression" made upon him by the phonograph that compels his obsession, as though he himself has been impressed and grooved like the soft cylinder wax.[16] Auditory metaphors pulse through the essay, suggesting that he is "played" by automated processes beyond his control. He notes the "rhythmic peculiarity of [his] imagination," emphasizing that he only acquires a skull once his fascination "reaches such a pitch" that he cannot resist it.[17] Rilke positions technical media as a communicative system connecting the human to both its own materiality and its evolutionary past. As Manuel De Landa points out, bone is the oldest material component of the human, that which "most readily crosses the threshold back into the world of rocks."[18] While the experimental phonograph makes audible an echo of the "indescribably immature" posthuman, it also enables retro-audition, listening back into this living record of both the human and matter more generally: Rilke imagines the stylus could be lifted from the coronal groove and placed upon any natural line or contour, thus playing and animating what has previously been a silent and dead world.

While Rilke "distrusts" his own imaginary experiment, the history of the gramophone, the phonograph, and other technical mediations of voice has depended upon assemblages of corpse and machine, as Kittler has discussed. Alexander and Melville Bell, for example, combined the larynx of a dead sheep with mechanical parts in order to make an early talking machine that eerily spoke the word "Mama"—an utterance perhaps appropriate for a nascent life-form. Alexander's later construction of a phonautograph (which was integral to his invention of the telephone) attached the ear of a human corpse and part of its skull to a stylus, which translated the sound vibrations of his voice into visible patterns when he shouted into the dead ear.[19] Losing his hearing later in life, Edison intuitively created an assemblage between his own skeleton and the phonograph: clamping his teeth onto the phonograph casing, he "listened" to cylinders by allowing the sound vibrations to act directly upon the bones of his skull. While Edison improvised out of necessity, his skull-audition foregrounds the way in which listening always involves the "primal" bodily materials of skull and bones and not only the socially constructed ear, pitched toward the articulation of language. Edison also articulates the phonograph's ability to reproduce, and thus to reanimate, the voices of the dead, providing a medium between living auditor and deceased speaker that extends the scope of the normative human life: "This tongueless, toothless instrument, without larynx or pharynx, dumb, voiceless matter, nevertheless utters your words, and centuries after you have crumbled to dust will repeat again and again to a generation that will never know you, every idle thought, every fond fancy, every vain word that you choose to whisper against this thin iron diaphragm."[20] Rather than advocating the disembodiment whereby the immortalized voice is "downloaded" onto the wax cylinder, Edison emphasizes the material continuum between the human and the machine so that the mutational processes of "becoming-dust" are succeeded by those of "becoming-machine," reanimating the "dumb, voiceless matter" of the phonograph.

Rilke's skull-stylus assemblage also anticipates recent experiments that use technology to access the "primal sound" of matter. In 2013, Josef Parvizi and Chris Chafe translated electroencephalogram recordings of both "normal" brain activity and epileptic seizure activity into sound recording in order to "hear" the human brain. In 2011, Bartholomäus Traubeck constructed a "record player" that translates the year rings of a tree into audible music. And in 2012, Mitchell Akiyama enacted the very experiment described in "Primal Sound," transferring the sound of the coronal suture onto a seven-inch record.[21] These different realizations of Rilke's experiment speak to an increasing sense of the unaided human sensorium's inadequacy to access the sensory data encoded within the material world.

Suggesting that the recording capabilities of technical media necessarily produce nonlinear histories, "Primal Sound" concludes by both enigmatically marking and obscuring the historical moment: "Soglio. On the day of the Assumption of the Blessed Virgin, 1919." The lapsed Catholics among us might not immediately place the date of the Assumption as August 15, only weeks following the signing of the Treaty of Versailles on June 28. Rilke's coded reference privileges the annular time of the Assumption, rather than the uncertain conclusion of the war, returning his attention to the experiment with the skull at the turn of the century, and then returning to the phonograph experiment fifteen years earlier, as though the recollection of a first encounter with media provides a way to traverse time by skipping from one groove to another, picking the stylus up from its present location and placing it down at an earlier moment. At the same time, moving forward or backward to a different track bears the echoing remains and sonic decay of what has already been heard. Encoded in the grooves of its own circular returns, "Primal Sound" suggests the impossibility of listening backward to a moment before the war amassed so many corpses—listening backward through corpses—without "hearing" an utterly transformed soundscape.

Situating his experiment with "primal sound" at the conclusion of World War I, Rilke inevitably, if surprisingly, aligns himself with dadaist sound poets and futurist noise artists whose practices are otherwise quite different from his own interest in the traditional lyric voice. The soundscape of World War I inspired futurist artists to directly "render the reality and the value of noises,"[22] as sounds produced by newly engineered machines guns, grenades, and explosive shrapnel, for example, altered modes of listening. Trench conditions also meant that war was often experienced primarily through auditory rather than visual senses; as Luigi Russolo notes: "In modern warfare, mechanical and metallic, the element of sight is almost zero. The sense, the significance, and the expressiveness of noises, however, are infinite."[23] Traditional poetic modes become inadequate, and the *"free words"* of futurist poetics are necessary to render the sounds of war, and thus the soundscape of modernity more generally. Russolo argues that the "noise" of futurist poetics, however, sought not only to convey the destruction of war but also to heal its wounds through a sonic flow not constrained by language: "Every manifestation of life is accompanied by noise. Noise is thus familiar to our ear and has the power of immediately recalling life itself. . . . Noise, arriving confused and irregular from the irregular confusion of life, is never revealed to us entirely and always holds innumerable surprises."[24] Modernist sound art thus finds its origins both in the new instruments of technology and in the "life" of a previously inaccessible dead material world.

Despite Rilke's euphoria about technologically accessing the "primal sound" of the skull, he ultimately recalls the posthuman potential of his experiment into the more traditional domain of the lyric rather than espousing the "free words" of the futurist. While the essay gives titular emphasis to "primal sound," Rilke's epiphany about the skull arrives not through sonic imagination but through visual reading of the coronal suture's line. He describes the "passing glance" that gives rise to the analogy and, making the importance of the visible line even more explicit, notes: "As will be seen, what impressed itself on my memory most deeply was not the sound from the funnel but the markings traced on the cylinder; these made a most definite impression." Rilke's emphasis on marks and traces suggests the inscriptive properties of the suture, and his obsession with the skull's "wavy line" elides into the poetic line, which is similarly encoded with all the material texture of the physical world if only the reader were able to liberate it.[25] The essay ultimately dismisses technology's ability to prosthetically extend the senses, noting that the telescope and the microscope "increase the range of the senses upward and downward" but that such isolated extensions cannot be "'experienced' in any real sense" because they fail to interpenetrate the full range of sense perception. The sensory novelty of the phonograph allows Rilke to imagine a synesthetic experience that would not just translate one sense into another but would "pass through the five gardens in one leap," thus decentering the "unique and risky center" of the human.[26] But Rilke claims such decentering as the domain of the poet rather than the posthuman. If the skull, the body, and materiality more generally can be "played" in such a way that they pass through "the five gardens" at once, such playing occurs, for Rilke, on the "supernatural plane, which is, in fact, the plane of the poem," rather than on an ontological plane where the instruments of technical media as we know them exist.[27] The technical stylus becomes, for Rilke, a figure for the work of the poet and the metaphorical connections whereby a negative fissure becomes a seam, as though the fissures of modernity could be sutured through writing. Rilke's engagement with phonography enforces writing's ability to rescript the meanings of technology, a kind of subsumption of the machine into the word; as Charles Grivel notes, "No sooner is the machine available than I rewrite it."[28]

In a remarkable synchrony with "Primal Sound," Loy's essay "Incident" also positions the cranial suture as the site of technical media's reconstruction of the human. Like Rilke, she locates the events of her essay in 1919, "just after World War I," suggesting that the twinned ruptures of war and media innovation entail a reimagination of the human. Loy describes crossing a Paris street with a friend, laughing with such enthusiasm that her skull fantastically dislocates from her spinal column and she suddenly finds herself "nowhere." Understandably anxious, Loy worries not that the separation of skull and spine implies death (her consciousness remains constant enough that she can chastise herself for losing her head) but that her consciousness has severed its relationship with the bodily form that becomes "merely an instrument with which to contact one's universe, rather than my whole, circumscribed 'self.'" Loy describes the "terror" of such a radical division between consciousness and matter: "consciousness, with, never again, anything to be conscious *of*" (36). For Loy, the body understood merely as an "instrument," rather than the material seat of consciousness, constitutes death. The "nowhere" of her disembodiment does not last long, however, as she describes the dawning of a new kind of perception: "Very gradually, very low down, on an horizon in profundity, a faint, dark light began to penetrate the nothingness; a sombre luminousness I compared to the bluish base of a steel J nib that had fascinated me in childhood" (37). Reversing the temporal trajectory of Rilke's essay, which subsumes the inscriptive power of technical media back into the earlier technology of the writer's stylus, Loy begins with the scene of writing, analogizing the dawning "dark light" with the "steel J nib," a familiar writing instrument of childhood.

In a strange limbo with cranium separated from spine, Loy intuitively reaches for the instruments of old media, as if to rewrite herself into embodiment, but she resists taking them up, trading the writing stylus for the instruments of emergent media. She notes that the "world" associated with the steel J nib "had *ceased*; the way a radio-television programme, once turned off, would no longer be conveyed to one" (37). While Rilke's return to the phonograph grooves of childhood attempts to listen back to a time before World War I—and his experiment with the skull perhaps attempts to listen, impossibly, to the lost worlds encoded within the skulls of the dead—Loy claims the impossibility of such retro-acoustics. Her postwar engagement with technical media emphasizes not the memory capabilities of the phonograph, which can repetitively replay the past, reanimating the dead with new life each time the stylus scratches new edges into the groove, but rather the live stream of radio and television, an incessant flow of sounds and images that can only be partially accessed, that is re-created with each new act of contact. Rather than the ghostly, layered (and ultimately writerly) metaphors of Rilke's essay, whereby suture is *like* groove, and memory is impressed upon *like* soft cylinder wax, each metaphorical iteration bearing the material residue of the others, Loy emphasizes the on-off action of an "annunciatory 'click'" (38).

This "annunciatory" switch signals the reanimation of the body in posthuman form: rather than mining the sensory data encoded within the coronal suture, Loy describes it reopening in order to admit an external electrical force into the body's organic structures. Separated from traditional sense organs, Loy nevertheless perceives the form of a "phosphorescent" "about-to-be-a-body" and, as its cranial suture opens, she simultaneously develops new phenomenological sensations that are radically open to technological forces:

> Suddenly, a shaft of rushing "force" with an impact-potential of incalculable tonnage descended from above upon that form. On its approach, I reflected, "The whole force of the universe! It will crush that body to infinitesimal fractions of atoms." I *knew* the form was about-to-be-a body, for although I had no organs of sense, I *saw* it out there in the dark, its contours so vaguely phosphorescent, just as I could *hear* the tornado-like thunderous onrush of, infinite force.
>
> I did not associate the body-contour, which had had no existence in my emptied universe prior to the annunciatory "click," with myself at all, as I waited, totally disinterested, for the expected collision; but as that shaft of force contacted the area on top of the cranium which at birth is open, at once ceasing to be cognisable by me, it slid easily, ethereally through the brain, down the spinal column, as lightning down a lightning rod, only, instead of running into the earth, it reanimated that body, now standing beside me not more than a yard away. (37–38)

Loy emphatically "sees" and "hears" this "about-to-be-a body" from a "totally disinterested" perspective, but these distanced perceptions lose their objectivity as Loy seems to pass bodily, phenomenologically through the reopened suture in a strange scene of posthuman birth. The "reanimated body" provides an eerie echo of *Frankenstein,* whose animation is also accomplished by "lightning down a lightning rod," and Loy emphasizes that such reanimation also involves a return from death. Loy finds herself "coming alive" again, and her companion, helpfully clearing up any doubt, notes: "All at once you actually became a corpse. It's inexplicable. There's no mistaking a corpse." But Loy describes this reanimated body not as a Frankensteinian patchwork of parts, a surface stitching together of the known, but as a body realized through rupture. Loy repeatedly emphasizes the sound of the "annunciatory 'click,'" the on-off switch that signals a leap into new form. Switched on, Loy awakens into a technologically mediated "Life," which, rather than being circumscribed to biological form, is "a sort of magnet to a sort of universal electricity" (39).

Loy's techno-phenomenology poses a marked contrast to the relative disembodiment of Rilke's essay. Despite the assemblages he creates between organic and technological materials, it is still some anonymous skull under experimentation rather than his own, and his visual examination of the skull is epistemologically consonant with the distanced position of the anatomy student at L'École des Beaux-Arts—itself an extension of the clinical "autoptic" gaze. In other words, Rilke's studied reconfiguration of the human does not involve an attendant reformulation of his own observational position. While Rilke subsumes the powers of phonography into the traditional writing stylus, Loy's reconfigured body is fitted to the tools of technical media rather than to older forms of inscription. She describes a "freezing" of her circulation, which concentrates into "a block of ice . . . neatly inserted in either elbow," as though her "reanimated" body is no longer a proper support for the authorial hand that might take up the "steel J nib" of the stylus (39). While Rilke concludes by referencing the infinite, circular time of "the day of the Assumption of the Blessed Virgin," placing his experiment with technology on a spiritual plane, Loy concludes by recounting a conversation with her child's nurse, emphasizing the embodied maternal rather than the spiritual virginal.

Enacting its own on-off switch, "Incident" ends somewhat abruptly, suspending the question of how such technologically reanimated but still specifically gendered "Life" might function, but other works by Loy critique technological enhancements of the body that exacerbate gendered forms of oppression. Her play *The Sacred Prostitute,* for example, critiques the "bad" posthumanism that grafts the sensory prostheses of technical media onto an otherwise unchanged male form. Satirizing Marinetti in the personified figure "FUTURISM," she describes the "x-ray eyes and ears of steel" that merely augment an unreconstructed masculinism whose primary aim is conquest. In this dialogue between FUTURISM and LOVE, for example, FUTURISM boasts:

> The Futurist has x-ray eyes, and ears of steel—He can see everything without looking at it, and stand any amount of noise—the evening breeze no longer reaches me, but the gentle vibrations of the *mitrailleuses* are still audible. *(loudly)* DARLING! *(gives her a thumping whack on the thigh—* LOVE. *jumps)* A-a-a-a-a a-h! You are just my type, for I have never seen anything like you before! *(very rapidly)* Will-you-love-me-will-you-love-me-will-you-love-me-love-me-love-me-love-me-me-ME—? ? ? I *must* have you—You see I have never had you before.[29]

Loy critiques the self-styled cybernetic figure whose embrace of technology seals his senses so that he "see[s] without looking" and "stand[s] any amount of noise." The female figure of "LOVE" experiences a sonic assault that permits no reply, reducing her to the self-echoing "Yes, dear" (and an occasional "Yes, dear?"). Unlike Rilke's imaginary experiment with technical media, which provides an encounter with "a new and infinitely delicate point in the texture of reality" (even if he ultimately forecloses this experiment as a somewhat unfortunate skeleton in his own closet), the futurist here experiences sensory death, reduced to a bluntly automated libido.

For Loy, the "primal sound" of much futurist sound poetry amplifies familiar forms of domination rather than allowing an unheard materiality to "speak." Closely approximating the onomatopoetic "telegraphic lyricism" of Marinetti's *Zong Toomb Toomb*, FUTURISM reads a sound poem to LOVE, but, as the title of his book, "Women I have had," suggests, such machine-inspired noise is deployed as a tool of conquest:

> Tatatata ta ta ta ta ta ta ta ta ta
> plum plam plam pluff pluff frrrrrr
> urrrrrrrrrrrrrraaaaaaaaaaaaa
> pluff plaff plaff gottgott gluglu
> craaa craaa
> cloc-cloc gluglu gluglu cloc-cloc gluglu
> scscscsc——

Do you feel that you could get into a more intimate relationship with me than you are *now*?[30]

Marinetti aspired toward, in his own terms, a "rapid, brutal, and immediate" poetics that would convey the "*taratatata* of the machine guns screaming" and the "*pluff-plaff* horse action *flic flac zing zing shaaack* laughing whinnies,"[31] but Loy critiques the futurist who projects the sound of an unreconstructed male voice, which is mistakenly imagined to resonate with the primal sound of materiality. No longer confined to the individual speaker, such sonic projection penetratively fills the world, silencing other voices, other sounds. Despite *Zong Toomb Toomb*'s claim that futurism is poetry "finally finally finally finally finally finally finally finally . . . being born," Loy suggests that its aims are, finally, oppressively familiar (and primal).[32]

Given Rilke's own claims for acoustic sensitivity, "Primal Sound" is also surprisingly dismissive of any voice other than his own. Toward its conclusion, the essay suddenly alludes to an anonymous "lady" who has served as an implicit auditor and whose interpretation Rilke is quick to correct once she shifts from auditor to speaker. When she compares the synesthetic experience of emergent media with erotic synesthesia, Rilke characterizes eroticism not as an engagement with otherness but, more strangely, as the self-reflexivity of "he [who] feels himself unexpectedly placed in the center of the circle."[33] The most acute listening in "Primal Sound" occurs not through the posthuman assemblage of stylus and skull but in the classroom, as the students hear the playback of "the sound which had been ours." Read in this way, it is hard not to regard "Primal Sound" as a somewhat euphoric description of male adolescence falling in love with the sound of its own voice. In Rilke's account, the male voice does not even have to engage with language in order to be "astonishing, indeed positively staggering" and to confer an authority that is "far greater than ourselves." While "Primal Sound" emphasizes the interpenetration of voice and machine, imagining the possibilities of a "new and infinitely delicate point in the texture of reality," it still traces a direct genealogical relation between the male voice produced in the classroom and the "primal sound" embedded in both the structure of the body and the natural world more generally.

Using "Primal Sound" as a seminal text, Kittler's *Gramophone, Film, Typewriter* reproduces Rilke's marginalization and correction of female voices, disqualifying them from sound recording's reconfiguration of "so-called Man." Female characters are afforded a limited role in Kittler's chapter on sound, "Gramophone," which develops its argument about sound recording through the following literary examples: the improper voice of Eliza Doolittle, whose dialect makeover is aided by vocal recording and playback; the audition of Anna Pomke, who eroticizes the "beautiful organ" of Goethe's voice and misses the philosophical complexity it conveys; and the "inhuman women whose hymn was wild and lustful like the scream of a crazed goddess" in Maurice Renard's "Death and the Shell"—hypersexualized voices that carry in concentrated form all the erotic potential of the female body so that simply hearing the voice becomes a form of sexual possession.[34] More generally, however, a perceived shift from alphabetic to technical media erases the need for these female figures altogether, as "literature defects . . . from red lips to white noise."[35] While Kittler ostensibly sympathizes with the marginal status of these characters (pointing out, for example, that Anna's erotic fixation on Goethe's voice is not unlike the devotion of "Nipper" the RCA dog to the voice of its master), the "voice" of his own essay replicates this disqualification, excluding from "Gramophone" any discussion of female authorship or recording artists, both in the Edison era of sound recording and in his culminating discussion of 1960s rock music.[36] In this way, the often virtuosic analytical voice of Kittler's writing is also a kind of echo, placing its stylus in Rilke's groove and replaying its commitments to a scene of male pedagogy.

While Kittler's discussion of the gramophone in literature emphasizes the correction, eroticization, and, ultimately, erasure of female voices and audition, Loy reminds us of a different literary scene: "the soggy atmosphere" of T. S. Eliot's *The Waste Land* in which the typist "fresh from the embraces of a stray acquaintance—turns on the gramophone and swallows her hairpins." Loy acknowledges that she is not quite replaying *The Waste Land* correctly. While Eliot's typist "smoothes her hair with automatic hand / And puts a record on the gramophone," an automation of the body implying that women can be played the same way that records can, Loy's typist finds the encounter much harder to swallow. Loy constructs audition as barbed critique rather than grooved automation, claiming: "The lover who was worsted by the gramophone probably had a uniform conception of either."[37] What music does *Loy's* female auditor hear when she puts a record on the gramophone?

Letters of the Unliving

Rilke and Kittler both suggest that the female ear is only able to "hear" a simple love story, but Loy's poem "Letters of the Unliving" positions female audition in very different relations to technical media. "Letters of the Unliving" is often interpreted as a lament for the lost Arthur Cravan, a nostalgic act of mourning the "dead language of amor." While Cravan might indeed be Loy's favorite track, "Letters of the Unliving" also functions, perhaps more interestingly, as an exploration of the "voices" that emerge from the living/unliving materiality of various media. "Letters of the Unliving" is "about" listening to words, voices, and sounds that have previously been recorded; but it is also "about" actively recording the experience of such listening, and thus engages in unusually layered acts of inscription (and reinscription). Kittler defines two conceptually different functions of the gramophone stylus: to record sound, translating vibration into visible grooves, and to retrace this groove in order to reproduce the original sound. While in "Incident" Loy rejects the traditional writing stylus as inadequate to write her own sensory experience with technology, in "Letters of the Unliving" she takes up a kind of second-order stylus in order to trace new marks into the still-impressionable grooves of an archival record—much as her rewriting of Eliot's typist creates an interior space in *The Waste Land* in which we might imagine an as yet unrecorded sound.

The speaker of "Letters of the Unliving" ostensibly attempts to bring new life to old love letters, referring to letters that were "left authorless . . . since the inscribing hand / lost life," but these letters are "covered with unwritten writing," which, in Kittler's terms, provides an allegorical definition for technical media inscription: "Ever since the invention of the phonograph, there has been writing without a subject."[38] Such automatic inscriptions proliferate in "Letters of the Unliving," as Loy emphasizes that which is not only "unliving" but also "unwritten," "unauthorized," and "unanswering"—but still recorded rather than simply absent. Loy also implicitly draws the analogy between written "letters" and sound recording, describing the "euphonious" past which, replayed in the present, is only a kind of "diminuendo." But in these acts of playback it is the materiality of inscription itself that sounds most powerfully, as "The hoarseness of the past / creaks / from creased leaves" and "This package of ago / creaks with the horror of echo / out of void." What "creaks" from the "creases," however, is not the human voice but a sonic assemblage that filters the human voice through an opaque nonhuman media so that it arrives trailing nonhuman echoes.

In this "unliving" sound we can hear not only acoustic decay but also the decay of media itself. Enacting a passage between the human and the nonhuman, media is endowed with its own forms of life—and its own forms of death. Kittler, in contrast, traces a distinct line between the "life" recorded by media and the dead forms it leaves in its wake. Valorizing a media revolution whereby the gramophone's powers to record sensory life supplant those of literature, Kittler claims, "Record grooves dig the grave of the author."[39] But they also dig the grave of the speaker, as the "immortal" recording inevitably circumscribes the mortal horizons of the one who speaks. The speaker dies, but the recorded voice lives on, according to Kittler, achieving a disembodied immortality. Gesturing toward a new technological pantheon, Kittler's history of sound recording culminates, on a rapturous note, with Jimi Hendrix's "And the Gods Made Love," a mediated enactment of immortality only previously dreamed of by literature.

Loy is not so interested in these gods. She, too, references an immortal—Adonis—but she rescripts this male god so that he is subject to decay (even as an allusion) rather than the infinite rebirth of replay: "The deathly handler / left no post-mortem mask — — — / only a callous earth made mouldy / your face excelling Adonis." "Letters of the Unliving" repeatedly regrooves its records or replicas of the human so that they similarly decompose: the "mask" that goes "mouldy," the "decoyed bloom" that "decay[s]," "life's imposture" that "implies no possible retrial." Rather than valorizing the transcendence of automated replay, Loy refers to the "horror of echo"; the following stanzas, for example, enact a form of sonic return whereby sounds recur with a difference, embodied through new signifiers:

Diminuendo
of life's imposture
implies no possible retrial
By my so now-while self
of my cloud-corpse
Beshadowing your shroud

the one I was with you
inhumed in chasms,

craters torn by atomic emotion
among chaos

No creator
reconstrues scar-tissue
to shine as birth-star.

Enacting a kind of "diminuendo" or sonic decay, the sound of "craters" returns in the different form of "creator," and "the one I was with you" is sonically condensed into "inhumed." Words (begin to) begin again— "imposture / implies"—but skip to unexpectedly different endings rather than enacting playback. When the poem is explicitly citational—the phrase "'As once you were,'" for example, is punctuated to indicate quotational playback of another's voice—it rearranges the replay so that "'As once you were'" becomes "the sweet once were we." Rather than emphasizing fidelity between the acoustic event and the record, "Letters of the Unliving" is replete with skips, scratches, echoes, sonic repetitions, and ambient silences, resuscitating the "unliving" status of the letter alongside other forms of technical media, vitalizing an alphabetically mediated voice from the grave to which Kittler and a host of others have consigned it.

When "Letters of the Unliving" explicitly asserts an "I," it is an "I" that is engaged with forms of nonhuman becoming rather than the "I" of a securely human position:

I am become
dumb
in answer
to your dead language of amor.

Given Loy's penchant for unusual words and the spatial emphasis she gives it, "dumb" is particularly notable here. I would suggest that we can regard "dumbness" not as the muteness of a silenced female voice, however, but the "dumbness" that has been associated with "dumb" things and "dumb beasts"—nonhuman life-forms that have their own modes of expression and answering. Just as, for Deleuze and Guattari, "the properly musical content of music is plied by becomings-woman, becomings-child, becomings-animal,"[40] "becoming-dumb" is a transformative affectivity by which the human voice enters into composition with a living environment of inhuman sounds, unintentional reverberations, decaying echoes, ambient silences—as well as the material form of media itself.

In this way, Loy's mediation of the voice has affinities with Rilke's experimental phonographic assemblage between the human and nonhuman, but Loy allows these strange assemblages to "speak" rather than recuperating them into a more familiar, and familiarly gendered, lyric voice. While the certainty of Rilke's stylus *describes* the ghostly echoes and decays that the sonic returns of "Letters of the Unliving" *enact*, Loy's poem operates not through vocal certainty but by maintaining the possibilities for aporias and the on-off "annunciatory" switch whereby the "speaker" of the poem might shift in order to register audition of the *un*spoken (but not disqualified or silent). "Letters of the Unliving" opens thus:

> The present implies presence
> thus
> unauthorized by the present[41]

"Letters of the Unliving" suggests that an opening presence, an opening *to* presence, can be performed "thus"—by halting its own voice and hearing what is "unauthorized by the present." Such openings, which are enacted in much of Loy's poetry through the incorporation of spaces and long trailing dashes, function like the cranial fissure in "Incident" whereby what was sutured and fully formed becomes undone, unwritten, and open to the new. For Loy, technical media entails a relation with materiality different from the "acoustic autopsies" enacted in Rilke's experiment with the phonograph and Marinetti's futurist poetics. While Rilke's penetrative listening is ultimately recuperated into the disembodied lyric voice and Marinetti's aspiration toward mechanical sound is motivated by the "will to penetrate" matter, Loy's own "Aphorisms on Futurism" explicitly resists anthropocentric manipulations of matter: "IN pressing the material to derive its essence, matter becomes deformed."[42] Loy's own futurism instead tunes the ear to the unheard present, allowing matter (including the matter of "unliving letters") to speak/creak from its creases in its own unfamiliar way.

It's Alive

While Loy's and Rilke's writings about the skull might be regarded as somewhat esoteric, the association between technical media and the coronal suture finds its popular culture analogue in the iconic figure of

Figure 10. Boris Karloff as the creature in *Frankenstein*, directed by James Whale (Universal Pictures, 1931).

James Whales's *Frankenstein* (fig. 10). Covered with stitched-together patches of necrotic skin, what does the seamed, reanimated skull-face of Whales's creature evoke if not the seams of the coronal suture, exteriorized and redrawn? These scars and stitches never heal, never disappear. If the coronal suture evokes that which has been sutured together as a "natural" stage of human development, the creature's stitches make visible that which will never cicatrize, signifying the human's ongoing openness to reconstruction by technical media as well as its receptivity to nonlocal forms of vision and audition.

Frankenstein's creature emblematizes the position of the early-twentieth-century subject who sutures together mediated experience from reanimated reproductions of that which is absent or dead. Appearing on the surface to be mutely inactive or corpse-like, this subject is nevertheless vivified through her interface with technical media and "needy for connection," to borrow Haraway's description of the cyborg.[43] Animated through the bolts protruding from the base of its skull—electrode terminals receptive to infusions of electrical, artificial "life"—the creature maintains a structural capacity (and arguably a need) for connection, even though those bolts serve no functional purpose in the film beyond the first scene of its creation. Aside from these electrodes, the creature is emphatically "natural" in its bodily construction. Like Rilke's phonograph made of paper, boar's bristle, and wax, the creature is a technological assemblage constructed entirely from organic materials, composed only of the dead body parts that acquire reanimation through their sutured contact with one another.[44] The creature's seams and scars thus signify technical media's reconstruction of the "organic" body, even if technology does not directly intervene into the body or rupture its apparent surface. Engagements with technical media trace new external lines of contact on the bodily surface, extending the scale of the singular human; just as Rilke claims that the phonograph amplifies the sound of something "far greater than ourselves," *Frankenstein*'s creature is, quite literally, "far greater than ourselves," towering over the human characters in the film—yet inexplicably so, given that it is composed only of human parts. Its size and characteristic guttural moans amplify the "primal sound" not only of the singular reassembled body but of the multiple bodies newly sutured and interfaced with one another through the networked capabilities of technical media. *Frankenstein*'s creature is also, in Rilke's terms, "indescribably immature," a nascent posthuman figure dazzled by rays of light in its first moments of perception, gesturing with a characteristic open-palmed gesture, "appealing to us as if seeking help," and connecting with the young girl Maria (before accidentally killing her in a moment of inexperienced misunderstanding about the operations of nature). As many critics have noted, audiences often sympathize more with the creature than with the human characters in the film, identifying with the experience of being continually reanimated into a technologically remade world.

The creature also specifically mirrors the filmic spectator-auditor's psychic position of "suturing" together the sound track and the images, which emanate from distinct sources in the theater, as well as the cuts and fissures that comprise the visual flow of the images themselves. A creation of light, shadow, cosmetics, prostheses, framing techniques, and the cinematic cut, *Frankenstein*'s creature embodies the recombinant properties of cinema and its seemingly magical powers of bestowing life. As James Heffernan notes, "film versions of *Frankenstein* implicitly remind us that filmmaking itself is a Frankensteinian exercise in artificial reproduction."[45] Scott Juengel similarly argues, "Whale's close-ups reveal a conspicuously constructed figure, the manifest stitches, seams, and folds announcing the face as assemblage, representation, narrative. . . . To gaze on Karloff is to participate in an endless visual reconstruction of the monstrous body."[46] The creature's inarticulate "primal sound" also conveys the sensory dissonance produced when sound film sutures the voice to the body for the first time. Released only a few years after 1927's *The Jazz Singer*, the first partial "talkie," *Frankenstein* addresses an audience relatively unaccustomed to hearing the onscreen body speak. Slavoj Žižek argues that the voice in film, far from "naturalizing" the onscreen body, always has an uncanny, "spectral" quality that "floats freely in a mysterious intermediate domain and thereby acquires the horrifying dimension of omnipresence and omnipotence."[47] In addition to evoking the "primal sound" of bodily matter, the creature's inarticulate moans thus amplify something excessive and "unnatural" about the voice in film, its supplementary, acousmatic quality, which never coheres with the onscreen body from which it purportedly emanates.

Frankenstein's introduction of the creature enacts a conflict between the linguistic mode of the "talkies" and the gestural language of silent film, which can be interpreted by viewers from different linguistic backgrounds. Dr. Frankenstein measures the creature's potential "humanity" by its ability to understand and respond to verbal commands (mostly "Sit down! Sit down!" as though taking a cue from dog obedience training), while the creature attempts to communicate through poignant but unreciprocated gestures, which "speak" more eloquently than Dr. Frankenstein's stunted verbal commands. In this way, the creature's "primal sound" emanates not from his vocal cords alone but from his body as a whole. Stitched together from the corpse materials of several different bodies, the creature is not a singular body but a multiplicity bearing the promise that the polyglot capabilities of multiple speakers might rematerialize in recombinant form. The European setting of the film also implies linguistic border-crossing, but the film forecloses this possibility, colonizing this setting with English dialogue. Rather than exploring the heteroglossic possibilities of technologically animated life, Dr. Frankenstein treats his creature like a grisly Eliza Doolittle whose guttural vocalizations must be disciplined into English. *Frankenstein* suggests that any voice reproduced from a distant shore transmits as noise rather than signal, even as its treatment of the reanimated body suggests that organic-technological assemblages yield only dead matter, as though we are hearing in the voice of the creature only the corpse larynx that Alexander and Melville Bell used in the creation of the talking machine, rather than the sound of a re-created human.

Frankenstein reinscribes the boundaries of the traditional human rather than exploiting the fresh seams that connect bodies in new ways and open its form to technology. Reinforcing an older fissure between mind and body, information and matter, the creature's murderous impulses are attributed to the "abnormal" brain that Dr. Frankenstein's assistant, Fritz, mistakenly chooses, as though the impulses of this mind survive intact to control the lifeless instrument of the creature's body. And, despite Dr. Frankenstein's ostensible commitment to expanding "life," the material processes of reanimating the corpse only highlight the hierarchies whereby some humans are routinely treated as less than human and less deserving of life. Dr. Frankenstein's first line in the film's opening scene is "Down, down, you fool!" as we see him pushing the physically "disfigured" Fritz into an offscreen space, emphasizing the position of social death that Fritz occupies. Although Dr. Frankenstein and Fritz both dig up the coffin in this opening scene, it is Fritz who does the real "dirty work," performing the unwanted task of cutting the executioner's rope suspending the corpse. While *Frankenstein*'s reanimation of the dead entails the possibility of a newly expanded recognition of the material continuum between the living and the dead, the human and the nonhuman, the film instead reifies these divides. It is perhaps for this reason that the creature's iconic image, marked with seams still rich in possibility, has acquired its own mutational "afterlife" outside the film, circulated and embodied in new contexts, providing a perennially popular "costume" through which people enact the posthuman forms of embodiment, sensation, and proprioception that are suggested but not realized by the film itself.

Ghosting Objects

While *Frankenstein* provocatively exteriorizes the sutures of the skull only to reassert a normativized human sensorium, Man Ray's "rayographs" blur the seams between the human and the nonhuman, entailing new modes of looking. Man Ray might be credited with giving modernism a "human face"; his photographic portraits of Gertrude Stein, H.D., Mina Loy, Ezra Pound, William Carlos Williams, T. S. Eliot, and many others created a pantheon of iconic modernist figures. At the same time, his visual work used collage and assemblage techniques to radically decenter the human figure, exploring the generative interactions between bodies and objects such as the printing press, the metronome, musical instruments, and the camera itself. His experimental "rayographs" in particular developed impersonal techniques to produce images in the absence of the human hand and eye, conjuring ghostly images of the skull through the juxtaposition of "dead" objects. Such images trouble the primacy of the human eye, involving synesthetic modes of looking that resolve into auditory and tactile impressions.

The technique of the rayograph entails placing objects on treated photographic paper and then exposing the objects to light—an "automatic" form of photography that allows the image to appear without the direct intervention of the photographer. The rayograph was also an "accidental" process resulting from a moment of distraction rather than a formulated intention. After mistakenly inserting unexposed paper into the developing tray, Man Ray "mechanically" placed a series of objects onto the treated paper, as though guided by a form of automation:

> As I waited in vain a couple of minutes for an image to appear, regretting the waste of paper, I mechanically placed a small glass funnel, the graduate, and the thermometer in the tray on the wetted paper. I turned on the light; before my eyes an image began to form, not quite a simple silhouette of the objects as in a straight photograph, but distorted and refracted by the glass more or less in contact with the paper and standing out against the black background, the part directly exposed to light. . . . Taking whatever objects came to hand—my hotel room key, a handkerchief, some pencils, a brush, a candle, a piece of twine—I made a few more prints.[48]

Like Rilke's construction of the phonograph from cardboard, boar's bristle, paper, and wax, rayographs replicate the operation of the camera without the apparatus of the camera itself or the direct authorial presence of the photographer. Although Man Ray assembles the objects on the treated paper—and, obviously, becomes more skillful and strategic at such assemblages after this first accident—the rayograph maintains an automated quality, distorting and inverting objects, and revealing, as the image develops, an etherealized form of the material world that is invisible to the "natural" human eye.

Rayographs challenge the epistemological certainty of vision, asking us to see materiality—and to see the process of seeing materiality—in new ways. At "first glance" the images resemble X-ray images, but rather

Figure 11. Untitled
rayograph, Man Ray,
1922–23. Copyright
Man Ray Trust/Artists
Rights Society (ARS), NY/
ADAGP, Paris 2016.

than dissolving the exterior of the body in order to penetratively gaze
into the interior structure, they remake the activity of the eye that would
move with certainty from surface to depth. When I look at the rayograph
in figure 11, for example, my eye flickers between recognition and uncertain exploration of that which has lost its familiar boundaries. I "see" the
form of the human skull remapped so that its rounded crown becomes
angular and the "eye" cavity becomes a jagged absence—an explosion of
negativity rather than an instrument of sight. The rayograph remaps the
whole body through the skull—shadowy hands seem to grasp the edges
of the ethereal skull, and *something like* a spectral navel slides across the
form of a mouth. Even as the rayograph reveals a tendency to anthropo-
morphize, an impulse to see an image of the human in the most defamiliarized presentation of objects, it remaps the human form to complicate such anthropocentrism. While the rayograph in figure 11 depicts
the elongated skull at an angle oblique to the viewer, the rayograph in

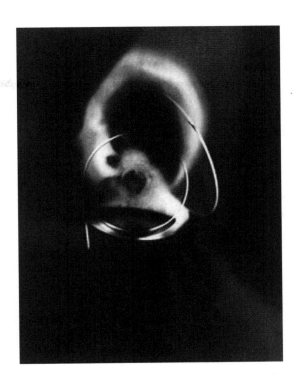

Figure 12. Untitled
rayograph, Man Ray,
1922. Copyright Man
Ray Trust/Artists Rights
Society (ARS), NY/
ADAGP, Paris 2016.

figure 12 directly plays on the traditions of human portraiture, producing a spectral image of the object relations that have historically enabled
and produced the human. Evoking a kind of ghostly primate, the rayograph also draws attention to the coiled wire and the object that form
the "mouth" of this proto-human, both of which press directly against
the surface of the photographic paper. The blurred abutting of objects
participates in polyse(a)my or code switching so that I see both the dead
become living and the living become dead. Vacillating between surface
and depth, my eye traces the boundaries of the collaged objects, even
as these seams dissolve into an etherealized whole—a kind of "cloud-
corpse," to use Loy's term—that is neither meat nor ghost. The rayographs also invite forms of looking that synesthetically resolve into other
sense perceptions. In figure 12, for example, the foregrounded "mouth"
conveys the possibility that objects might "speak," placing the viewer
in the "becoming-dumb" position of imaginatively hearing the primal

sound of matter. The rayograph redistributes the familiar apertures of the skull—openings to vision, audition, and speech—so that the human is no longer the secure perceptual center of the phenomenal world. Susan Laxton usefully characterizes Man Ray's rayographs through the term "flou," or "blur." In an aesthetic context, "flou" is a critical assessment of a photograph that is unintentionally out of focus, but as Laxton discusses, the rayographs also involve ontological and representational forms of "flou": "Rayographs are in every way a visual manifestation of this tendency toward indeterminacy. Like shape shifters, they fluctuate between abstraction, description, imagination, and materiality: between art and its others."[49] Laxton argues that rayographs allow the viewer to gaze upon something that escapes "the limits of physical reality itself," given that the spectral images no longer conform to the original objects Man Ray places on the treated paper. Like Rilke's improvised phonograph, the power of the rayograph lies not in its mimetic reproduction of the physical world but in its ghostly remaking of matter, generating, in Rilke's terms, "a new and infinitely delicate point in the texture of reality." The medium of the rayograph itself, as Laxton notes, participates in this encounter with an ontologically unfamiliar but nevertheless insistently material form:

> As contact prints produced by placing objects directly onto treated paper, they are unique images made without the technological mediation of the camera lens. Thus they excuse themselves from the critical discourse that grasps photography as a *mechanical* means of reproduction. This is no small thing, as the elimination of the mediating negative means that rayographs are unique, "original" objects eligible to retain the aura of traditional works of art.

Because the rayographs are original works, rather than reproductions, Laxton argues that traditional forms of "mastery and authorship remain intact," along with "all the attendant implications of signature, agency, and direct access to expression."[50] I would suggest, however, that authorship of the rayographs is subject to its own kind of "flou." As the play on his own pseudonym suggests, "rayographs" imply both autobiographical signature and erasure, an intentional eliding of the authorial hand of "Man" in favor of writing with light rays. Rather than signature, agency, and expression, the artist's role is to create the conditions in which elements of the material world can interact with one another in new ways, in which light can trace its own transformative material signature not only through objects but through a field of newly sutured things. Like early spirit photography's fixation with using the medium of film to capture ghostly images, rayographs exploit technology's ability to make the invisible visible, to transcend the limits of the human sensorium and capture what the human eye alone cannot see.

Rayographs provide a compelling example of "hauntology," Derrida's term for the ontological uncertainty that haunts our engagement with things, the "blurred" aporia between the commoditized representational appearance of objects and the things themselves. In this way, Man Ray's ghostly images—and even the imagination of ghosts more generally—do not escape from the world of lived relations, but instead offer a way to conceptualize relationships with matter that is never fully *present*. Akin to representation, ghosts give matter back to itself in attenuated form, not simply marking the reappearance of the past but signifying the temporal difficulty of matter itself, disturbing our sense of the presence of things, and compelling us toward unrealized possibilities. Derrida asks:

> *What is* a ghost? What is the *effectivity* or the *presence* of a specter, that is, of what seems to remain as ineffective, virtual, insubstantial as a simulacrum? Is there *there*, between the thing itself and its simulacrum, an opposition that holds up? Repetition *and* first time, but also repetition *and* last time, since the singularity of any *first time*, makes of it also a *last time*. Each time it is the event itself, a first time is a last time. Altogether other. Staging for the end of history. Let us call it a *hauntology*.[51]

For Derrida, the ghost signifies the destruction of time, simultaneously marking repetitive returns and uneasily conjuring an end of history haunted by experiences that were never realized. The rayographs, too, operate through a temporal as well as an ontological "flou," marking the re-presentation or return of elusive forms of matter, as well as a glimpse into an adjacent history of objects that only becomes visible through technologically produced forms of perception. Such technological representation is necessarily *post*human, an automatic mode of image production that comes "after" the human authorial hand has withdrawn its influence.

We might thus reverse the truism about pursuing "the ghost in the machine" and instead regard the machine itself as an embodiment of the ghostly past, the elusive present, and an uncertain posthuman future. Derrida claims:

For there to be a ghost, there must be a return to the body, but to a body that is more abstract than ever. The spectrogenic process corresponds therefore to a paradoxical *incorporation.* Once ideas or thoughts *(Gedanke)* are detached from their substratum, one engenders some ghost by *giving them a body.* Not by returning to the living body from which ideas and thoughts have been torn loose, but by incarnating the latter in *another artifactual body, a prosthetic body.*[52]

The ghost is thus never simply disembodied but implies a re-incarnation into a changed materiality—Rilke listening through the skulls of World War I, Loy's imagination of the coronal fissure opening to admit a spontaneously electrified body, the reanimation of dead parts in *Frankenstein,* and Man Ray's ghostly depiction of both a primal ur-human and its future technologically mediated sensorium. Ghosts and skulls are media through which the human engages with technology and a consequently rearranged material world.

Skull Control

In each of these texts, sutures and grooves mark mediated engagements between the traditional human form and technology; my discussion concludes, however, by moving outside the frame of the printed text, the film, and the photograph in order to consider the lived performance of such sutures. In her quotidian acts of performance art, Baroness Elsa von Freytag-Loringhoven embodied the posthuman possibilities of bodily assemblage, treating her own shaved skull as a site of material suture.[53]

Shortly after her arrival in the United States in 1910, the Baroness was arrested for the perceived outrage of walking the streets wearing men's clothing and smoking. Undeterred by this encounter with the law, her public promenades only became more spectacular, a kind of street theater that transgressed not only normative boundaries defining gendered modes of dress but also boundaries between humans and machines, humans and objects, and humans and animals. Humachine, humaterial, humanimal: the Baroness treated her body as an element in a collage, grafting onto her bodily form an array of technological tools, found objects, commodities, and even animals. She famously shaved her head, painting it with bright colors and attaching objects such as an airplane propeller, a sardine can, and feathers. Her head-shaving exposed the structure of the skull, treating its covering skin as a canvas to be repainted and its underlying form as a site of material connection. The Baroness had skull control.

While there are regrettably few surviving photographs of the Baroness, Irene Gammel gives the following vibrant account culled from various descriptions written by her contemporaries:

> Her head: shaved and occasionally shellacked in striking colors like vermil-ion red. Her makeup: yellow face powder, black lipstick, and an American stamp on her cheek. Her jewels: utilitarian, mass-produced objects like tea-spoons as earrings or large buttons as fingers rings. Her accessories: tomato cans and celluloid rings adorning her body; the hem of her skirt decorated with horse blanket pins. An electric battery taillight decorated the bustle of her black dress in imitation of a car or bicycle. She also used live animals as part of her street performance: a wooden birdcage around her neck hous-ing a live canary; five dogs on her gilded leash as she promenaded up Fifth Avenue. Her outrageous costumes made her a New York landmark at sub-way stations, in public offices, in museums, at exhibitions, in department stores, and on the major thoroughfares. With each new day, she added new twists to her repertoire of makeup, headdresses, and costumes that were frequently made from junk objects collected in the streets.[54]

Walking the public streets that are historically perilous spaces for women, the Baroness makes herself spectacular, both drawing attention to the parts of her body that conventions of female "modesty" typically con-ceal and redrawing the body so that it transcends conventions of gen-der presentation altogether. With teaspoons in her ears, a battery taillight in her bustle—and suggestively nonfunctional buttons and pins wait-ing to hook the world into novel forms of connection—the Baroness's body-assemblages exemplify Deleuze and Guattari's discussion of the "desiring-machines" whose multiple openings, closures, and connec-tions resist psychoanalytic definitions of the singular body and its pre-dictable oedipal economies: "Everywhere *it* is machines—real ones, not figurative ones: machines driving other machines, machines being driven by other machines, with all the necessary couplings and connec-tions. An organ-machine is plugged into an energy-source-machine: the one produces a flow that the other interrupts."[55] The live animals and technological objects make her a kind of ambulatory menagerie, a living *Wunderkammer* suggesting that the human is an assemblage in minia-ture of the things with which it interacts.[56] The Baroness's street perfor-mances treat the body itself as an emergent media form.

Aside from the visual impact of her altered body, one might also imagine the sonic impact of her movements through the street, as the clatter of objects interacting with her body announced her presence far in advance of her arrival. The artist George Biddle described the Baroness as adorned with "some sixty or eighty lead, tin, or cast-iron toys: dolls, soldiers, automobiles, locomotives, and music boxes," objects that seem selected for both their representational and their sonic properties.[57] Attaching these metallic figures to her dress, the Baroness transforms her body into a sonic machine, and the "primal sound" of the human gait is made audible through its interaction with the cast-iron objects. As iron locomotive and doll clatter against one another, the acoustic "signature" of the human step is rewritten, suggesting the way in which modern transportation systems not only move the body through space at accelerated speeds but also transform the rhythms of ambulation itself. Wearing "sixty or eighty lead, tin, or cast-iron toys," the Baroness also presents herself not as a singular subject but as a multiplicity, an embodied emblem of the crowds of Europeans who came to the United States in the wake of the war.

The Baroness's shaved, painted-red head also inevitably evokes blood, figuratively turning the skull inside out and making visible the typically invisible circulatory networks of the body. In this way, the circulatory flows of the singular body connect with the larger networks of migratory flows in the early twentieth century. Decorating her painted cheek with an American postage stamp, the Baroness also connects these blood networks to other communicative networks, semiotically conceiving her body as an address to the United States, a corporeal message to be read through acts of self-circulation. Djuna Barnes notes that the Baroness's signature stamp (a kind of posthuman beauty mark) was just as often a "foreign postage stamp—cancelled" and that she ornamented her body with "strands from a cable once used to moor importations from far Cathay."[58] Defining identity through transnational circulation rather than national origin, the Baroness situates herself as a nodal point within a prosthetic nervous system that extended communication and perception across the Atlantic and the Pacific.

Despite the futury of the Baroness's bodily performance, her abandonment of traditional modes of female—or even human—dress, Barnes also situates her in relation to the past, describing her as "an ancient human notebook on which has been written all the follies of a past generation."[59] In this way, the Baroness's self-fabricating "skull control" positions her body as a medium sensitive to external inscription, much like Rilke using the stylus to play the skull, or Man Ray using the inscriptive power of light rather than his own authorial hand to make the rayograph image appear. Receptive to such inscription, the Baroness's futurist fashioning of the body is not just a marginalized performance but an integral "human notebook" written with the "follies" of the past. Gammel characterizes her body as "inscribed" with the trauma of World War I in particular:

> Written on her body was the trauma of earlier experiences including the tension of perpetual conflict and emotional violence at home. . . . In the midst of youthful America, by 1917 the Baroness came to represent Old Europe, associated with old age, decadence, and destruction. For America and its young modernist poets and authors, including Williams Carlos Williams, Hart Crane, and Wallace Stevens, her body was the unsettling body of Europe at war. Although Greenwich Village and America's young modernist poets and painters were far from the trench warfare in Belgium, far from the smell of chlorine gas, and far from close contact with corpses, for the exiled Europeans the reality of the war they had escaped was always close by. For Americans, the memory of Old Europe was inscribed on her flesh and used to terrorize a young generation of artists.[60]

Walking the streets of New York with her shaved head painted blood-red, the Baroness is a kind of living corpse bearing witness to the atrocities of war and its unassimilated trauma. If the Baroness conceived of her body as participating in both transatlantic and transpacific networked communication systems, these early-twentieth-century systems are inevitably developed in tandem with the needs of war, thickened with commands that produce corpses and with reports that convey body counts. Even as the Baroness's remaking of the body marks a futurist performance of what a body can be and, in a Spinozan sense, what a body can *do*—Marcel Duchamp remarked, "She's not a futurist. She is the future"—this futurity acknowledges that the instruments of technology and media, such as the telegraph, the radio, and the airplane propeller affixed to her own head, often have their origins in war and bear a trail of corpses in their wake.[61]

The Baroness's poetry also performs bodily assemblages, such that writing functions as a prosthetic extension of the body and, conversely, as an inhuman force reciprocally acting upon the body. Her 1920 poem "Blast," for instance, imagines the writing instrument not as a tool guided by human articulation but as a blunt scalpel penetrating the skull, performing a kind of alternative autopsy. Incapable of carving out a space separate from the war, the pen retraces its explosive "blasts," hollowing out the skull and evacuating the familiar form of the human:

Take spoon — scalpel —
scrape brains clear from you —
how it hurts to be void![62]

"Blast" specifically correlates the violence of war with the gendered topographies of the body, describing in martial terms the besieged "twin hillocks" of the Earth and the embattled relations between a "pranked mother" and "stark kings." While the intertwined masculinist conquests of war and heteronormative sexuality leave the speaker as an uninhabited shell, this "void" is still an embodied, phenomenological site of pain—"how it hurts to be void!" In place of such "barren" conquests and "voided" phenomenologies, the Baroness's poetry often foregrounds a more androgynous joining of body with machine. In "A Modest Woman," for example, the speaker rejects the female modesty implied by long skirts and instead exposes the body not through metaphors of erotic display but through the language of functional technological assemblage, asking: "Why should I — proud engineer — be ashamed of my machinery — part of it?"[63] The Baroness's signature dashes both unpredictably join and unpredictably separate the elements of the "I," the "engineer" and "my machinery," and she describes neither the autonomous "I" nor a hierarchical "engineer" who controls the instrumentalized machinery of the body, but rather a Deleuzo-Guattarian plane of unity: "Everywhere *it* is machines . . . machines driving other machines, machines being driven by other machines." Becoming a connective "part of it" is not only a thematic question in the Baroness's poetry; she imagines technology as a "teacher" that comprises "half" of her poetics: "Machine teaches / Precision. It has to be / Half of genius."[64]

"A Dozen Cocktails—Please" exemplifies this Deleuzo-Guattarian plane of consistency, an *"itness"* whereby the wireless and invisible networks of technical media corporeally trace new grooves into the machinery of the human and its vocalizations. Posing the question "What's radio for—if you please?" the poem works toward a corporeal definition of "broadcasting":

What's radio for—if you please?
"Eve's dart pricks snookums upon
Wirefence"
An apple a day—
It'll come———
Ha! When? I am no tongueswallowing yogi.
Progress is ravishing—
It doesn't *me*—
Nudge it—
Kick it—
Prod it—
Push it—
Broadcast———
That's the lightning idea![65]

The poem rejects the notion that wireless broadcast simply replicates disembodied voices, beginning with the citational, disembodied echo of "Eve's dart" but turning away from this gendered story with a distinctly embodied "Ha!" claiming, "I am no tongueswallowing yogi." Rather than the generative position of "becoming-dumb," in which the auditor enters into composition with nonhuman affectivity, the "tongueswallowing yogi" evokes bodily control and asceticism, as well as "swallowing" her own native tongue as a German speaker translated into the United States. "A Dozen Cocktails" accordingly refuses the ascetic, silenced position of "tongueswallowing" in favor of technological "progress" that is corporeally "ravishing," suggesting the possibilities of euphoric intensities. For the Baroness, progress is "ravishing" not because it moves toward technologically determined forms of disembodiment but because the advances of technical media inevitably entail a corporeal remaking, requiring the participatory, embodied activity of the human—the nudge, the kick, the prod, the push. Her peculiar syntactic emphasis on the "it" includes the reformulation of matter more generally, as the "thinginess" of an unnamed "it" is nudged, kicked, prodded, pushed, and, finally, broadcast. This reformulated matter remakes or "ravishes" the human in turn; "It doesn't *me*—," the Baroness claims, rejecting the familiar sense of a singular identitarian "me." The poem's celebration of the "lightning idea" thus refers not to the distanced, rationally disembodied force that brings the Frankensteinian corpse back to uncanny life only to reject such life as unlivable, but rather to the transformative "idea" that materializes through the body, putting the *me* under negation in favor of an unknown but emphatically embodied posthuman future.

Written for vocal performance, the Baroness's sound poetry directly deploys the sensory faculties of voice and audition, treating the skull itself as a resonant medium. Taking scalpel to skull, her sound poetry aspires to access the "primal sound" encoded within the body and matter, but unlike Marinetti's sheerly onomatopoetic sound poetry, which is motivated by a humanist "will to penetrate" the life of material things, her poetics acknowledges the embeddedness of objects within semiotic systems, such that the denotative properties of human semiotics coexist with the sounds of matter.[66] For example, her sound poem "Teke / Heart (Beating of Heart)" (a title that implies the violent extraction or "taking" of the heart just as it connotes the more idiomatic notion of "comfort") onomatopoetically captures the rhythms of the body even as it moves across a multilingual spectrum of connotative associations. The following stanza sonically evokes the rhythmic "ticking" of the heartbeat (aligned with the pulsing "machinery" of both the body and poetic meter) and linguistically evokes the "ache" that is metaphorically associated with emotions of the heart:

> Acke flasse — qvmk. Teke
> Achm — té
> Ackm — tk — kté![67]

"Teke / Heart," however, simultaneously decenters the "Beating of Heart" as the primary engine of emotion, reorganizing the body and its traditional metaphorical associations. Requiring the embodied use of the voice in order to be fully realized, the repetition of "Orkmmm — orkmm — mmm — —" also evokes the sense of taste, followed by the more enveloping evocation of "heat" through repetition of the Swedish-derived "Hirre — héta / Hetta — hett." Vacillating between sheer sound and indirect signification, invented words operate as sensory objects moving in a thickened soundscape. The poem evokes tears, for example, through a play on "lacrimosa," repeating the related sounds "jachmosa — / Mosa—achmosa," falling words and sounds that perhaps indirectly mourn the unspoken dead. The Baroness's sound poetry thus not only replicates the sounds of objects but also uses sound to create the possibility of a renewed sensory relationship with objects—and the language that represents them.

The Modernist Skull

Assembling these various modernist skulls (or perhaps, in Frankenstein-ian fashion, stitching new connective seams between them) invites a cumulative question about modernism. In each of the texts I examine, technical media produces not the disembodied replication of that which is dead or absent but, on the contrary, a reconfiguration of bodily mate-riality and a reconsideration of the skull in particular as a material sub-stance. How, then, does the materializing skull in these modernist texts challenge conceptions of literary modernism's preoccupation with *interi-ority*? That is, if modernism has often been understood through its explo-ration and delineation of *consciousness*, how do the modernist artists I have discussed shift our attention, quite literally, from what is "inside" the skull to its material surface, exploring the skull as a site of extrinsic suture, connection, and assemblage?

In imagining a modernism that turns us inside out, however, it is not my intention to linger over the distinction between interior and exterior, given that such a distinction still upholds the metaphorics and metaphys-ics of materializing container and disembodied cognition. If the skull is an exteriorizing surface, it is, after all, a complicated surface, rich with its own depths of somatic data and accessible only through the prior pene-tration or decomposition of the skin (itself a layered, unruly boundary). The modernists I examine are also interested not in the skull *alone* but a "modernist skull" that serves as a site of assemblage. It is useful, then, to consider a strain of modernism that challenges not only the bound-ary between the interior and exterior of the human but also, according to the overarching terms of my book, the metaphysics of "dead" material container and "lively" interior subject such that matter and conscious-ness are continually reconfigured through one another along a common vitalist plane.

Georges Bataille argues that while the skull is perhaps the most imme-diately legible reminder of death, it has also traditionally kept death at bay, presenting an artifact of death that obscures the material processes of decomposition and decay:

> [W]hen the bones are bare and white they are not intolerable as the putre-fying flesh is, food for worms. In some obscure way the survivors perceive in the horror aroused by corruption a rancour and a hatred projected towards them by the dead man which it is the function of the rites of mourning to

appease. But afterwards they feel that the whitening bones bear witness to that appeasement. The bones are objects of reverence to them and draw the first veil of decency and solemnity over death and make it bearable; it is painful still but free of the virulent activity of corruption.

These white bones do not leave the survivors a prey to the slimy menace of disgust. They put an end to the close connections between decomposition, the source of an abundant surge of life, and death.[68]

In this way, skulls and bones have historically circumscribed the living human not only from death but also from what Bataille terms the "abundant surge of life" enacted through decomposition. The skull becomes a paradoxical prophylactic against this "surge of life," providing a way to see, touch, and handle that which is otherwise too gruesome to experience, an object through which even the horror of Poor Yorick becomes the occasion for philosophical speculation and soliloquy. While Rilke focuses on the materiality of the skull, he similarly overcomes the "virulent" and viral materiality of death, positioning the skull as an "object of reverence," suitable for candlelit study and contemplation. Even as he places the stylus in the suture, the "appeasement" of bones separates biological matter from the dead instruments of technical media, rather than understanding their living unity.

Bataille's discussion of bones as a "veil of decency" suggests not only a horror and disgust *for* "putrefying flesh" but also a horror and disgust for flesh itself *as* putrid. In this way, the desire to escape the "slimy menace" of the corpse has affinities with Moravec's transhumanist aspiration to transcend the "jelly" of the body. In Rilke's and Kittler's writing, the "menace" of flesh is invariably gendered, as Rilke seeks to extricate the lyric voice from the erotic synesthesias proposed by his mostly silent female auditor and as Kittler valorizes technologically engineered "white noise" over materially embodied "red lips." But the texts I discuss in this chapter also locate the "modernist skull" not on the "supernatural plane of the poem," as Rilke does, but on the "natural plane" of material assemblage between gendered flesh and technology. Loy's imagination of the cranial suture as a site that is "open at birth" and reopened by technology, for example, challenges the traditionally procreative body. Here the skull is living and elastic matter with its own generative capabilities rather than the ossified future "testament" that emerges in the wake of the human. With her skull painted red, the Baroness similarly performs the living unities among skull, flesh, and media, evoking the pulse and flow of blood rather than the "white" and "whitening" properties of the skull or the disembodied "white noise" of technical media. The Baroness refashions the female body as a medium of living broadcast through its androgynously productive "machinery" rather than its reproductive imperatives. While the skull thus seems to provide a gender-neutral form of materiality, its reconceptualization as a medium simultaneously invites the posthuman reconceptualization of gender, sexuality, and procreation. In *Frankenstein*, the creature's technologically assembled body similarly poses a challenge to patriarchal authority: Dr. Frankenstein's father closes the film by raising a toast "to a son, to the House of Frankenstein!" reasserting the traditions of heteronormative family and birth that are threatened by "monstrous" forms of technological birth. Man Ray's rayographs also use the technological assemblage of objects to remap the body through the sensory apertures of the skull, suggesting new forms of tactility, perception, and bodily passage. In this way the "modernist skull," exteriorized through technological assemblage and thickened with living, gendered flesh, is not a separating boundary between the interior and exterior of the subject but rather a living medium of transmission between the human and the nonhuman—a memento vivere rather than a memento mori.

4 LOVE AND CORPSES

Djuna Barnes's Queer Posthumanism

"She said, 'I shall die beneath you, yet from my body you shall garner
ten sons, and they shall be harnessed of terribleness, and you shall
bury me quickly, for I am burst asunder at their way within me, for they
come marching, and I rejoice and go from this hour no further.' And
she charged him well, saying: 'When you have dragged them forth by
their iron locks, smite them with rain-water, and put my name on their
tongues, and tell them thenceforth nothing of me, nor picture me to
them in any way, saying, "She was tender-hoofed and her breasts were
ten." For I am, and soon shall be as I am not, and they must know no
deception. Nor cut their wings on the right side, nor cut their wings on
the left side, nor metal their hoofs, for they are shod of me, at the forge
of my heart, and they are!'

"And so it was that Thingumbob rose up in the dawn and plucked his
sons from her belly, and carried them to his nest, and there daylong and
nightlong he sits above them, the smoke of his sorrow boiling above the
trees, his eyelids shaking under, for he knows her gift to him was the
useless gift of love."

"Is that all?" said Julie.

DJUNA BARNES, *RYDER*

DRAWN FROM AUTOBIOGRAPHICAL EXPERIENCE of her own family,
Djuna Barnes's *Ryder* contains a macabre fairy tale about love between
"the Beast Thingumbob" and the faceless creature known simply as "the
Cheerful." While the Beast seems to reside primarily in the trees and
Cheerful is associated with the fecundity of the earth, both are hybrid
creatures who resist classification: the Beast "had wings . . . as well as
paws, feathers as well as fur," and Cheerful has spent "many æons of

moiling and fuming about in fur and feather." It is precisely this strangeness, this sense of being singular and unclassifiable according to familiar taxonomies, that causes Cheerful and the Beast to fall in love. Their love is encompassing and painful because it feels unprecedented; as the narrator notes, "when a great Beast like Thingumbob suffers the pangs of love . . . it has no planned way, but must go what way it can."[1]

Despite the singularity of their love (and of the Beast and Cheerful as creatures), the relationship unfolds according to recognizably gendered tropes. Cheerful enacts a familiar narrative of self-sacrifice, giving up her life in support of the patriarchal project of producing ten sons. Cheerful is a kind of Earth goddess, while the Beast's association with the trees gives him hierarchical power over other creatures. The Beast is triumphant among the animal species because he has "murdered the murder in others." And while Cheerful and the Beast are both hybrid creatures with human characteristics, these characteristics are unevenly distributed and associated with gendered norms. The Beast, for example, is gifted with language—in Barnes's illustration, it is his name that radiates in the sky like an ambiguous sun—but Cheerful's human traits are located in her body. With the exception of her "thinly hoofed" feet and her "face [which] was not yet," Cheerful has recognizably human physical traits, and even an excess of such traits, given her five rows of breasts and her darkly outlined groin, which provides a focal point for the illustration.[2] The illustration (see fig. 13) seemingly depicts the moment immediately before the Beast "plucked his sons from her belly," an act that accomplishes Cheerful's death, but the image is ambiguous.[3] In the absence of what Levinas terms the "living presence" of the face, it is impossible to know whether she is living or dead; the hasty dash of her eyebrows offers only an ambiguous punctuation to the otherwise blank expanse of what "was not yet." Without a face, Cheerful's body acquires the semiotics of a corpse, inert flesh that is *for* others' use; as Levinas notes, "The skin of the face is that which stays most naked, most destitute. . . . At the same time, the face is what forbids us to kill."[4] Cheerful's absent face also poses certain insurmountable problems in terms of her relation to language and her own narrative: How is she known as "the Cheerful" if she does not have a face that telegraphs emotion? How is she able to deliver the self-sacrificial speech about their ten sons, asking the Beast to "put my name on their tongues," given that she herself does not have a tongue with which to speak? While the hybrid creatures in *Ryder* seem to offer a model of love that escapes the boundaries of the

Figure 13. "The Beast," from *Ryder*, Djuna Barnes, 1928. Copyright The Authors League Fund and St. Bride's Church, as joint literary executors of the Estate of Djuna Barnes.

human, this hybridity paradoxically enables traditional forms of gender to be inscribed all the more emphatically because specific aspects of the human are selectively valorized or suppressed.

When Julie, a figure for the young Barnes herself, asks "Is that all?" at the end of the fairy tale, she precociously conveys her sense that the Beast's maudlin tears are an inadequate response to the "useless gift" of Cheerful's love, but she also perhaps conveys her disappointment in the tale itself, which replicates familiar tropes of love, childbirth, and death. Given the exotic apparati with which Barnes equips the Beast and Cheerful—wings, hooves, fur, feathers, extra breasts—why does their love story end with such a predictable affirmation of heterosexual reproduction and the reproduction of the family? Surely "many æons of moiling and fuming about in fur and feather" would yield something more transformative, more *posthuman* than this affirmation of heteronormativity? Julie's response critiques the predictable humanism of the fairy tale, in which the putative "differences" of the Beast and Cheerful can be overcome through the humanizing force of love. Heteronormative reproduction in the name of family prevails even if the Beast has to "pluck his sons from [Cheerful's] belly," creating a corpse in the process.

Despite the surface exoticism of their bodies, the parodic tale of Cheerful and the Beast thus perpetuates the myth of a "Family of Man," which, in Barthes's critique, positions the supposedly universal and natural properties of birth and death as the unifying, immutable bookends of the human experience. Discussing "The Family of Man," an international photography exhibition curated by Edward Steichen in 1955, Barthes argues that the myth of a human family is produced in two ways: "First the difference between human morphologies is asserted, exoticism is insistently stressed, the infinite variations of the species, the diversity in skins, skulls and customs are made manifest. . . . Then, from this pluralism, a type of unity is magically produced: man is born, works, laughs and dies everywhere in the same way." Such a mythical "family" of man, which provides "an alibi to a large part of our humanism," privileges the unexamined category of "nature" over the distinctions of history, denying the radically different ways in which birth and death occur.[5] Barthes offers the example of Emmett Till, lynched at the age of fourteen, whose death, far from unifying him with a larger "Family of Man," tragically exemplifies the historically specific disqualification of those deemed less than "fully human." The myth of the "Family of Man," as Barthes argues, is often selectively deployed to further a white colonial agenda, eliding the specificity of cultural differences that impede such an agenda and then retracting sympathetic claims of universal kinship when they no longer have utility. Predicated upon "the solid rock of a universal human nature,"[6] the mythic "Family of Man" also ignores the historically contingent processes by which medicine and technology construct the phenomenologies, materialities, and temporalities of birth and death as well as the social conditions that allow access to such technologies. The twofold process Barthes identifies—whereby superficial, exoticized forms of "difference" are asserted only to be recuperated into a bedrock understanding of "Man"—applies across a range of cultural contexts. Claiming that even cultural imaginations of extraterrestrials conform to this pattern, Neil Badmington quotes Barthes: "Probably if we were to land in our turn on the Mars we have constructed, we should merely find Earth itself, and between these two products of a same history we should not know how to disentangle our own."[7] Just as cultural representations of extraterrestrials often discover that they are a lot like humans after all, Barnes's tale of Cheerful and the Beast emphatically asserts their exoticism only to recall it into a universal story of family.

The myth of the "Family of Man" necessarily positions the heteronormative family as the legitimate and universal channel through which the naturalized phenomena of birth and death occur. This emphasis on the family as the primary organizing principle of human existence concretizes the binary structure of gender as central to the humanist "Family," marginalizing those who exist outside the mandates of what Michael Warner terms "reprosexuality."[8] My goal in opening with this tale from *Ryder* is thus not simply to rehearse the gender dynamics between Cheerful and the Beast—the horror of a "Cheerful" female self-sacrifice is so pronounced it hardly needs to be articulated—but to consider how this gender relation is a necessary component of the tale's residual humanism, its failure to conclude in any way other than replicating the traditional family (even if the Beast mourns his loss from a nest, rather than a more "human" setting). While this book has thus far focused on definitions of humanism that presume a normatively gendered white male at its center, Dana Luciano and Mel Y. Chen point out that humanism is often implicitly structured according to a "hetero-gendered pair." In this way, humanism often presumes not only an implicitly masculinized subject who is "rational, bounded, integral, sovereign, and self-aware" but also his feminized counterpart, who is characterized by her sympathetic, "humane" capacity "to feel for others, to love and to grieve and to respond to the suffering of others," but who is nevertheless still "self-regulated, limited in scope and function." Even if they are not literally embodied by male and female subjects, respectively, these two defining principles of humanism often function in interactive cooperation so that the "cognitive-rational" principle does injury through its dehumanization of the other, while the "sympathetic-emotional" counterpart devotes itself to reparations of such damage—all the while maintaining the overarching structure of human center and dehumanized margin.[9] In the same way, the Beast's "rational" murder in the name of family and Cheerful's "sympathetic" self-sacrifice to the life of her sons enact the binary dynamics of this hetero-gendered humanism. Despite the posthuman possibilities of "moiling and fuming about in fur and feather" the hetero-gendered union prevails, resulting in an excess of family, rather than an excess of sexuality.

Ryder's tale of Cheerful and the Beast anticipates the interrelated tropes of love, corpses, and species transformation in *Nightwood*, whose original title was *Night Beast*. Like Cheerful, *Nightwood*'s Robin Vote exists in a state of species liminality, described as "a woman who is beast turning human" and an "eland coming down an aisle of trees, chapleted with orange blossoms and bridal veil."[10] While Robin is thus figuratively vivified, she is also a corpse-like figure, introduced in a state of unconsciousness, unaware of the animal visions she inspires, her human face, like Cheerful's, an illegible absence. Unlike Cheerful, however, Robin refuses to sacrifice herself to motherhood, first threatening to murder her son, then leaving her family and beginning a relationship with Nora Flood. Serving as the focal point of both male and female desire, Robin's queer sexuality undoes the universalism of heterosexual reproduction in the novel, but it is also involved in the larger project of undoing the human and humanist conceptions of the bi-gendered "Family of Man." Her reciprocal engagements with corpses, animals, plants, and other forms of nonhuman life exceed a bounded emphasis upon the species perpetuation of the human, defining her as a generative source of life that flourishes where traditional forms of reproduction fail in the novel.

While this discussion of gender and family focuses on *Nightwood* in particular, it also provides a necessary concluding chapter for the book as a whole, given that heteronormative conceptions of gender and procreation are so deeply embedded in a species conception of the "Family of Man." The previous chapter's discussion of Loy and the Baroness specifically examined the role of emergent media in reconceptualizing the gendered and reproductive body, but many of the texts I have discussed in this book challenge the dominant paradigm of the heteronormative family. In *Cane*'s "Portrait in Georgia," for example, the African American body is lynched as a paranoid protection of white female "purity" and the boundaries of the white heteronormative family. Many of *Cane*'s serial vignettes involve thwarted or traumatic forms of sexuality, demonstrating the exclusionary force of the white heteronormative family. Faulkner similarly critiques the way in which the boundaries of the human and the nonhuman are adjudicated through the boundaries of the family, as Henry Sutpen's murder of his multiracial and "illegitimate" half brother attempts to protect the "sanctity" of the Sutpen family. And in *As I Lay Dying,* human-nonhuman intersections are enacted through the context of family: when Vardaman claims that "My mother is a fish," for example, he challenges not only the species distinctions that define the human but also the family norms through which the species is perpetuated.

In addition to this consideration of the heteronormative family, my discussion of *Nightwood* poses larger questions about the role that queer love and sexuality might play in unseating the suzerainty of the human. What would it mean to love in a queer, posthuman way, given that love has traditionally been regarded as a humanizing force, or even the pinnacle of human sensibility? If love has often been understood as a universally "human" phenomenon, an experiential domain from which animals, plants, minerals—in short, the whole of nonhuman life—are excluded, how might the "useless gift" of queer, posthuman love alter the social structures associated with humanism and the exclusionary "Family of Man"? In posing these questions, I write with an acute awareness of the challenges and risks involved in theorizing queer sexuality from the perspective of the posthuman and, more particularly, the posthumous. If queer subjects have often been regarded as less than "fully human" or cast into the positions of both symbolic social death and tragically realized fatality, what is potentially risked, reinscribed, or erased in thinking about queer sexuality's associations with the nonhuman and the corpse? Yet, as Jeffrey Cohen and Todd Ramlow note, to reduce the boundary-crossing potential of queer sexuality to "the merely human frame within which queer theory has sometimes allowed its ambit to be circumscribed" is also to risk replicating the very forms of humanism that continue to define queer life as precarious life.[11]

Nightwood's relentless pursuit of the nonhuman has posed a critical challenge to its commentators, who have often sought to recuperate the novel into more familiar humanist expressions. In her preface to the 2006 edition (which I very much admire), Jeanette Winterson notes, for example, that Barnes "writes into the center of human anguish" (xvi). Writing in a different vein in his 1936 introduction, T. S. Eliot nevertheless makes a similar case for the novel's universal humanism, arguing, "To regard this group of people as a horrid sideshow of freaks" is to miss the novel's "profounder significance," namely, its depiction of "the human misery and bondage which is universal" (xxi–xxii). To merely relocate the characters whom Eliot regards as "sideshow freaks" onto a main stage of universal human experience where actions of "profounder significance" unfold, however, is to reinforce a tautological sameness of human experience, replicating the twofold process Barthes describes, whereby "exotic" forms of difference are asserted, only to be recuperated into a universalized "Family of Man." Rather than understanding queer sexuality within a "merely human frame," *Nightwood* explores forms of queer relationality that embrace the generative, volatile, and sometimes destructive forces of the nonhuman, transgressing the species boundaries that define "Man" through his universal sameness.

My approach to *Nightwood* follows the work of theorists who similarly theorize queer sexuality—and sexuality in general—as an unmaking of the humanist subject. In "Is the Rectum a Grave?" for example, Leo Bersani understands sexuality as performing the "breakdown of the human itself in sexual intensities" rather than that which can be recuperated by liberal humanism.[12] Lee Edelman argues, similarly, that if heteronormativity has consigned queer sexuality to the grave, such morbidity should not be redeemed but celebrated in its potential to "bury" idealized and masculinized conceptions of the subject: "It is we who must bury the subject in the tomb-like hollow of the signifier."[13] "Burying" the singular subject, in turn, repositions death, so that it functions not as "an individualized, judicial event" but a materially distributed phenomenon that, in Cohen and Ramlow's terms, "opens up the queer to spaces that suddenly cease to stand as final resting places filled only by silence."[14] In this way, queer openings to the nonhuman entail generative possibilities that exceed the tautological replication of humanist ascendency. Judith Butler argues that undoing heteronormativity and the gendered forms upon which it is predicated involves "embrac[ing] the destruction and rearticulation of the human in the name of a more capacious and, finally, less violent world, not knowing in advance what precise form our humanness does and will take."[15] Similarly emphasizing the anticipatory possibilities of posthuman, queer sexuality, Luciano and Chen's "Has the Queer Ever Been Human?" asserts that to explore queer engagements with the nonhuman is not to erase or replicate a history of dehumanization but to "ask about other forms, other worlds, other ways of being that might emerge" from such engagements.[16]

Exploring such "other ways of being," *Nightwood* often depicts queer love through figures of the corpse, which functions as an emblem neither of social death nor of the psychological death drive that has traditionally defined the erotic life of the human, but as an archae-corporeal site through which characters experience nonhuman, prehuman, and posthuman forms of "life."[17] Such engagements with the corpse redraw the boundaries of both the monadic self and the other, who no longer serves as a secure "object" of desire. *Nightwood* instead describes a complex interplay between self and other so that it is not simply the "personal" body of the other that one desires and experiences through eroticism, but the body's sedimented histories, its decompositional lines of flight, and the material traces of its relations with animals, plants, minerals, and nonhuman things. Like the fairy tale in *Ryder*, whose hybrid creatures enact a familiar story about the gendered dynamics of love, *Nightwood* couples its fantastic descriptions of posthuman bodily transformation with a relatively uncomplicated story about characters who fall in love, and then lose love, in a series of triangulated exchanges. If love seems like a failed project in the novel, however (such that the love plot is more like a burial plot), *Nightwood* also invites modes of reading that do not simply replicate a heteronormative emphasis on the births and deaths, beginnings and endings that define the universal life arc of the "Family of Man," but instead depict the "life" of queer sexuality through an alinear, punctuated series of deaths, passages, and becomings. Critiquing this humanist "Family" is, however, in no way intended to devalue the often profound forms of support and nurturing that individual experiences of family provide; my critique is, instead, targeted toward the reproductive family as a transcendent ideal upon which definitions of the human are often predicated, devaluing and excluding not only individuals, relationships, and community alliances that exist outside the normative family but also experiences of becoming that escape its purview. As Cohen and Ramlow argue, "Beginnings and endings are two points that capture a trajectory of becoming and entrap it within a diminishing closed circuit, as if the world were a small place, as if an infinite *intermezzo* were inconceivable."[18]

"Burying" the subject as a singular entity, *Nightwood* shifts attention away from the centrality of unified characters who serve as representative agents of human fate, modeling the possibilities of queer love through the relentless generation of posthuman bodily forms, even if such bodies never fully materialize as characters within the plot. As Cary Wolfe points out, posthumanism invites us not only to think in terms of plots, characters, and themes, but also to think *differently*.[19] *Nightwood* similarly encourages readers to divest reading of its deeply ingrained investments in the fate of the human and to consider the possibilities of queer sexuality beyond its allegorical representations through plot and character. For each instance in which *Nightwood* asks us to consider the becoming-animal or becoming-earth of the human, there is a reciprocal instance in which the becoming of the animal or the earth is also at stake, a becoming whose possibilities are lost if we attend only to the human. Such transgressive becomings cross from text to reader as well, decentering the humanist commitments of the reader and asking her to adopt a posthuman position in turn. Just as Cheerful asks the Beast to put her name on the tongues of their sons, even though she herself does not have a tongue with which to speak, *Nightwood* often places language on the tongue of a (not entirely human) reader engaged in her own becoming. When Julie asks "Is that all?" after hearing of Cheerful's death, her question critiques the Beast's inadequate response to Cheerful's "useless gift of love," but it also draws attention to that which is incompletely narrated, the anticipation of a future form, which, like Cheerful's own face, "was not yet." In this way, Cheerful's blank face is not simply a marker of gendered subjugation but also a fertile blankness that escapes the inscriptive power of the human's traditionally gendered binaries.

Imposing a universal sameness to the diverse faces represented in the photographic "Family of Man" exhibition, Carl Sandburg commented, "If the human face is 'the masterpiece of God' it is here then in a thousand fateful registrations."[20] Resisting such signifying constraints placed on the human face, Cohen and Ramlow note, "This visage, this *faciality* as privileged marker of 'humanness,' is the very thing that Deleuze insisted one must lose. He argued that 'One has to lose one's identity, one's face . . . One has to disappear, to become unknown.'"[21] This chapter similarly develops an approach to posthuman love that resists the "fateful registrations" of a universal face, suggesting an unrealized possibility that refuses to replicate the "Family of Man," and that, like Cheerful's blank face, cheerfully turns toward something as yet unknown.

The Inhuman of Love

Nightwood is set primarily in the postwar period of the 1920s, but it opens, "Early in 1880," describing Hedvig Volkbein's birth of Felix Volkbein, one of the main characters. Hedvig gives birth, names him Felix, and then promptly dies in the novel's opening paragraphs:

> Hedvig Volkbein—a Viennese woman of great strength and military beauty, lying upon a canopied bed of a rich spectacular crimson, the valance stamped with the bifurcated wings of the House of Hapsburg, the feather coverlet an envelope of satin on which, in massive and tarnished gold threads, stood the Volkbein arms—gave birth, at the age of forty-five, to an only child, a son, seven days after her physician predicted that she would be taken.
>
> Turning upon this field, which shook to the clatter of morning horses in the street beyond, with the gross splendour of a general saluting the flag, she named him Felix, thrust him from her, and died. (3)

Nightwood opens with a kind of parody of the human life cycle in miniature; thrusting Hedvig out of the narrative as definitively as she thrusts away her newborn child, the novel suggests that the value of Hedvig's "life" is exhausted once she passes it along to Felix. Yet the details of this opening scene also mark a significant departure from the universal "Family of Man" that Barthes critiques. Birth and death occur here not as naturalized phenomena but in a historically contextualized social space. The "spectacular crimson" bed and its valance "stamped with the bifurcated wings of the House of Hapsburg" establish the military context of the Austro-Hungarian Empire and provide, like the "envelope of satin," a lushly material enveloping exterior that inscribes the social world of Hapsburg onto the surface of Hedvig's hollowed-out body. Barnes's depiction of birth and death is also, unlike constructions of a universal "Family," notably anti-sentimental. The violence and drilled precision with which Hedvig "named him Felix, thrust him from her, and died," suggest that birth and death are automatic reflexes dictated by the closely circumscribed world she inhabits, rather than occasions for emotion. And, rather than adherence to the gendered norms that define the "Family of Man," this opening scene depicts birth as an act of gender rebellion. Strikingly alone in the opening tableau, Hedvig dies with the "gross splendour of a general saluting the flag." Her delivery also defies medical prescription, occurring "seven days after her physician predicted that she would be taken." This excess of "seven days" recalls Genesis, casting the birth in mythic terms and substituting female creation for biblical creation. Despite everything that is unconventional about this life cycle of birth and death, however, the mandate of reproduction prevails. The gender inversion involves no true *transgression* or "*pleasure* in the confusion of boundaries," to quote Donna Haraway,[22] but instead upholds the mandate of a binary gender system whose meanings are determined by military, medical, and religious authority. As though she is rehearsing the humanist straits of only vacillating between two gendered norms, Barnes describes the drilled inevitability of heterosexuality that fails to risk what Bersani describes as the ontological "breakdown of the human."

If *Nightwood* aligns the beginning of the narrative with biological birth, however, it quickly decouples narrative time from the progression of the heteronormative life cycle, instead describing disorienting spatiotemporal shifts that resist being understood through their linear progression. After a long description of two portraits that Guido acquires in order to represent a faux aristocratic family lineage, the novel abruptly notes: "At this point exact history stopped for Felix who, thirty years later, turned up in the world" (10); after a "sideshow" episode in Berlin with circus folk, Felix then "turned up in Paris" without narrative motivation (33). Following these disorienting spatiotemporal shifts, Barnes introduces Robin in an unconscious state, lost to space and time.[23] Unlike Hedvig, whose body and subsequent corpse are fixed firmly in social time, the elaborate figurative language through which Robin "lives," despite being unconscious, escapes the immediate social context of postwar Europe, describing her material connection with plant and ocean life as well as organic matter such as fungi and amber:

> The perfume that her body exhaled was of the quality of that earth-flesh, fungi, which smells of captured dampness and yet is so dry, overcast with the odour of oil of amber, which is an inner malady of the sea, making her seem as if she had invaded sleep incautious and entire. Her flesh was the texture of plant life, and beneath it one sensed a frame, broad, porous, and sleep-worn, as if sleep were a decay fishing her beneath the visible surface. About her head there was an effulgence as of phosphorous glowing about the circumference of a body of water—as if her life lay through her in ungainly luminous deteriorations—the troubling structure of the born somnambule, who lives in two worlds—meet of child and desperado. (38)

Robin's transcorporeal engagement with nonhuman life produces a range of sensory effects, evoking all the tactility and phenomenological sensation that is absent from Hedvig's socially determined body. Transgressing the taxonomic categories of terrestrial, aquatic, and aerial life, Robin is unclassifiable according to any of these and is instead a site of "becoming-woman, becoming-child; becoming-animal, -vegetable, or -mineral; becomings-molecular of all kinds, becomings-particle."[24] As Carrie Rohman notes, "She is a supremely primordial and elementary being whose subjectivity, rather than being impermeable and distinct, is characterized by seepage and overlapping."[25]

Nightwood's introductions of Hedvig and Robin thus juxtapose the different temporalities of *bios* and *zoë*: the social time of *bios*, in which the normative human life cycle and its production of a "human family" exist, and the alternately slow and fast temporalities of *zoë*, in which the becoming-body participates. The ambient but palpably material "perfume" that Robin's body emits is produced through the layered, variable speeds of *zoë*—the particular speed of fungi, the slow-time condensations of amber, as well as the attenuating temporalities of "decay" and "deterioration" that seem opposed (or at least adjacent) to the punctuated birth-and-death of Hedvig's opening scene. Despite the highly figurative language that marks Robin's relation with the nonhuman, "the troubling structure of the born somnambule" evokes a mode of physical becoming and not merely the dream world associated with symbols and the unconscious. Understanding sleep as a form of becoming with its own particulate properties, Deleuze and Guattari similarly describe the deterioration through which Proust's Albertine enters into assemblage with the nonhuman: "Albertine can always imitate a flower, but it is when she is sleeping and enters into composition with the particles of sleep that her beauty spot and the texture of her skin enter a relation of rest and movement that place her in the zone of a molecular vegetable: the becoming-plant of Albertine."[26]

When Robin momentarily awakens, her engagement with the nonhuman disrupts the social world into which she emerges. In its perhaps most frequently discussed passage, *Nightwood* describes Robin as "a woman who is beast turning human," as though the unstable process of "turning human" that emerges from her involvement with animal and vegetable life refuses to reside securely within the gendered category of "woman." Occasioned by Felix's first sight of Robin and the genesis of his desire for her, the "beast turning human" simultaneously evokes and ruptures the heteronormative structure of wedding customs:

> Sometimes one meets a woman who is beast turning human. Such a person's every movement will reduce to an image of a forgotten experience; a mirage of an eternal wedding cast on the racial memory; as insupportable a joy as would be the vision of an eland coming down an aisle of trees, chapleted with orange blossoms and bridal veil, a hoof raised in the economy of fear, stepping in the trepidation of flesh that will become myth; as the unicorn is neither man nor beast deprived, but human hunger pressing its breast to its prey.
>
> Such a woman is the infected carrier of the past: before her the structure of our head and jaws ache—we feel that we could eat her, she who is eaten death returning, for only then do we put our face close to the blood on the lips of our forefathers. (41)

The eland "chapleted with orange blossoms and bridal veil" produces an "insupportable" joy not only by disrupting heteronormative customs but also by opening the human to other unrealized becomings: in Deleuzo-Guattarian terms, the eland-bride "bear[s] witness to *'an inhumanity immediately experienced in the body as such,*' unnatural nuptials 'out-side the programmed body.'"[27] While *Nightwood*'s critics have discussed Robin's association with the animal here,[28] what has not quite been drawn out of this passage is the way the processes of becoming-animal describe not only Robin but also the desire and attendant phenomenological sensations produced through perception of Robin—and perhaps not Robin in particular but "such a person" as Robin. As vivid as the passage is, it departs from the materiality of Robin's body, describing her movements as "an image of a forgotten experience; a mirage of an eternal wedding cast on the racial memory" of the one who perceives her. The sequential transformations of the eland-bride coincide with an unraveling of the deeply ingrained perceptual modes that define "racial memory," finally positioning perception in a more primordial position of "human hunger pressing its breast to its prey." Such primordial "hunger," however, does not simply slide backward along a predictable evolutionary scale, but defines a lateral transgression of boundaries. Barnes defines Robin as an "infected carrier of the past," suggesting that the "past" is transmitted as contagion, as virus, as mutation, crossing from carrier to carrier and mutationally altering the bodies it invades.

This "infection" also crosses from text to reader. When the narrator claims that "we feel that we could eat her," it is worth asking who (or perhaps *what*) is speaking, and to whom (or to *what*). Articulating a desire to "eat" Robin places language in the mouth of a becoming-animal, unsettling what we might have presumed to be a (more or less) human narratorial perspective. This desire to "eat" Robin is not just metaphorical but emphatically phenomenological, so pronounced that "the structure of our head and jaws ache." Becoming-animal thus occurs not only "within" the frame of the fictive world, on the side of that which is represented, but also through the reader interpellated into the "we" whose "head and jaws ache," as though there were an invisible bestial form straining to emerge from our own containing human frame. This account of desire unseats "us" from a securely human position, and the effect of the novel is not so much to humanize—to model human consciousness and behavior through a set of recognizable traits and affects—but to animalize. *Nightwood* thus provides a striking example of what it might mean to read "in a posthuman way," which entails "read[ing] against one's self, against one's own deep-seated self-understanding as a member or even representative of a certain 'species.'"[29] Reading "against one's self" here significantly entails passing not only between the human and the nonhuman but also between the living and the dead: it is only through eating "she who is eaten death returning" that we "put our face close to the blood on the lips of our forefathers." Suggesting an inverse prosopopoeia, "our face" becomes a radically uncertain face, as "we" ingest "eaten death returning"—an incorporated form of death. Robin's association with the posthumous thus interrupts an anthropocentric valuation of life, which Jami Weinstein describes as the "remnants of humanism buried in the concept *life itself*."[30]

While the reader encounters "she who is eaten death retuning," Felix paradoxically regards the posthuman potentiality that he senses, but does not fully recognize, as a force to vivify enervated humanist traditions. Immediately after the introduction of Robin and "our" desire to eat her, the narrator claims that only "something of this emotion came over Felix" (41), that the fantastic mutations of Robin are occasioned by, but not identical with, Felix's perception. Dr. Matthew O'Connor (typically referred to as just "the doctor") "know[s] that Felix had experienced something unusual," but Felix immediately rechannels the unusual into the usual, claiming, in response to Robin's unconscious state, that "he wished a son who would feel as he felt about the 'great past'" (42). Rather than an encounter with otherness, Felix experiences desire as a form of self-replication. This replicative desire for sons is modeled, in turn, upon the impulses of his own father, Guido, whose paternity is described almost as a kind of cloning, or "prepar[ing] out of his own heart for his coming child a heart, fashioned on his own preoccupation" (5). Replicating himself, his father, and the "Family of Man" that precedes them, Felix is drawn to Robin's "quality of the 'way back'" (44) but attempts to rechannel the "deep time" experience of tasting "blood on the lips of our forefathers" into a more palatable version of human history. Robin is charged with producing a son but also, more importantly, with retroactively producing an ersatz aristocratic lineage whereby Felix would be inscribed within official versions of human history. Felix identifies Robin as an ideal partner in his reproductive endeavor, because "with an American anything can be done" (42).

This entitled belief that "anything can be done" with (or to) Robin suggests that Felix can adopt a kind of curatorial relationship to his own blood, crafting his lineage into whatever form he desires.[31] When Felix later asks the doctor, "Why did she marry me? It has placed me in the dark for the rest of my life," the doctor indirectly answers by reintroducing Robin's engagement with the nonhuman, which Felix fails to experience:

"Take the case of the horse who knew too much. . . . She was in mourning for something taken away from her in a bombardment in the war" (121). Felix's desire, however, is not to experience the processes of becoming-animal or becoming-posthumous by incorporating "she who is eaten death returning," but to escape death altogether by creating an unbroken family lineage that would connect him with both the humanist past and its future. Even if Felix misrecognizes the posthuman potential of "the beast turning human," however, his apparently "straight" desire is motivated by a current of inhuman life roiling below this placid surface. Rather than positioning queer sexuality in the marginalized space of social death, *Nightwood* suggests that the inhuman transgressions of queer erotics subtend the "tomb-like hollow" of the heteronormative subject. *Nightwood* thus models not only queer love but also the *becoming-queer of love* that passes through an array of micro-gendered, micro-sexed, and micro-specied associations.

Reciprocal Effects

If my reading of *Nightwood* thus far has anthropocentrically focused on the becoming-animal and its potential implications for the human, *Nightwood* also asks us to consider the reciprocal becoming of the animal from *its* position. Deleuze and Guattari argue that the processes of becoming are always reciprocal, that for every "becoming-animal" of the human there is a reciprocal deterritorialization and becoming of the animal. They illustrate this reciprocity through the example of the wasp and the orchid, whose interactions deterritorialize (and reterritorialize) insect and plant alike:

> How could movements of deterritorialization and processes of reterritorialization not be relative, always connected, caught up in one another? The orchid deterritorializes by forming an image, a tracing of a wasp; but the wasp reterritorializes on that image. The wasp is nevertheless deterritorialized, becoming a piece in the orchid's reproductive apparatus. But it reterritorializes the orchid by transporting its pollen. Wasp and orchid, as heterogeneous elements, form a rhizome.

Considering the "wasp-orchid," which uncannily takes the visual form of the wasp, and even produces the pheromones of the female wasp in order to attract the pollination of the male wasp, Deleuze and Guattari argue that such relationships should be understood not simply "in a signifying fashion" as imitation or lure "but a capture of code, surplus value of code, an increase in valence, a veritable becoming, a becoming-wasp of the orchid and a becoming-orchid of the wasp."[32] In the same way, how might the human and nonhuman exchanges in *Nightwood* be understood not only "in a signifying fashion" but also through their capture and production of code, much as Robin, as an "infected carrier," facilitates exchanges that are coded, mutational, and viral?

When Robin leaves Felix and Guido, disappearing for several months and then reappearing in Nora's company, Barnes only indirectly narrates the beginning of their relationship, instead foregrounding the mediation of a nonhuman perspective and interrogating the reciprocal exchanges between the human and the nonhuman. While Felix's first meeting of Robin occurs through the fantastic mutation of Robin into an "eland-bride," Robin and Nora's meeting positions the human and the animal in very different relationship, as their intimacy arises spontaneously through interaction with a circus lioness rather than through a human-to-human interface. They are strangers before the lioness prostrates herself in front of Robin, but they leave the circus arena physically connected:

> Then as one powerful lioness came to the turn of the bars, exactly opposite the girl, she turned her furious great head with its yellow eyes afire and went down, her paws thrust through the bars and, as she regarded the girl, as if a river were falling behind impassable heat, her eyes flowed in tears that never reached the surface. At that the girl rose straight up. Nora took her hand. "Let's get out of here!" the girl said, and still holding her hand Nora took her out. (60)

While Felix misrecognizes the becoming-animal of Robin as belonging only to her, Robin and Nora are mutually implicated in their experience with the lioness. More importantly, while Felix attempts to translate the energy of becoming-animal into the traditional human channels of family, the lioness experiences her own processes of becoming rather than being subordinated in the figurative representation of the human (Robin as eland-bride). The circus encounter is mutual in that animal regards human as much as human regards animal—it is the lioness's "furious great head with its yellow eyes afire" that dominates the scene. Seeking escape from various forms of human entrapment, the lioness thrusts her paws through the bars of her cage, using her body to disrupt the boundaries separating human and animal. The lioness's unshed "tears," markers of emotion that are typically attributed only to humans, are described

as "a river falling behind impassable heat," emphasizing the fluid qualities of becoming that connect human and animal rather than the hierarchical relationship that has reduced her to living in a circus cage. Robin
is similarly depicted as wearing a superficial animal "hide" that moves
across fluidly connected forms of "life," her beauty characterized as a
"sort of fluid blue under the skin, as if the hide of time had been stripped
from her, and with it, all transactions with knowledge" (143). Abruptly
rejecting the humanist hierarchy that reduces the lioness to a cage ("Let's
get out of here!" Robin cries, in one of her few lines in the novel), Robin
and Nora's relationship emerges through their mutual recognition of the
currents that run between human and animal.

Attending to the position of the animal and the reciprocal experience
of *its* becoming also provides a new approach to the final chapter, "The
Possessed," which has perplexed, if not overtly troubled, many of the
novel's critics. "The Possessed" abruptly shifts from its setting in Europe
to the United States, but it is a de-realized United States. Robin's primary
activity is "wandering without design" through spaces that are notably
depopulated, "pulling at the flowers, speaking in a low voice to the animals," engaged with "something unseen" (176, 177). Robin's country is
a nonhuman country. "Wandering without design," she nevertheless
"circled closer and closer" to Nora's property, which "had its own burial
ground and a decaying chapel," drawn there as if by an instinctual pull
(55). Robin sleeps alternately in the woods and the chapel, engulfed by
the forces of the nonhuman, which "obliterat[e] her as a drop of water is
made anonymous by the pond into which it has fallen" (177). It is Nora's
dog, rather than Nora, who detects Robin's presence, leading Nora toward
the chapel, a traditional site of weddings, funerals, and christenings. The
scene of human reunion, however, is interrupted as Nora blindly collides
with the wooden jamb of the chapel's threshold, and Robin and the dog
face off on all fours with one another.

Nightwood's conclusion is troubling if we approach it from a humanist perspective of identifying with character and its fate within the plot,
which is understood to allegorically model the outcomes of behavior.
That is, if *Nightwood* advocates the non-normative potentials of queer
love and of becoming-animal, what does it mean that the characters
find their conclusion in an abandoned site of decay, ambiguously "going
down" in what might suggest devolution or madness?[33] The encounter
between Robin and animal becomes quite different, however, if we regard
it not from an anthropocentric position but from the position of the ani-

mal.[34] Here the animal is not a signifier of devolution but an actant in its own right. The dog and Robin occupy positions of physical reciprocity, with Robin "barking in a fit of laughter, obscene and touching," and the dog "cry[ing] then, running with her, head-on with her head." *Nightwood* abandons its fantastically metaphorical voice in this final chapter, instead emphasizing forms of expressive but nonlinguistic communication. It is an animal tongue, rather than a human tongue gifted with speech, that dominates the end of the novel: the dog's "tongue slung sideways over his sharp bright teeth" forming "a stiff curving terror in his mouth" (179). The dog's gesture also produces the final image of the novel; located in front of "a contrived altar, before a Madonna" (178), the dog lies down next to Robin, "his eyes bloodshot, his head flat along her knees" (180). Posed in a kind of posthuman reconfiguration of the *Pietà*, the dog corporeally disrupts an iconic scene predicated upon virgin birth, the transcendence of physicality and sexuality, and the inviolate status of the family as the basis for spiritual transcendence. The novel's final tableau thus describes the trans-specied "birth" of something unknown and rich with possibility between the human and the nonhuman. Rather than reaching a narrative conclusion that reinforces the determinative meaning of death in the normative human life span, *Nightwood* radically opens the final chapter to unrealized unions between the human and the nonhuman. "The Possessed" thus asks us to consider the "fate" of queer love not by measuring Nora and Robin's relationship according to its similarity to or difference from heteronormative couplings but by posing more trenchant questions about how queer love is involved in a reconfiguration of the "Family of Man."

The Family Grave

While "The Possessed" is potentially nihilistic from a humanist point of view, the destruction of the heteronormative family inherent in this chapter is also valuable in its own right, achieving an openness to the unknown by "embrac[ing] the destruction and rearticulation of the human in the name of a more capacious and, finally, less violent world," to return to Butler's claim. *Nightwood* pursues such destruction and rearticulation of the human through forms of becoming-posthumous. When Robin appears in Nora's dreams as a harbinger of death, for example, she accomplishes an important burial of the heteronormative family and the signifying traditions that locate the subject within a bigendered familial lineage. Nora claims that her love for Robin entails "enter[ing] my dead," an entry into her genealogical past that inevitably reconfigures its hierarchical relationships:

> Was I her devil trying to bring her comfort? I enter my dead and bring no comfort, not even in my dreams. There in my sleep was my grandmother, whom I loved more than anyone, tangled in the grave grass, and flowers blowing about and between her; lying there in the grave, in the forest, in a coffin of glass, and flying low, my father who is still living; low going and into the grave beside her, his head thrown back and his curls lying out, struggling with her death terribly, and me, stepping about its edges, walking and wailing without a sound; round and round, seeing them struggling with that death as if they were struggling with the sea and my life; I was weeping and unable to do anything or take myself out of it. There they were in the grave glass, and the grave water and the grave flowers and the grave time, one living and one dead and one asleep. (158)

This remarkable passage describes not only the death of the grandmother and the figurative death of the father but also the absolute mortification of a natural world that they might have inhabited, tattooing "the grave" upon the material world through repetitive emphasis upon "the grave glass, and the grave water and the grave flowers and the grave time." This misapplication of signifiers hollows out language's ability to represent the world, such that the dark opacity of the "grave" uncertainly joins with, and thus undoes, a range of materials and concepts: the brittle transparency of glass, the fluidity of water, the botanical life of the flower, and the philosophical conception of time. In redundantly assigning "the grave" to each of these materials, the signifying power of language is evacuated, providing no stable "ground" on which the grandmother and the father can exist. For the reader, who knows the father and the grandmother only as these "graved" figures with no other attributes, characteristics, or actions outside of Nora's dream, the primacy of these family positions is undone, along with their ability to prescribe the meanings of subjecthood more generally. Just as Bersani charges queer sexuality with "bury[ing] the subject in the tomb-like hollow of the signifier," Nora's love for Robin buries the signifiers that would dictate gendered identity and their roles within a larger humanist "Family." While this "grave world" might appear enervated, *Nightwood*'s redistribution of mortality across "the grave glass, and the grave water and the grave flowers and the grave time" paradoxically extends the horizons of what counts as "life" rather than positioning death as life's inert other.

Nightwood also enacts the deterioration of the heteronormative family through Nora and Robin's exchange of the doll, which, in its mimetic yet hollow form functions as a material emblem of the "tomb-like hollow of the signifier." When Robin gives Nora a doll (and later crushes it under her heel), Nora initially interprets the doll through the heteronormative paradigm of family, claiming, "We give death to a child when we give it a doll—it's the effigy and the shroud; when a woman gives it to a woman, it is the life they cannot have, it is their child, sacred and profane" (151). For Nora, the doll is an emblem of nonprocreative sexuality, connoting the deathly space outside the heteronormative mandate that Edelman terms "reproductive futurism"—a relentless championing of reproduction and the child, who bears the promise of a redemptive future, despite the atrocities of the past.[35] Understanding queer sexuality as excluded from this heteronormative narrative of progress, Nora regards her relationship with Robin as a site of death, deprived of "the life they cannot have." *Nightwood* suggests, however, that such figurative associations with death are not an exclusionary effect of the reproductive mandate but are produced by heteronormativity itself. When Nora reflects that "we give death to a child when we give it a doll," she identifies the deathliness of imposing upon a child the expectation that she herself must inevitably produce a child one day, thus defining "life" as the always-deferred future that belongs to the generation to come. When the child is given a doll and expected to rehearse the future position of unreconstructed parental care in relation to this mimetic representation of herself, the child is interpellated into a heteronormative narrative whereby "the future is mere repetition and just as lethal as the past."[36] *Nightwood* accordingly describes Felix and Robin's son as an "addict to death" (114), suggesting the mortifying exploitation inherent in using the child to project a social order that is always progressing toward some more optimistic, but inevitably deferred, future.

Although Nora identifies the deathliness of imposing a reproductive mandate upon the child, the doctor defines the doll as an active "weapon" with which to reconceptualize the human. The doctor imagines that children's "play" uses the doll as a focal point to undermine the gender norms they represent, claiming the doll as the favored object of "the girl who should have been a boy, and the boy who should have been a girl."

In this way, the doll acts as a kind of "weapon" in a queering machine that deterritorializes the gendered rules of the family. The doctor ascribes an inverse relation between gender-queering and the mimetic properties of the doll, claiming that the doll "resembles but does not contain life," while the "third sex . . . contains life but resembles the doll." While Robin is temporarily confined in this inert rehearsal of family roles, often dressed in boys' clothing and rocking the doll, which Nora describes as "our child," she eventually destroys this oedipal substitute, crushing it beneath her heel, leaving its "china head all in dust" (157), and rejecting gendered and sexual possibilities that are confined only to the family and familiar human forms.

Love's Remains

If heteronormative marriage, binding couples "'til death do us part," reinforces death's finality as the horizon of human life, queer love in *Nightwood* complicates this linear temporality and its ability to define the human form. Barnes positions queer desire through a generative return from death, introducing Robin as "she who is eaten death returning," and Nora claims that queer love unfolds not in a linear progression toward conclusion but through a dilatory foreknowledge of death: "Love is death, come upon with passion; I know, that is why love is wisdom" (146). Queer love's ability to love in the face of death (and perhaps to survive love itself) implies an incorporation of death, an ability to be "she who is eaten death returning," redefining death not as the limit that demarcates the subject but as a series of engagements with otherness that continually punctuate the subject's experience. Such engagements with the otherness of death are generative of transcorporeal forms of life not confined to the autonomous subject. The doctor describes Robin and Nora's relationship, for example, not only as the interaction between two subjects but through the contagious, transcorporeal agency of a "pox," claiming that if the beloved "were dying of the pox, one would will to die of it too, with two feelings, terror and joy, wedded somewhere back again into a formless sea where a swan (would it be ourselves, or her or him, or a mystery of all) sinks crying" (146). Just as Deleuze and Guattari argue that becomings entail "a capture of code, surplus value of code," the becoming-queer, becoming-other of love implies the surplus, contagious, agential movements of code. In this way, Barnes describes queer love not through the normative life span predicated upon the "universal" experiences of birth and death but rather through molecular processes such that "sharing a life" with the beloved implies particulate, viral exchanges across a range of material and social boundaries. Such contagious exchanges challenge the unity of a social body that hygienically privileges only those bodies deemed most suitable for reproduction. As Weinstein notes, "Microbes, like queers, women, and people of color, both disturb and reinforce established notions of purity and ontologically hygienic portraits of the human and its handmaiden, life."[37] Sharing the beloved's "pox" implies a contagious, transcorporeal generation that challenges this "hygienic portrait of the human," producing not a mimetic echo of the eternal human but, much more improbably, a swan. In the doctor's account, the resultant "wedding" of terror and joy produces a posthuman entity beyond gendered assignations ("would it be ourselves, or her or him, or a mystery of all") whose environment is an unrealized "formless sea."

As Robin leaves Felix, then Nora, then Jenny, returning finally to Nora's property only to engage with the nonhuman forces there, *Nightwood* disrupts linear narratives of love, but it also questions what love leaves in its wake. Barnes suggests that even love's "remains" are generative, such that the "death" of love is imbricated in a larger redefinition of the horizon of life. Unable to "keep" Robin, who wanders the streets of Paris night after night, Nora figuratively incorporates Robin into her own body as a kind of "fossil" or "intaglio":

> Love becomes the deposit of the heart, analogous in all degrees to the "findings" in a tomb. As in one will be charted the taken place of the body, the raiment, the utensils necessary to its other life, so in the heart of the lover will be traced, as an indelible shadow, that which he loves. In Nora's heart lay the fossil of Robin, intaglio of her identity, and about it for its maintenance ran Nora's blood. Thus the body of Robin could never be unloved, corrupt or put away. Robin was now beyond timely changes, except in the blood that animated her. . . . Nora would wake from sleep, going back through the tide of dreams into which her anxiety had thrown her, taking the body of Robin down with her into it, as the ground things take the corpse, with minute persistence, down into the earth, leaving a pattern of it on the grass, as if they stitched as they descended. (61–62)

Nora's encryption of Robin's fossilized form seems to make her own body into a tomb, but even this incorporation requires the circulation of her own vital blood, which both "animates" Robin's form and deterritorializes her own. Just as the orchid "deterritorializes by forming an image, a tracing of a wasp," Nora forms a "tracing" or "intaglio" of Robin's identity, her own body then reterritorialized and resurging into the vital life that circulates around this tracing. It is not so much that Nora "keeps" Robin, then, but that she experiences "becoming-Robin," which inaugurates a series of other becomings: the passage concludes not where it begins, in an abstracted, private "tomb," but in a material space of becoming-earth. The earth then forms a tracing and "pattern" of the corpse upon the visible surface, but is reterritorialized through the subterranean return of the corpse to the larger "life" of *zoë*. The becoming-earth of the corpse shifts the passage away from the circumscribed human corpse, describing the animated activity of the "ground things [that] take the corpse with minute persistence." This active taking and almost intentional "minute persistence" of becoming-earth redefines life in terms of its agency rather than its finitude. As Jussi Parikka notes in his discussion of Braidotti, "Life is intensive, creative, and infinite in the Spinozan take, in which life became a subject as well."[38] While *Nightwood* thus associates queer love with death, such association is part of a larger repositioning of life and death as adjacent, rather than oppositional, vital forces resistant to the punctuated beginning and endings of the heteronormative life cycle.

Love's Circulations

Nora's body is deterritorialized through the circulation of her blood around the incorporated "intaglio" of Robin, but in *Nightwood,* love also participates in a larger network of circulations—not of partners necessarily, but, less materially, of affects, fleeting sensations, material traces, and linguistic exchanges. We interact not only with the beloved as a singular subject but also with what circulates through her in the form of information, images, stories, works of art, and networks of other people. As Robin moves from Felix to Nora to Jenny, for example, this somewhat predictable plot about love gained and lost is deemphasized in favor of a proliferation of exchanges among these various characters and the mediation of these exchanges through the commentary of the doctor. When Nora tracks Robin through Paris, the city becomes an environment imprinted with Robin's traces, and Robin's body, reciprocally, becomes a map marked by the movements, flows, and gestures of Paris as a collective: "Looking at every couple as they passed, into every carriage and car, up to the lighted windows of the houses, trying to discover not Robin any longer, but traces of Robin, influences in her life (and those which were yet to be betrayed), Nora watched every moving figure for some gesture that might turn up in the movements made by Robin" (66). Pursuing Robin in this way is a painful experience for Nora, but *Nightwood* simultaneously models a map of queer exchanges and networks that have thus far gone unrecorded in what Felix describes as "the great past."[39]

The densest nodal point in this network is "Dr. Matthew-Mighty-grain-of-salt-Dante-O'Connor" (87), who has no autonomous "life" of his own in the way that other characters do but instead facilitates connections among the characters and proliferates discourse. He introduces characters to one another, serves as confessor about their relationships, and offers indirect advice through parables peopled (and unpeopled) with fantastic figures. The doctor is a gynecologist, and we learn, indirectly, that he is an abortionist, but *Nightwood* also separates him from these biological forms of birth and death. "The doctor" is, more equivocally, a "middle-aged 'medical student'" with an "interest in gynaecology" (17), and his primary role is not to preside over naturalized birth and death but to serve as a kind of midwife who continually brings forth fragmentary tales of unusual bodies rich in possibilities.[40] Midway through the first chapter, he takes control of the party through the unopposable volume of his voice, simultaneously assuming narrative control of the novel.[41] When Nora is introduced, he claims, "Flood, Nora, why, sweet God, my girl, I helped to bring you into the world!" suggesting not so much that he was present at her physical birth but that he helps to "bring [her] into the world" of the novel (21). Large sections of *Nightwood* consist of sham Socratic dialogues between the doctor and characters seeking deliverance from the pain of desire; he also makes statements that associate him with the authorial position, asking, "And must I, perchance, like careful writers, guard myself against the conclusions of my readers?" and claiming, "I have a narrative, but you will be put to it to find it" (101, 104). Transgressing the boundary between narrator and character, *Nightwood* encourages us to read "the doctor" not solely through the representational lens of personhood but as a generative locus in a pattern of recurring narratives, tropes, and images.[42]

The "action" of the novel might be said to culminate in the chapter "Watchman, What of the Night?" when Nora visits the doctor's apartment unannounced at three in the morning, discovering him in bed wearing a wig, cosmetics, and traditionally female dress. The doctor's apartment is appropriately situated "between the court and the church" at the meeting point of several tramlines, marking the intersection between different forms of social power and traffic flows; as Ann Kennedy notes, "A more Foucauldian positioning of him could hardly be possible."[43] Disrupting Foucauldian power structures through his position as both "the doctor" and a cross-dresser, Matthew has unique access to the body both in terms of medical knowledge and gender performance, biological matter and cultural "expression." And if the doctor is a midwife figure, he is also engaged in a form of self-delivery; defying the gender prescriptions of traditional medicine, his cross-dressing implies an active reconfiguration and delivery of his own body. Surprised by his transvestism and diverted from her own purpose, which is seeking advice about Robin, Nora details the various instruments of the doctor's trade: "a rusty pair of forceps, a broken scalpel, half a dozen odd instruments that she could not place, a catheter, some twenty perfume bottles, almost empty, pomades, creams, rouges, powder boxes and puffs" (85). His collection contains both medical instruments for penetrating the bodily surface and cosmetic instruments for altering and masking that surface. The unhierarchized list, however, which slides from catheter to powder puff as if there is no difference, complicates the distinction between the material substance and the cultural performance, suggesting that the "rusty forceps" and "broken scalpel" of traditional medicine are no longer adequate tools to penetrate into the body's hidden recesses and that cosmetics might just as well translate information about the interior.

While Baroness Elsa von Freytag-Loringhoven is often cited as an "inspiration" for Robin's character, it is perhaps more compelling to trace her materialization in *Nightwood* not through the human figure of Robin but through the collection of prosthetic objects that extend the boundaries of Matthew's body and populate his room. As I discussed in the previous chapter, the Baroness used an array of objects, animals, and technological instruments to reformulate the "machinery" of her body, and we can similarly understand the doctor not only through transgenderism but also through a form of transmaterialism.[44] Such intertwining of the body and matter challenges Nora to alter her modes of perception, as the doctor transitions not from one gender to another but from a state of illegibility to one of "alchemical" possibility.

Nora initially characterizes the doctor's room through its "incredible . . . disorder" and his accoutrements as a form of death: "it was as if being condemned to the grave, the doctor had decided to occupy it with the utmost abandon" (84). But she quickly revises her perceptions so that this "grave" becomes "the grave dilemma of his alchemy" (86), as though transvestism has the "alchemical" ability to produce something beyond the binary components of gender and the discourses that define the body through either its bounded interiority or its exterior surface. Nora's first flashing insight about the doctor accordingly understands cross-dressing not as a transgression of gender categories but as a transgression of *species* categories: "God, children know something they can't tell; they like Red Riding Hood and the wolf in bed!" (85). When she formulates her thoughts more carefully, she still characterizes cross-dressing not in terms of gender but as an engagement with the "extremities" of the human: "Is not the gown the natural raiment of extremity? What nation, what religion, what ghost, what dream, has not worn it—infants, angels, priests, the dead; why should not the doctor, in the grave dilemma of his alchemy, wear his dress?" (86). Rather than confining him to the social margins, the doctor's "natural raiment of extremity" intimately stitches him into the fabric of various humanist institutions as he shares the dress that attires national, religious, and legal figureheads; his dress simultaneously unravels these institutions, however, connecting him to the posthumous and to the ethereal realm of ghosts and spirits—that which occupies a shadowy space excluded by Enlightenment rationalism.

Anticipating Butler's discussion of gender-queering and queer sexuality in "Beside Oneself: On the Limits of Sexual Autonomy," Nora's final reflection upon the doctor's cross-dressing is, "He dresses to lie beside himself" (86). Butler argues that becoming gendered is "always, to a certain extent, becoming gendered *for others*," and that gender and sexuality should not be understood primarily as questions of identity but as *"modes of being dispossessed."*[45] Gender and sexuality emerge as constitutive "fields of desire and physical vulnerability"[46] that cast us toward others and, as Butler argues, toward a reconstitution of the human form. In the same way, the doctor "dresses to lie beside himself," engaged in the processes of becoming-gendered for the one who has yet to arrive. The doctor's body is instead given over to Nora, who receives his corporeality not as a unitary entity but as involved in a queer ecology of matter, which includes the wolf, the gown, the forceps, and "half a dozen odd instruments that she could not place." The doctor's queer body marks a mode of dispossession from the human as well as the displacement of matter from its traditional function. In this way, Barnes's description of the doctor's trans-species, trans-material body exemplifies Butler's claim that the task of queer politics is "no less than a remaking of reality, a reconstituting of the human, and a brokering of the question, what is and is not livable."[47] Nora's reception of the doctor's body is significantly involved in brokering "what is and is not livable." Rather than regarding Matthew as "condemned to the grave," Nora, too, *redresses* her position in order to "lie beside herself," entertaining the "grave alchemy" whereby his gender transgression remakes the category of the human, rather than simply recuperating transvestism into the normative paradigms of gendered binaries and gender imitation. In Butler's terms, Nora's response "lives with its unknowingness about the Other in the face of the Other, since sustaining the bond that the question opens is finally more valuable than knowing in advance what holds us in common, as if we already have all the resources we need to know what defines the human, what its future life might be."[48]

Speaking from a position "beside himself," the doctor's soliloquies in "Watchman, What of the Night?" produce a fantastic catalog of bodies that operate according to their own rules of subtle arrangement and purpose, resisting the universalism of the "Family of Man." Taking a discursively wandering approach, he describes a "Town of Darkness," a liminal space between dreaming and waking, animated by its corporeal particles, circulations, and exchanges (87).[49] This vast signifying city obscures the edges that separate human, animal, and vegetable worlds: alongside his consideration of human dreams, the doctor asks: "And what of the sleep of animals? The great sleep of the elephant, and the fine thin sleep of the bird?" (92). Rather than being defined through birth and death, the doctor's "Town of Darkness" is populated by bodies marked with different apertures and closures, seeping out of their containing borders, weeping, bleeding, sweating, and liquidly flowing in exchanges with the environment. He describes, for instance,

> The criers telling the price of wine to such effect that the dawn saw good clerks full of piss and vinegar, and blood-letting in side streets where some wild princess in a night-shift of velvet howled under a leech; not to mention the palaces of Nymphenburg echoing back to Vienna with the night trip of late kings letting water into plush cans and fine woodwork! (88)

He emphasizes the body's traces and fluid passages, its porosity to outside materials, describing, for instance, the figure who "can trace himself back by his sediment, vegetable and animal, and so find himself in the odour of wine in its two travels, in and out" (91).[50]

The doctor's speech finds an obscure focus through narration of "the night of nights," when he introduces Robin to Jenny (and indirectly betrays Nora); the motive for his "Town of Darkness" is thus love and infidelity, but his wandering discourse suggests that love must be situated within the larger movements and flows through both Paris and more liminally uncertain terrains. At one point Nora interjects, "I'll never understand her—I'll always be miserable" (92), but "understanding" Robin entails entering the networks of human and nonhuman forces in which Robin exists. Matthew's narration of such networks unwrites forms of history that have selectively recorded the life of the body. He urges Nora to imagine "the hand, the face, the foot" outside visual forms of illumination, and he advocates a form of "history at night" that has never been "countenanced or understood to this day" (92). He details the marginalized bodies of "those who turn the day into night, the young, the drug addict, the profligate, the drunken and that most miserable, the lover who watches all night long in fear and anguish." Despite his descriptive detail, such bodies "begin to have an unrecorded look," losing, much as "the Cheerful" does, the human countenance that marks participation in the traditional "Family of Man" (101). The doctor's own body is implicated in such networked exchanges, as he describes his peregrinations through "history at night," "haunt[ing] the *pissoirs*" and "thumping the dock with a sailor" (97). When he eventually narrates the meeting of Robin and Jenny, he focuses not on their personal interaction but their relations with the crowd and the material infrastructure of Paris. Their romance begins during a carriage ride that takes them "down the *Champs Elysées,*" "straight as a die over the *Pont Neuf,*" and "whirled around into *rue du Cherche-Midi*" (110). Even as he describes the origin of a relationship that implicates Robin, Jenny, Nora, and, to some degree, himself, he uses the seemingly irrelevant details of these physical sites to produce a wandering verbal map of Paris, describing the history of an unrecorded queer circulation through the city as well as a queering *of* history and the historical archives. Resisting a linear model of history dominated only by human figures perceived through an epistemologically certain human sensorium, the doctor argues that history at night "can't be thought of unless you turn the head the other way, and come upon thinking with the eye that you fear, which is called the back of the head; it's the one we use when looking at the beloved in a dark place, and she is a long time coming from a great way" (89).

The doctor also transforms "the grave" to which Nora initially condemns him by imagining transvestism as a kind of "autopsy" that functions through creative making rather than eviscerating dissection:

> What an autopsy I'll make, with everything all which ways in my bowels! A kidney and a shoe cast of the Roman races; a liver and a long-spent whisper, a gall and a wrack of scolds from Milano, and my heart that will be weeping still when they find my eyes cold, not to mention a thought of Cellini in my crib of bones, thinking how he must have suffered when he knew he could not tell it for ever. (107)

Rather than understanding the body as a unitary entity defined by long-established social gazes, the doctor describes communication between his own corporeal organs and different historical objects, remapping the body as itself a living archive that emerges through transcorporeal relations with other materialities. As Judith Scherer Herz suggests, the doctor's "autopsy" enacts a form of metempsychosis, which posits a life force that moves indiscriminately among material forms sharing a vitalist unity.[51] Herz compares the corporeal migrations of this autopsy to John Donne's discussion of metempsychosis in *Infinitati Sacrum,* in which the "soul" moves across a spectrum of human and nonhuman forms, including an emperor, a horse, a spider, a melon, and an apple. Earlier in his narration of "history at night," the doctor explicitly cites one of Donne's sermons: "We are all conceived in close prison, in our mothers' wombs we are close prisoners all . . . all our life is but a going out to the place of execution and death" (103). Read in relation to the doctor's creative autopsy, his allusion to Donne suggests liberation not only from the "close prison" of the reproductive family and its gendered roles but also from the "prison" of the human; "going out to the place of execution and death" describes a departure from the strictly human form and a willingness, in Butler's terms, "to allow the human to become something other than what it is traditionally assumed to be."[52]

The doctor's creative autopsy unsutures the eye from normative social gazes and instead approaches the queer body by "coming upon thinking with the eye that you fear." The "eye that you fear" decouples vision from knowledge, instead entertaining uncertainty and, in Butler's terms, "unknowingness about the Other in the face of the Other." The doctor claims, "my heart . . . will be weeping still when they find my eyes cold" (108), emphasizing the networked vitality and the circulatory reach of the heart rather than the epistemological certainty of the eye. But even this "cold" eye is significantly reconfigured. The doctor's "cold eye" is not the gaze of a "newly dead eye," which Descartes claimed as a model for objective looking, the only gaze not "tainted" by the deceiving influences of the other senses. Nor is this "cold eye" the eye of traditional autopsy, which becomes the basis for a generalized model of looking and knowing the body, in which knowledge is the privilege of the disembodied viewer, and corporeality becomes the inert other of life. The doctor's alternative autopsy instead imaginatively *sees through* the "cold eye" of the corpse, a model of looking that requires us to rehearse perhaps the most extreme form of identification with otherness, just as Nora revises her perspective so that what was initially "condemned to the grave" becomes the occasion for an expanded engagement with posthuman life. Undoing the socially constructed eye that seeks classificatory understanding, *Nightwood* proposes that we remake the human by looking through the gaze of an untried, "cold eye," the rehearsal of otherness that is *love's eye*—"the one we use when looking at the beloved in a dark place, and she is a long time coming from a great way."

CODA

In Kind Cuts: Gertrude Stein's Tender Buttons
and the Nonhuman Corpse

Gertrude Stein, it seems to me, is already effectively dead as a writer.
Nobody really reads her, but everybody continues to talk knowingly and
concernedly about her. Her "importance" is a myth. . . . Later ages will
gather about the corpus of her work like a cluster of horrified medical
students around a biological sport.

B. L. REID, *ART BY SUBTRACTION: A DISSENTING OPINION
OF GERTRUDE STEIN*

B. L. REID's *Art by Subtraction* (1958) does not take kindly to Gertrude
Stein. Characterizing her as a "recording mechanism, a camera that
somehow utters words rather than pictures," Reid objects to the automated processes by which Stein's writing "subtracts" from literature the
humanist qualities of beauty, elevated thought, and moral contemplation; he writes, "This is not art; this is science."[1] Reid implies that those
who "really read" Stein are themselves not fully human but are, instead,
"Nobody." I am opening by quoting Reid, however, not in order to rehearse
his critique of Stein's automated "difficulty" (although it is a critique that
is reiterated in less *personal* terms by many of Stein's commentators) but
to pose questions about his claim for the future "corpus" of her work,
attended to by the "horrified" students reduced to dissecting a particularly bizarre body that seems recalcitrant to the rules of human anatomy.

Analogies between the dead body and the artistic "body of work" are
common and, indeed, are etymologically implied by the term *corpus*. But
what kind of body is a text? What kind of relation exists among living readers, writers, and the "corpses" of literary works? Examining a range of different "corpse poems"—poems that specifically represent the speech of
the dead—Diana Fuss argues that literature's animation of "dead letters"

is always the speech of the dead: "Is not every literary utterance a speaking corpse, a disembodied voice detached from a living, breathing body?" In this way, Addie is a speaking corpse in *As I Lay Dying,* but so is the text itself, which comes to readers as an animated voice severed from the "living, breathing body" that produced it. Describing the relation between the living and the dead as an uncertain, reversible passage, however, Fuss also positions the text as the nonhuman force that "animates the living": "Poets are not serving as mediums for the dead; they are themselves dead without the poem to give them voice. Death thus animates the living, not the other way around."[2] For Fuss, it is poetry that *makes* the poet and brings the poet to "life." Catharine Stimpson further complicates this living-nonliving status of the text by considering the role of the author's death in *remaking* the text. Stimpson claims that Stein's death, like that of many artists, necessarily initiates a different kind of critical attention, as death simultaneously produces both the corpse of the author and a "corpus" of work. If the author's death seems to finalize the "body of work" left behind, however, Stimpson also describes the afterlife of Stein's work and her posthumous reputation as an interactive "dependency" between the living and the dead: "If the reality of her work and the memory of her life were to survive, others would now have to secure her fame. . . . Dead, Stein had become a dependent."[3]

In *Tender Buttons* (1914), however, Stein's own conceit for the way we relate to the "corpse" of the text is not necessarily predicated upon the human corpse that presents the reader with an opaque mirror of herself or that animates the reader or the author into a recognizably human form. Evacuated of discernible human subjects, *Tender Buttons* describes not a human corpse but, in Deleuzo-Guattarian terms, a "zone of indiscernibility" where living humans and the corpses of animals, objects, and the textual "corpus" itself come into contact. And, if the text is a corpse, we engage with it not through the "scientific" processes of subtraction and dissection occurring in an unfamiliar space of cold remove, to return to Reid's metaphors, but through the domestic space of lived relations with "OBJECTS," "FOOD," and "ROOMS," the three sections that comprise *Tender Buttons.* Everyday corpses, rather than the "biological sport" that Reid describes.

Turning from the human to the nonhuman corpse is necessary to this project's overarching interrogation of the boundary between the living and the dead, given that nonhuman corpses are routinely assembled with and incorporated into the living body in the form of instrumental bodily extensions and edible matter. In "FOOD" in particular, Stein explores the processes whereby nonhuman bodies become granular and particulate, assimilated into the human body to literally constitute the human as a "zone of indiscernibility" between living and nonliving matter. Jane Bennett argues that edible matter discloses "what Deleuze and Guattari called a certain 'vagabond' quality to materiality,"[4] and in *Tender Buttons* human and nonhuman bodies are similarly vagabond in nature, open to the transitory movements of matter. But how might the textual body, too, be a vagabond body, a vagabond form of matter? "FOOD" describes passages from one form of matter to another, but these passages are also linguistically enacted. As the title suggests, *Tender Buttons* is replete with "tender" matter, "soft" objects that move through transformational states, resisting the fixity of verbal and rational categories—"Melting and not minding," as nouns slide into the role of verbs.[5] Stein writes, "And so in *Tender Buttons* and then on and on I struggled with the ridding myself of nouns, I knew nouns must go in poetry as they had gone in prose if anything that is everything was to go on meaning something."[6] Making nouns *go*, Stein often severs the relation between the referential properties of the signifier and the matter it represents, as nouns often unexpectedly shift into the position of agents. *Tender Buttons*'s repetition of "cut," which slices through the text, for example, enacts a linguistic play that cuts across cases, simultaneously noun, verb, and adjective, troubling the differences between bodies and actions. Where, then, are the boundaries between the human body and its activity when we engage with the human-nonhuman body of the text and *its* particular forms of life?

Carl Van Vechten notes that *Tender Buttons* focuses on the quotidian forms of materiality that "fasten our lives together,"[7] but the fastenings of "our lives" are inevitably assemblages between the human and the nonhuman. The first OBJECT in *Tender Buttons*, "A CARAFE, THAT IS A BLIND GLASS," for example, opens with the phrase "A kind in glass and a cousin" (11), immediately yoking "glass" and "cousin," the nonhuman and the human, but also posing taxonomic questions about kind, kin, and kinship, and perhaps, from an ethical perspective, kindness—terms that are distributed throughout the text.[8] More disturbingly, perhaps, *Tender Buttons* also explores the way that human bodies are often "fastened" to animal corpses, problematizing a more homogeneously defined category of "life" that can be separated from death. While the human corpse is an exceptional, taboo body demarcated from the world of the living, non-human corpses are seamlessly assimilated into both the living body and the life of material culture, paradoxically regarded as sources of vitalism rather than mortalism. *Tender Buttons* relentlessly probes the species differences in "kind" between humans and animals, living and nonliving, as well as the transformative processes of disassemblage and incorporation whereby these ontological differences are obscured. In "ROASTBEEF," for example, Stein writes:

> The time when there are four choices and there are four choices in a difference, the time when there are four choices there is a kind and there is a kind. There is a kind. There is a kind. Supposing there is a bone, there is a bone. Supposing there are bones. There are bones. When there are bones there is no supposing there are bones. There are bones and there is that consuming. The kindly way to feel separating is to have a space between. This shows a likeness. (38)

The passage evokes the moment when consuming the cultural, culinary construct of "ROASTBEEF" yields to a more direct ontological encounter with the animal and its bones: "When there are bones there is no supposing there are bones." The repetitive emphasis on unidentified "bones" confuses the classificatory distinctions of "kind," drawing attention to the ontological "likeness" of the ossified structural form shared by humans and animals. Perhaps calling for an ethical—or at least phenomenological—response to such ontological confusion, the passage concludes by questioning the "kindly way to feel" about such likeness. If "the kindly way to feel separating is to have a space between," however, *Tender Buttons* describes the conceptual or phenomenological suppression of the ontological "kinship" we have with meat that is necessary in order to preserve the fiction of "a space between" the human and the animal. The verbal relay between "kind" and "kindness" is interlaced throughout "ROASTBEEF," even when Stein discusses different "kinds" of animals: "In kind, in a control, in a period, in the alteration of pigeons, in kind cuts and thick and thin spaces, in kind ham and different colors" (36). The wordplay is evocative, questioning, and open-ended: What constitutes a "kind cut" when referring to the "alteration of pigeons" into "FOOD"? What are the "thick and thin spaces" that separate, and fail to separate, the human and the nonhuman, the reader and the text?

Upton Sinclair's *The Jungle* (1906) influentially describes the modernized processes of automated slaughter whereby the animal is disassembled to produce "meat," but it also shows how such slaughter disassembles the human. Just as the animal is broken down into "cuts" of meat, the human is broken down into its separate components through localized industrial injuries: fingers damaged by acid, thumbs reduced to "lump[s] of flesh" after repetitive engagements with knives, rheumatism resulting from work in chilling rooms, and hands severed in moments of distraction at the stamping machines.[9] There are also zoonotic transfers between the human and the nonhuman: germs, contagious diseases, and blood poisoning acquired through the "maze of cuts" marking human hands (120). *Tender Buttons* explores the further processes of disassemblage that necessarily occur within the household economy of the kitchen—and even at the level of the plate. "FOOD" is riddled with "cuts" of various kinds, which Stein often connects with uncertain forms of sensation. *Tender Buttons*'s description of carving into beef, for example, includes "pleasure" and "wailing" that seem to belong both to the carver and the meat: "Please be the beef, please beef, pleasure is not wailing. Please beef, please be carved clear, please be a case of consideration" (39). The passage evokes the suppressed pain and "wailing" embedded within the beef, as well as the wish that this seepage of pain into the domestic space might be suppressed—bloodlessly "carved clear" in a "case of consideration." Despite this wish for meat to be "carved clear," however, "FOOD" often describes the bleeding, "reddening" processes of cutting into edible matter. In "ROASTBEEF," Stein writes, "In the inside there is sleeping, in the outside there is reddening" (35). Imploring us to "read redder," "red" flows through "FOOD," drawing attention to the fluid processes whereby the vitality of edible matter is translated into the vitality of the human (39). Questioning the process of this material incorporation, Bennett asks: "*How is this transfer possible?* . . . What is actually happening when *these* bodies mix with *mine?*"[10] *As I Lay Dying* poses similar questions about such material transfers, as Vardaman repeatedly reflects upon the life of the dead fish that will be "Cooked and et. Cooked et."[11] The ingestion of edible matter demonstrates that the human body is neither autonomous nor bounded but rather a product of its continual physical exchanges with the environment; as Bennett notes, "In the eating encounter, all bodies are shown to be but temporary congealments of a materiality that is a process of becoming, is hustle and flow punctuated by sedimentation and substance."[12]

I acknowledge here that it is perhaps my own form of embodied readership, my own sense of the ethical stakes of "hustle and flow" with other bodies, that compels me to put pressure on questions of "kinship" and "kindness" in the eating encounter between humans and animals. I am strategically slicing into "ROASTBEEF" in order to "read redder" and to draw attention to the potential "wailing" of the animal behind the "pleasure" of consumption. But I am certainly not suggesting that Stein "herself" advocates a vegetarian sensibility. Stein writes about "ROASTBEEF" with too much apparent relish—and perhaps with the semiotic luxury of "playing with one's food" rather than with an ethical urgency. Stein's appetites are apparent both "inside" and "outside" her writing; as Mabel Dodge Luhan noted, "Gertrude was hearty. She used to roar with laughter, out loud. She had a laugh like a beefsteak. She loved beef."[13] Luhan describes various convergences of the human and nonhuman—oral consumption and oral expression, Stein's "hearty" body and the body of the beef. In this way, "Please be the beef" precludes the reciprocal processes of assemblage and exchange with the animal in favor of simply "being" the beef: you are what you eat. But if "being" the beef falls back into the solidity of nouns rather than the transformative processes of becoming, Stein never allows nouns to rest for long. For Stein, the technique of "making nouns go" implies not just "ridding" the text of nouns but making them *go* and move, hustle and flow.

As many critics have noted, "cow" is coded language for sexual pleasure in Stein's writing. "I hope she has her cow," Stein writes (27). Making nouns *go*, "Please be the beef, please beef, pleasure is not wailing," acquires very different connotations. Moving away from the secure referentiality of the noun, "beef" is not simply "beef" (or "cow" for that matter), and *Tender Buttons* evokes different kinds of "pleasure" and "wailing" than my reading has thus far suggested. When "MUTTON" seems to confuse the substance by referencing "light curls very light curls," and "silk and stockings" that were "not present," Stein evokes not only the ontological breakdowns involved in eating MUTTON but also the ontological breakdowns of sexuality (41). Read in these different ways, the body of the text is, in Fuss's terms, "a speaking corpse, a disembodied voice detached from a living, breathing body"—an autopoetic body that "speaks" to me (and through me) in one tongue, and an extension of Stein's own "living" body that speaks in another. As Stimpson notes in her discussion of Stein's "somagrams," Stein's literary reputation is constructed both from the "corpus" of her writing and from her own corporeal image, which asserted not only a female body but also a monumental, and monumentally queer, body that was unapologetic about its appetites and occupation of "ROOM." Such assertion of a prodigious body and body of writing perhaps informs Reid's objection to the troubling "myth" of Stein's "importance," as well as his sense that Stein's literary corpus ought to be properly dissected rather than incorporated, assimilated, or "really read."

Questioning who and what we typically endow with the capacity for "tenderness," *Tender Buttons* explores the differences that cut across various "kinds" of human and nonhuman bodies. In "FOOD," vegetable matter is no less "red" or filled with blood than animal bodies are: vegetables are also corpse bodies ferried from one assemblage to another. Stein begins "VEGETABLE," by asking, "What is cut. What is cut by it. What is cut by it in" (53). In shifting from "What is cut" to "What is cut by it" she alludes to the reciprocal processes of the cut, the concomitant breakdown of the vegetable and the human who consumes it. As Deleuze and Guattari note, "When knife cuts flesh, when food or poison spreads through the body, when a drop of wine falls into water, there is an *intermingling of bodies*."[14] Stein also evokes the "unequal scream" and "little ins and red" that would seem to result from cutting the animal rather than the vegetable: "It was a cress a crescent a cross and an unequal scream, it was upslanting, it was radiant and reasonable with little ins and red" (53). "FOOD" confuses vegetable and animal matter, perhaps, quite literally, in the way that some meals intermingle vegetable and meat items so that, once ingested, they become inseparable from the living "red" of the human body. In other instances, however, descriptions of vegetables are marked by the intrusion of something more jarringly visceral. In "SALAD DRESSING AND AN ARTICHOKE," for example, Stein writes, "Please pale hot, please cover rose, please acre in the red stranger, please butter all the beef-steak with regular feel faces" (59). The sudden reference to "all the beef-steak with regular feel faces"—in the middle of the salad course—marks the return of the animals Stein describes earlier, confronting the eater (and the reader) with the "feel faces" of the animal but also suggesting the inherently social aspect of eating, the confrontation not only with the "red stranger" of one's own material vitality but also the others sharing or deprived of sharing food—the "feel faces" of those who are not even at the table. "One never eats entirely on one's own," Derrida notes, arguing that eating is "*learning* and *giving* to eat, learning-to-give-the-other-to-eat."[15]

Although we know that much of the human diet consists of animal corpses (even if we tend to suppress the "feel faces" behind the meat), *Tender Buttons* also seems to evoke the animal corpses that are more covertly embedded in everyday objects. Animals often surprisingly emerge from Stein's OBJECTS, or OBJECTS come to life as animals. We can understand these transformations strictly as verbal play, but they also coincide with the material processes by which animal bodies are transformed into objects. To return to *The Jungle*, Sinclair writes:

> Out of the horns of the cattle they made combs, buttons, hairpins, and imitation ivory; out of the shin bones and other big bones they cut knife and toothbrush handles, and mouthpieces for pipes; out of the hoofs they cut hairpins and buttons, before they made the rest into glue. From such things as feet, knuckles, hide clippings, and sinews came such strange and unlikely products as gelatine, isinglass, and phosphorus, bone black, shoe blacking, and bone oil. They had curled-hair works for the cattle tails, and a "wool pullery" for the sheep skins; they made pepsin from the stomachs of the pigs, and albumen from the blood, and violin strings from the ill-smelling entrails. When there was nothing else to be done with a thing, they first put it into a tank and got out of it all the tallow and grease, and then they made it into fertilizer. (50–51)

While such totalizing usage of the animal is laudable from a certain perspective, given that nothing is wasted, it also produces "strange and unlikely products" that are, for most people, defamiliarized as derived from the animal. We might envision corpse parts in the mad science laboratory of *Frankenstein* or even in Alexander and Melville Bell's early experiments with technology, but most of us fail to recognize the corpses that comprise our everyday relations with objects. The music of the violin, the photographic print made with albumen, the purity of the soap bar, the hygienic utility of the toothbrush, the ornamental neatness of the button: all these seem to be a world away from the "rivers of hot blood and carloads of moist flesh" required to produce them (328–29). *The Jungle* reveals how invisibly permeated throughout human culture the nonhuman corpse is, rendered into products that infiltrate many aspects of human life, literally providing the "glue" that holds material culture together. If *The Jungle* describes the process whereby the animal is deconstructed, its flesh and viscera rendered into the defamiliarized form of *the button*, for example, *Tender Buttons* disassembles the hard discretion of objects once again. In "A BOX," Stein writes, "Out of kindness comes redness and out of rudeness comes rapid same question, out of an eye comes research, out of selection comes painful cattle" (13). What comes "out of the BOX" is not another object but, much more alarmingly, the "redness" and "rudeness" associated with "painful cattle."

Tender Buttons evokes the processes by which the bodies of objects and corpses are invisibly nested in one another such that material culture is corpse culture.

Evoking the startling "redness" of the often invisible corpse life that enables human vitality, *Tender Buttons* is not only a vagabond body but also a body that is difficult to "ingest" or "assimilate." Rather than depicting reading as a disembodied process, "FOOD" suggests that our engagement with the text and, more generally, the processes of mental life are predicated upon the material ingestion and difficult breakdown of matter. "ROASTBEEF," for example, characterizes "education" as a "difference in cutting" (36), and in "MUTTON" Stein reflects that "Students, students are merciful and recognised they chew something" (40). "FOOD" thus foregrounds the close relation between information and matter, the analogies between mental and material forms of rumination, digestion, and assimilation. But what do we "digest" when we read a text like *Tender Buttons,* which, like many modernist texts, emphasizes opacity, difficulty, uncertainty, and linguistic play? For example, what is it that we consume when Stein follows her description of "pain soup" with the following sequence of sounds: "A no, a no since, a no since when, a no since when since, a no since when since a no since when since, a no since, a no since when since, a no since, a no, a no since a no since, a no since, a no since" (59)? As students of Stein, we "recognize we chew something," but what? Sianne Ngai notes that Stein's metaphors of incorporation might take us out of the human realm, as Stein's "meta-taste concept seems to demand not only the representation of delectable objects but the image of something less easily consumable—a blistered, toothy, and staggering something that we would not want to put in our mouths at all."[16] What is this "blistered, toothy, and staggering something" that is perhaps not only inhuman but also bears the possibility of biting back? Reading *Tender Buttons* requires an uncertain material and sensory engagement with the text, a yielding to the "difference in cutting" that the text performs. But what kind of alteration is achieved "in kind cuts"? Where do we cut the boundaries of the human, either from the body of the text or a larger body of matter? As Derrida notes in his dialogue on eating, "We know less than ever where to cut—either at birth or at death. And this also means that we never know, and never have known, how to *cut up* a subject."[17]

Embracing the uncertainty of not knowing "how to *cut up* a subject" is a marked departure from the epistemological cuts of the clinical gaze and the attendant forms of autoptic vision that extract an idealized human from other dehumanized or mortified forms of material life. Stein's verbal play cuts across the categories that allow for such certain extractions: "Cut a gas jet," "Cut the grass" (46), "Cut the whole space into twenty-four spaces" (47), "Cut up alone the paved way which is harm" (48). In this way, *Tender Buttons* performs an alternative autopsy that continually recuts not only the human figure but also the conceptual categories that understand matter through ontologically discrete forms. The experimental techniques of modernism often foreground such alternative conceptual and formal cuts—the cuts of the surrealist "exquisite corpse," the chance operations of the dadaist "cut-up," the editing techniques of the cinematic cut, the poetic fragment and the jarring line break, the disassemblage of traditional novelistic and literary forms, the reassemblage of voices and perspectives that, like Fuss's "speaking corpses," are detached from a "living, breathing body." Through such modernist experimentation, the human figure, too, is cut into by the body of the text—surface cuts, calculating incisions, "kind cuts," a "maze of cuts" by which the human as a unitary figure dies in favor of that which is remade through the recombinant powers of cutting.

More generally, Stein's emphasis on education as a "difference in cutting" suggests that reading might always be a kind of *posthumous* and *posthuman* activity, as the living cuts of readership animate, and reanimate, the text that otherwise exists in a state of dormancy, if not death. Stein claims that such "cuts" are always reciprocal: "What is cut. What is cut by it. What is cut by it in" (53). Reading cuts both ways. Such reciprocity compels me to consider the cuts that my own reading has performed by placing the corpus of modernism in relation to the emergent discourses of posthumanism, the interpretive practices by which I have cut up, cut into, extracted, cited, recirculated, and reassembled the texts discussed in this book. Reading cuts across time periods, as my position within an early-twenty-first-century context of bodies, machines, and materials inevitably informs my reading of modernism—even as modernism not only imaginatively anticipates but also arguably constructs the materials of our current posthumanist moment. In this way, we might regard the text not as the fixed and lifeless body around we which gather to perform what Reid terms the "biological sport" of a detached analytical autopsy, but rather as the vital "talking corpse" that speaks to us, through us, and cuts into us, in kind.

"Corpse" is not a term that appears in *Tender Buttons,* but it appears in the lyrics of the title track from Broadcast's 2005 album, *Tender Buttons,* itself a remaking and recutting of Stein's 1914 text. When I teach Stein, I often begin by playing a track from this album, tuning *Tender Buttons* for contemporary ears, regarding Stein's text not as the disembodied voice severed from the body and material context that produced it but as a living broadcast that reemerges into new sensory, material, and technological fields. Trish Keenan's lyrics in the concluding stanza of "Tender Buttons" (which have acquired their own poignant afterlife since Keenan's untimely death in 2011) perhaps reflect upon her own engagement with the varied *corpus* of Stein, alluding to the process by which reading continually "cuts" into the nonhuman bodies of texts, allowing us to make and remake the "likeness" of both a continually emergent text and the continually emergent posthuman figure cut by such reading:

The corpse
The likeness

Die cut
Die cut
Die cut
Die

      cut

          Die

               cut

                   Die

                       cut . . . [18]

NOTES

Introduction

1 Ernest Hemingway, *The Sun Also Rises* (New York: Scribner, 2006), 200.

2 F. Scott Fitzgerald, *The Great Gatsby* (New York: Scribner, 2004), 162.

3 The publication of photographs depicting corpses was carefully controlled during the war, but they were circulated in the years following; Ernst Friedrich's *War against War* (1924), including photographic captions in four languages, offered a particularly graphic representation of World War I death and injuries.

4 See Mark Goble's insightful discussion of modernism and media archives (Goble, *Beautiful Circuits: Modernism and the Mediated Life* [New York: Columbia University Press, 2010]).

5 Rosi Braidotti, *The Posthuman* (Cambridge: Polity Press, 2013), 66.

6 W. J. T. Mitchell, "The Rights of Things," foreword to *Animal Rites: American Culture, the Discourse of Species, and Posthumanist Theory,* by Cary Wolfe (Chicago: University of Chicago Press, 2003), xiii.

7 In this way, my project's focus on the corpse and the terrestrial would productively resonate with Matthew A. Taylor's recent book examining the posthuman cosmological in American literature. Taylor identifies a paradox in contemporary posthumanism: if the humanist self is predicated upon the exclusion of the nonhuman, the posthumanist self potentially includes the nonhuman so that it "serves our all-too-human agendas" and "becomes ourselves" (Taylor, *Universes without Us: Posthuman Cosmologies in American Literature* [Minneapolis: University of Minnesota Press, 2013], 7). Taylor turns to a cosmological dimension of the universe that is more recalcitrant to such inclusion. Taking his (and others') critique of the way in which the nonhuman might simply "becomes ourselves," my project distinguishes between reconfigurations of the human that serve humanist agendas and those that involve a more radical engagement with nonhuman otherness.

8 See John Troyer's discussion of the various nineteenth-century technologies that conspired to produce "a timeless human corpse that resisted organic decomposition and visual degradation" (Troyer, "Embalmed Vision," *Mortality* 12, no. 1 [2007]: 23).

9 See, for example, Hans Moravec, *Mind Children: The Future of Robot and Human*

Intelligence (Cambridge: Harvard University Press, 1990) and *Robot: Mere Machine to Transcendent Mind* (Oxford: Oxford University Press, 1999); and Ray Kurzweil, *The Age of Spiritual Machines: When Computers Exceed Human Intelligence* (New York: Penguin Books, 2000) and *The Singularity Is Near: When Humans Transcend Biology* (New York: Penguin Books, 2006).

10 Moravec, *Mind Children*, 116.

11 N. Katherine Hayles, *How We Became Posthuman: Virtual Bodies in Cybernetics, Literature, and Informatics* (Chicago: University of Chicago Press, 1999), 3, 5.

12 Ibid., 5.

13 Braidotti, *The Posthuman*, 120.

14 Following Braidotti and Deleuze, Margrit Shildrick's work on assisted suicide argues, "Without doubt, *my* death signals the cessation of myself but nonetheless the event of dying is a further opening, another moment of becoming. In that sense, the individual instance of dying celebrates the flux and flow of becoming, and death itself is negated (Shildrick, "Death, Debility, and Disability," *Feminism & Psychology* 25, no. 1 [2015]: 158). Jami Weinstein argues that attending to "posthumous life" counters the "pernicious and trenchant humanist assumptions" embedded in an unreconstructed vitalist emphasis on *"life itself"*: "Whereas the posthuman is theorized on the basis of the death of Man (or human), the posthumous is meant to capture a broader and more comprehensive repudiation of humanism involving the death of life in its humanistic forms. Posthumous life, then, pushes the envelope of posthumanism by renouncing the vestiges of humanistic life still present and deeply entrenched in our ontological and ethical presuppositions even after 'the death of Man'" (Weinstein, "Vital Ethics: On Life and In/difference," in *Against Life*, ed. Alastair Hunt and Stephanie Youngblood [Evanston: Northwestern University Press, 2016], 96).

15 Characterizing corpses as "ambiguous protagonists," David Sherman notes that they "organize plots which begin with a biological perishing and involve a search for ritual and hygienic care, marks of identification, and secure state of rest that accomplish death as a culturally intelligible event" (Sherman, *In a Strange Room: Modernism's Corpses and Mortal Obligations* [Oxford: Oxford University Press, 2014], 108).

16 I am indebted here to Jane Bennett's discussion of "thing-power," "the curious ability of inanimate things to animate, to act, to produce effects dramatic and subtle" (Bennett, *Vibrant Matter: A Political Ecology of Things* [Durham: Duke University Press, 2010]).

17 Gilles Deleuze and Félix Guattari, *A Thousand Plateaus: Capitalism and Schizophrenia*, trans. Brian Massumi (Minneapolis: University of Minnesota Press, 1987), 257.

18 For discussion of the "lives" of celebrity, political, and other corpses that act in the public sphere, see Katherine Verdery, *The Political Lives of Dead Bodies: Reburial and Postsocialist Change* (New York: Columbia University Press, 1999); and Margaret Schwartz, *Dead Matter: The Meaning of Iconic Corpses* (Minneapolis: University of Minnesota Press, 2015).

19 Jani Scandura and Michael Thurston, "America and the Phantom Modern," in *Modernism, Inc.: Body, Memory, Capital,* ed. Scandura and Thurston (New York: New York University Press, 2000), 3.

20 Michel Foucault, *The Order of Things: An Archaeology of the Human Sciences* (New York: Routledge, 2002), 422.

21 Jacques Derrida, "The Ends of Man," in *Margins of Philosophy,* trans. Alan Bass (Chicago: University of Chicago Press, 1972).

22 Deleuze and Guattari, *A Thousand Plateaus,* 254.

23 Gilles Deleuze and Félix Guattari, *Anti-Oedipus: Capitalism and Schizophrenia,* trans. Robert Hurley, Mark Seem, and Helen R. Lane (Minneapolis: University of Minnesota Press, 1983), 285–86.

24 Ibid., 4.

25 Deleuze and Guattari, *A Thousand Plateaus,* 266.

26 Ibid., 30.

27 Fitzgerald, *Gatsby,* 137.

28 Deleuze and Guattari, *Anti-Oedipus,* 335.

29 Tim Armstrong, *Modernism, Technology, and the Body: A Cultural Study* (Cambridge: Cambridge University Press, 1998), 98.

30 Judith Butler, *Undoing Gender* (New York: Routledge, 2004), 1.

31 Stefan Herbrechter, review of *The Posthuman,* by Rosi Braidotti, *Culture Machine* 14 (April 2013): 3.

32 Stefan Herbrechter and Ivan Callus, "What Is a Posthumanist Reading?" *Angelaki* 13, no. 1 (April 2008): 95.

33 Stefan Herbrechter, *Posthumanism: A Critical Analysis* (London: Bloomsbury Academic, 2013), 7.

34 Michel Foucault, *The Birth of the Clinic: An Archaeology of Medical Perception,* trans. Alan Sheridan (New York: Pantheon Books, 1973), 125. Foucault argues that although this eighteenth-century perception of the cadaver is exaggeratedly benighted, it nevertheless functions as a kind of truth in the nineteenth century.

35 Karen Jacobs, *The Eye's Mind: Literary Modernism and Visual Culture* (Ithaca: Cornell University Press, 2000), 1–2.

36 Ibid., 27, 19. Robyn Wiegman argues, similarly: "Through the Foucauldian framework, 'race' emerges as the effect of specific organizations of Western knowledge in which scientific and aesthetic approaches to vision, as well as philosophical delineations of (dis)embodiment, assume prominent roles" (Wiegman, *American Anatomies: Theorizing Race and Gender* [Durham: Duke University Press, 1995], 10).

37 René Descartes, *The Philosophical Writings of Descartes,* vol. 1, trans. John Cottingham, Robert Stoothoff, and Dugald Murdoch (Cambridge: Cambridge University Press, 1985), 166.

38 Friedrich Nietzsche, *The Will to Power,* quoted in Jonathan Crary, *Techniques of the Observer: On Vision and Modernity in the Nineteenth Century* (Cambridge: MIT Press, 1922), 40.

39 Ibid., 43.

40 Julia Kristeva, *Powers of Horror: An Essay in Abjection*, trans. Leon S. Roudiez (New York: Columbia University Press, 1982), 3.

41 Foucault, *Birth of the Clinic*, 142.

42 Cary Wolfe uses the term "triumphant disembodiment" to characterize Hayles's account of posthumanism in *How We Became Posthuman*, which, he claims, positions the posthuman in opposition to embodiment, information in opposition to matter, and processes such as mutation as external forces that act on the body (Wolfe, *What Is Posthumanism?* [Minneapolis: University of Minnesota Press, 2009], xv).

43 Seth Moglen, *Mourning Modernity: Literary Modernism and the Injury of American Capitalism* (Stanford: Stanford University Press, 2007); Walter Kalaidjian, *The Edge of Modernism: American Poetry and the Traumatic Past* (Baltimore: Johns Hopkins University Press, 2005).

44 Sherman, *In a Strange Room*, 10.

45 Quoted in Herbrechter, *Posthumanism*, 60.

46 Wolfe, *What Is Posthumanism?* xvi.

47 Herbrechter notes, "Literature—this humanist invention—might be seen as a privileged cultural practice that engages in this representational negotiation between the human and the inhuman" (*Posthumanism*, 57).

48 William Carlos Williams, *Spring and All* (New York: New Directions, 2011), 8–9.

49 Williams often rejects spelling conventions in *Spring and All*. His preference for "occured" here perhaps plays with the notion that species extinction is a difficult "cure" for the ailments of *Homo sapiens*.

50 Ibid., 11.

51 Ibid., 10–11.

52 Giorgio Agamben, *Homo Sacer: Sovereign Power and Bare Life,* trans. Daniel Heller-Roazen (Stanford: Stanford University Press, 1998), 4.

53 Braidotti, *The Posthuman*, 121.

54 Agamben, *Homo Sacer,* 7.

55 Braidotti, *The Posthuman*, 121.

56 Ibid., 129.

57 Agamben, *Homo Sacer,* 8.

58 See Walter Benn Michaels's critical discussion of Williams's materialist poetics and exclusionary forms of American identity (Michaels, "American Modernism and the Poetics of Identity," *Modernism/modernity* 1, no. 1 [1994]: 38–56).

59 William Carlos Williams, *In the American Grain* (New York: New Directions, 2009), 115.

60 Ibid., 73–74.

61 Jeff Webb, "William Carlos Williams and the New World," *Arizona Quarterly* 56, no. 1 (Spring 2000): 65–88.

62 Wolfe, *What Is Posthumanism?* xvii.

63 Elizabeth McAlister, "Slaves, Cannibals, and Infected Hyper-Whites: The Race and Religion of Zombies," *Anthropological Quarterly* 85, no. 2 (2012): 472.

64 Victor Halperin, *White Zombie* (United Artists, 1932).

65 William Faulkner, *As I Lay Dying* (New York: Vintage International, 1990), 44.

66 Diana Fuss, "Corpse Poem," *Critical Inquiry* 30, no. 1 (Autumn 2003): 30.

67 Deleuze and Guattari, *A Thousand Plateaus,* 159–60.

68 Herbrechter and Callus, "What Is a Posthumanist Reading?" 95.

69 Bill Brown, "Thing Theory," *Critical Inquiry* 28, no. 1 (Autumn 2001): 12.

1. Inhuman Remains

1 Gilles Deleuze and Felix Guattari, *A Thousand Plateaus: Capitalism and Schizophrenia,* trans. Brian Massumi (Minneapolis: University of Minnesota Press, 1987), 160.

2 Maurice Blanchot, *The Space of Literature,* trans. Ann Smock (Lincoln: University of Nebraska Press, 1982), 256.

3 Ibid., 259.

4 See David Sherman's discussion of "the burial plot's dangerous powers of expansion and excess" in *As I Lay Dying* (Sherman, *In a Strange Room: Modernism's Corpses and Mortal Obligations* [Oxford: Oxford University Press, 2014], 131). Sherman argues that Faulkner's protracted burial plot critiques the modernization of death and its devaluation of the dead.

5 William Faulkner, *As I Lay Dying* (New York: Vintage, 1991), 143. Hereafter cited parenthetically by page number.

6 Blanchot, *The Space of Literature,* 259. See also Daniel Tiffany's compelling discussion of Blanchot, the corpse, and the image in Ezra Pound's poetry (Tiffany, *Radio Corpse: Imagism and the Cryptaesthetic of Ezra Pound* [Cambridge: Harvard University Press, 1995]).

7 Ibid., 257, 258.

8 Martin Jay, "Returning the Gaze: The American Response to the French Critique of Ocularcentrism," in *Perspectives on Embodiment: The Intersections of Nature and Culture,* ed. Gail Weiss and Honi Fern Haber (New York: Routledge, 1999), 175.

9 Michael Foucault, "Nietzsche, Genealogy, History," trans. Donald F. Bouchard and Sherry Simon in *The Foucault Reader,* ed. Paul Rabinow (New York: Pantheon, 1984), 83.

10 Judith Butler, "Foucault and the Paradox of Bodily Inscriptions," *Journal of Philosophy* 86, no. 11 (1989): 603.

11 Judith Butler, *Bodies That Matter: On the Discursive Limits of Sex* (New York: Routledge, 2011), xiv.

12 See, for example, Cary Wolfe's discussion of mutation (Wolfe, *What Is Posthumanism?* [Minneapolis: University of Minnesota Press, 2009]).

13 R. L. Rutsky, "Mutation, History, and Fantasy in the Posthuman," *Subject Matters* 3, no. 2–4, no. 1 (2007): 111.

14 Ibid., 104.

15 John K. Simon notes that Addie is "treated as a corpse before her unobtrusive demise and as a sort of strangely living entity afterwards" (Simon, "The Scene and Imagery of Metamorphosis in *As I Lay Dying,*" *Criticism* 7, no. 1 [Winter 1965]: 20); Eric Sundquist claims that "dying maintains a figurative power far succeeding the literal event of Addie's death" (Sundquist, *Faulkner: The House Divided* [Baltimore: Johns Hopkins University Press, 1983], 30).

16 Michel Foucault, *The Birth of the Clinic: An Archaeology of Medical Perception*, trans. Alan Sheridan (New York: Pantheon Books, 1973), 125.

17 Michel Foucault, *The History of Sexuality, Volume 1: An Introduction*, trans. Robert Hurley (New York: Random House, 1978), 138.

18 Foucault, *Birth of the Clinic*, 149.

19 Quoted in Akira Mizuta Lippit, *Atomic Light (Shadow Optics)* (Minneapolis: University of Minnesota Press, 2005), 47.

20 Donald M. Kartiganer's discussion of verticality and horizontality in *As I Lay Dying* associates the figurative language used at the Bundren farm with verticality, metaphor, and Being, and that during the journey with horizontality, metonymy, and Becoming. Kartiganer aligns these oppositions with de Saussure's diachronic and synchronic, Jakobson's metaphor and metonymy, New Criticism's the miraculous and the mundane, de Man's symbolic and allegorical, and Lacan's Imaginary and Symbolic. Rather than invoking these axes of signification, my discussion is interested in the novel's use of vertical and horizontal images first to situate the body in a predictably mappable visual field and then to disrupt this field through reconfiguration of the human (Kartiganer, "The Farm and the Journey: Ways of Mourning and Meaning in *As I Lay Dying*," *Mississippi Quarterly* 43, no. 3 [Summer 1990]: 281–303). See also Hortense J. Spillers's provocative discussion of Faulknerian "geography as a living agent," in which "the subjective component of space turns it into an infinite series of authorships" (Spillers, "Topographical Topics: Faulknerian Space," *Mississippi Quarterly* 57, no. 4 [Fall 2004]: 548, 535).

21 Jay, "Returning the Gaze," 175.

22 Deleuze and Guattari, *A Thousand Plateaus*, 520.

23 Peter Brooks, *Body Work: Objects of Desire in Modern Narrative* (Cambridge: Harvard University Press, 1993), 88.

24 Brooks notes, "The window, like the mirror, is a traditional metaphor of realist vision directed at the world" (ibid., 89). See also Homer B. Pettey, who includes the window within the "metaphorical frames" that "serve as sites of death" in the novel (Pettey, "Perception and the Destruction of Being in *As I Lay Dying*," *Faulkner Journal* 19, no. 1 [2003]: 27).

25 Henry James, *The Art of the Novel*, ed. R. P. Blackmur (New York: Scribner, 1934), 46.

26 Brooks, *Body Work*, 88. Simon compares the novel's disjunctive points of view to "a movie scenario where we watch a character's back as he walks into a house and then see him coming towards us as he enters from outside." He argues that, despite the disruption of vision, the external world of the novel remains autonomous and "fundamental" ("Scene and Imagery," 3, 5).

27 N. Katherine Hayles, *How We Became Posthuman: Virtual Bodies in Cybernetics, Literature, and Informatics* (Chicago: University of Chicago Press, 1999), 37–38.

28 Tracing the afterlife of Freud's emphasis on vision, Wolfe notes, "Freud's valorization of the human who sees at the expense of the animal who smells is sustained (even if transvalued) in the figure of vision that runs from Sartre's discourse on the look in *Being and Nothingness* through Foucault's anatomy of panopticism in *Dis-*

cipline and Punish" (Wolfe, *Animal Rites: American Culture, the Discourse of Species, and Posthumanist Theory* [Chicago: University of Chicago Press, 2003], 3).

29 See Michael Kaufmann's discussion of the interplay between narrative events and "paginal space" (Kaufmann, "The Textual Coffin and the Narrative Corpse of *As I Lay Dying*," *Arizona Quarterly* 49, no. 1 [Spring 1993]: 99–116).

30 Drawing upon Akira Mizuta Lippit's discussion of animal discourse and "animetaphor," Christopher T. White argues, "*As I Lay Dying* re-situates language within a continuum of signifying practices that are *a*human" (White, "The Modern Magnetic Animal: *As I Lay Dying* and the Uncanny Zoology of Modernism," *Journal of Modern Literature* 31, no. 3 [Spring, 2008]: 82).

31 See Dorothy J. Hale's discussion of Bakhtinian heteroglossia in relation to *As I Lay Dying* (Hale, "*As I Lay Dying*'s Heterogeneous Discourse," *Novel: A Forum on Fiction* 23, no. 1 [Autumn 1989]: 5–23.

32 M. M. Bakhtin, "Discourse in the Novel," in *The Dialogic Imagination: Four Essays*, trans. Caryl Emerson and Michael Holquist (Austin: University of Texas Press), 293.

33 Ibid., 292.

34 Ibid., 332.

35 Ibid., 341.

36 See Hale's discussion of the way in which the "sayable" functions as the verbal negotiation of a public self in *As I Lay Dying* ("*As I Lay Dying*'s Heterogeneous Discourse," 12).

37 See Karen Jacobs's discussion of the relation between corporeality and vision (Jacobs, *The Eye's Mind: Literary Modernism and Visual Culture* [Ithaca: Cornell University Press, 2001]).

38 My discussion follows John T. Matthews, who argues that the "play of Faulkner's language" opposes the notion that the experience of external reality precedes language (Matthews, *The Play of Faulkner's Language* [Ithaca: Cornell University Press, 1982]).

39 See, for instance, Sundquist, *Faulkner*, and Simon, "Scene and Imagery." André Bleikasten comments, "The animate and the inanimate, the human and the nonhuman are brought into a relationship of reciprocal metaphor, and so are Faulkner's language and Faulkner's 'world,' one mimicking the other without allowing us to determine which is 'one' and which the 'other'" (Bleikasten, *The Ink of Melancholy: Faulkner's Novels from "The Sound and the Fury" to "Light in August"* [Bloomington: Indiana University Press, 1990], 168).

40 Deleuze and Guattari, *A Thousand Plateaus*, 391.

41 Jani Scandura and Michael Thurston, *Modernism, Inc.: Body, Memory, Capital* (New York: New York University Press, 2001), 5. See also Jessica Baldanzi and Kyle Schlabach, who argue that the "outrage" prompted by Addie's corpse represents a failure of such encryptment; the corpse "thwarts all attempts to close off our personal and national narratives" (Baldanzi and Schlabach, "What Remains? (De)composing and (Re)covering American Identity in *As I Lay Dying* and the Georgia Crematory Scandal," *Journal of the Midwest Modern Language Association* 36, no. 1 [Spring 2003]: 52).

42 Gilles Deleuze, *Difference and Repetition*, trans. Paul Patton (New York: Columbia University Press, 1994), 134.

43 Bleikasten refers to this passage not in narrative terms at all, but as a "pure kinetic poem" (*Ink of Melancholy*, 165).

44 Deleuze and Guattari, *A Thousand Plateaus*, 240.

45 Ibid., 273.

46 Ibid., 240.

47 Sundquist, *Faulkner*, 40.

48 Foucault, *Birth of the Clinic*, 142.

49 Deleuze and Guattari, *A Thousand Plateaus*, 249.

50 Foucault, *Birth of the Clinic*, 142.

51 Deleuze and Guattari refer specifically to Sarraute's discussion of Proust, who explores both the molecular properties of matter and its existence within the molar "envelope" of character (Deleuze and Guattari, *A Thousand Plateaus*, 267).

52 William Faulkner, *Absalom, Absalom!* (New York: Vintage, 1990), 12. Hereafter cited parenthetically by page number.

53 See Christopher J. Cunningham's discussion of Sutpen and the "unmaking" of the myth of the "self-made man." Drawing upon both Mark Seltzer's and Walter Benn Michaels's discussions of the paradox of the "self-made man," Cunningham argues that the conflict between "self-production" and "gynophobic" forms of male reproduction represent "violently incoherent ideologies of what it means to be American" (Cunningham, "Sutpen's Designs: Masculine Reproduction and the Unmaking of the Self-Made Man in *Absalom, Absalom!*" *Mississippi Quarterly* 49, no. 3 [Summer 1996]: 563).

54 See Patricia Tobin's discussion of the novel's delayed description of Sutpen's "human origins" (Tobin, "The Time of Myth and History in *Absalom, Absalom!*" *American Literature* 45, no. 2 [May 1973]: 252–70).

55 See Alex Vernon's discussion of Darwinian themes and language in *Absalom, Absalom!* and of the novel itself as a "'cross-breed' of several literary forms" (Vernon, "Narrative Miscegenation: *Absalom, Absalom!* as Naturalist Novel, Auto/Biography, and African-American Oral Story," *Journal of Narrative Theory* 31, no. 2 [Summer 2001]: 155).

56 Jonathan S. Cullick argues that Sutpen's "inability to maintain his patriarchal design is a reflection of his inability to maintain a narrative design" (Cullick, "'I Had a Design': Sutpen as Narrator in *Absalom, Absalom!*" *Southern Literary Journal* 28, no. 2 [Spring 1996]: 48). See also Bernhard Radloff, "*Absalom, Absalom!* An Ontological Approach to Sutpen's 'Design,'" *Mosaic* 19, no. 1 (January 1986): 45–56.

57 Manuel De Landa, *A Thousand Years of Nonlinear History* (Boston: MIT Press, 2009), 26–27.

58 Jane Bennett, *Vibrant Matter: A Political Ecology of Things* (Durham: Duke University Press, 2010), 11.

59 See Tim Bielawski's discussion of "monumental rhetoric" and "the image of text as embalmed corpse" in *Absalom, Absalom!* (Bielawski, "(Dis)Figuring the Dead:

Embalming and Autopsy in *Absalom, Absalom!*" *Faulkner Journal* 24, no. 2 [Spring 2009]: 29).

60 Rebecca Saunders discusses Judith's purchase of the gravestones as part of a larger pattern of "lamentation" that is characterized by "the transfer of property, the redistribution of possessions, and the remapping of territorial boundaries" (Saunders, "On Lamentation and the Redistribution of Possessions: Faulkner's *Absalom, Absalom!* and the New South," *Modern Fiction Studies* 42, no. 4 [Winter 1996]: 732).

61 Walter Benn Michaels, *Our America: Nativism, Modernism, and Pluralism* (Durham: Duke University Press, 1995), 2.

62 For other discussions of Faulkner and incest, see Karl F. Zender, "Faulkner and the Politics of Incest," *American Literature* 70, no. 4 (December 1998): 739–65; Constance Hill Hall, *Incest in Faulkner: A Metaphor for the Fall* (Ann Arbor: UMI Research Press, 1986); Sundquist, *Faulkner;* and John T. Irwin, *Doubling and Incest/Repetition and Revenge: A Speculative Reading of Faulkner* (Baltimore: Johns Hopkins University Press, 1975).

63 See also David Krause's discussion of Bon's letter (Krause, "Reading Bon's Letter and Faulkner's *Absalom, Absalom!*" *PMLA* 99, no. 2 [March 1984]: 225–41).

64 This image of the corpse bleeding on Judith's wedding dress is Rosa's conceit; however, I am placing pressure on it here because it provides a striking, problematic image that the novel as a whole arguably works to interpret.

65 Norman W. Jones argues that Quentin's *"I dont"* marks the simultaneous acknowledgment and denial of homosexual desire; while Jones's discussion does not explicitly engage with questions of the human and the nonhuman, his argument importantly defines a mode of sexuality that is outside that of the normative white patriarchal male (Jones, "Coming Out through History's Hidden Love Letters in *Absalom, Absalom!*" *American Literature* 76, no. 2 [June 2004]: 339–66). See also Erin Pearson's discussion of the Sutpen house as a kind of "cryptic closet" (Pearson, "Faulkner's Cryptic Closet: Forbidden Desire, Disavowal, and the 'Dark House' at the Heart of *Absalom, Absalom!*" *Mississippi Quarterly* 64, nos. 3–4 [Summer–Fall 2011]: 341–67).

66 William Faulkner, *The Sound and the Fury* (New York: Vintage, 1990), 95.

2. Autopsy-Optics

1 James Allen, *Without Sanctuary: Lynching Photography in America* (Santa Fe: Twin Palms, 2000), 201.

2 While my chapter focuses specifically on the lynching of African Americans by whites, I would like to acknowledge the broader racial context of lynching in the United States during this period.

3 "An Appeal to the Conscience of the Civilized World" (New York: National Association for the Advancement of Colored People, 1920).

4 Quoted in Amy Louise Wood, *Lynching and Spectacle: Witnessing Racial Violence in America, 1890–1940* (Chapel Hill: University of North Carolina Press, 2009), 212.

5 See, for example, Dora Apel, "Memorialization and Its Discontents: America's First Lynching Memorial," *Mississippi Quarterly* 61, nos. 1–2 (Winter–Spring 2008): 217–35; Jacqueline Goldsby, *A Spectacular Secret: Lynching in American Life and Literature* (Chicago: University of Chicago Press, 2006); and Wood, *Lynching and Spectacle.*

6 Shawn Michelle Smith, *Photography on the Color Line: W. E. B. Du Bois, Race, and Visual Culture* (Durham: Duke University Press, 2004), 127.

7 For discussions of lynching in *Cane,* see Kimberly Banks, "'Like a Violin for the Wind to Play': Lyrical Approaches to Lynching by Hughes, Du Bois, and Toomer," *African American Review* 38, no. 3 (Autumn 2004): 451–65; Susan Edmunds, "The Race Question and the 'Question of the Home': Revisiting the Lynching Plot in Jean Toomer's *Cane,*" *American Literature* 75, no. 1 (March 2003): 141–68; and Jeff Webb, "Literature and Lynching: Identity in Jean Toomer's *Cane,*" *ELH* 67, no. 1 (Spring 2000): 205–28.

8 Jean Toomer, *Cane* (New York: Norton, 2011), 38. Hereafter cited parenthetically by page number.

9 Walter Benn Michaels, *Our America: Nativism, Modernism, and Pluralism* (Durham: Duke University Press, 1995), 62. Michaels further argues, "Thus lynching no longer attempts to enforce the taboo against 'racial intermingling'; it actualizes the racial difference that makes the intermingling possible" (62). Goldsby argues, similarly, "the scene of lynching [is] a composite of the mortification of black flesh and the sanctification of white femininity" (*Spectacular Secret,* 290).

10 See Karen Jacobs, *The Eye's Mind: Literary Modernism and Visual Culture* (Ithaca: Cornell University Press, 2001).

11 Mark Whalan makes a different argument about the body in *Cane.* He suggests that Toomer's interest in physical culture and bodybuilding, which are reflected in "Bona and Paul," allows for a redefinition of identity. "Physical culture," he writes, "promised a selective erasure of history and heredity, two of the factors which white discourse had used to assign black bodies a hierarchical place" (Whalan, "'Taking Myself in Hand': Jean Toomer and Physical Culture," *Modernism/modernity* 10, no. 4 [November 2003]: 611).

12 I am indebted to Smith's *Photography on the Color Line* both for introducing me to Du Bois's "Georgia Negro Exhibit" and for its insightful, extensive discussion of the materials. As Smith notes, there has been surprisingly little critical attention paid to Du Bois's groundbreaking exhibit. For additional discussions, see Michelle H. Phillips, "The Children of Double Consciousness: From *The Souls of Black Folk* to the *Brownies' Book,*'" *PMLA* 128, no. 3 (May 2013): 590–607; and David Levering Lewis and Deborah Willis, eds., *A Small Nation of People: W. E. B. Du Bois and African American Portraits of Progress* (New York: Amistad, 2003).

13 The question of the unity or progression of *Cane*'s three sections has been a divisive topic for critics. Arna Bontemps notes of its contemporary reception: "Reviewers who read it in 1923 were generally stumped. Poetry and prose were whipped together in a kind of frappé" (Bontemps, "Commentary on Jean Toomer and *Cane,*" in *Cane,* ed. Darwin T. Turner [New York: Norton, 1988], 187 [here-

after cited as *Cane,* ed. Turner]). More recent criticism, however, has been divided about whether the "frappé" of *Cane*'s fragments constitute a kind of narrative. Michael Krasny and Todd Lieber argue that the text has a progression, such that the first section describes the beauty and lyricism of the South while the second describes an alienation from this vital source (Krasny, "The Aesthetic Structure of Jean Toomer's *Cane,*" *Negro American Literature Forum* 9, no. 2 [Summer 1975]: 42–43; Lieber, "Design and Movement in *Cane,*" *College Language Association Journal* 13 [1969]: 35–50). Toomer, on the other hand, argues that the second section departs from the "sadness" and "futility" of the South, imagining a "wholly new life" in the North. He notes of the final section, "And Kabnis is *Me*" (Toomer, "To Waldo Frank, n.d., late 1922 or early 1923," in *Cane,* ed. Turner, 151). Other critics argue that there is little difference between the social oppression in the North and the South; see, for example, Janet Whyde, "Mediating Forms: Narrating the Body in Jean Toomer's *Cane,*" *Southern Literary Journal* 26, no. 1 (Fall 1993): 42–53; and Patricia Watkins, "Is There a Unifying Theme in *Cane*?" *College Language Association Journal* 15 (1972): 303–5. Jennifer M. Wilks emphasizes the "aesthetic fusion of South and North, African American and American" (Wilks, "Writing Home: Comparative Black Modernism and Form in Jean Toomer and Aimé Césaire," *Modern Fiction Studies* 51, no. 4 [Winter 2005]: 808). Bowie Duncan takes a somewhat different approach, comparing *Cane* to a "jazz composition" that is "continually in process" (Duncan, "Jean Toomer's *Cane*: A Modern Black Oracle," *College Language Association Journal* 15 [1972]: 323).

14 Michel Foucault, *The Birth of the Clinic: An Archaeology of Medical Perception,* trans. A. M. Sheridan Smith (New York: Pantheon Books, 1973), 144.

15 Eugene Arnold, "Autopsy: The Final Diagnosis," in *Images of the Corpse: From the Renaissance to Cyberspace,* ed. Elizabeth Klaver (Madison: University of Wisconsin Press, 2004), 15.

16 Ibid., 3.

17 Ibid., 4.

18 Stefan Hirschauer, "The Manufacture of Bodies in Surgery," *Social Studies of Science* 21, no. 2 (May 1991): 299, 300.

19 Ibid., 314.

20 Fatimah Tobing Rony, *The Third Eye: Race, Cinema, and Ethnographic Spectacle* (Durham: Duke University Press, 1996), 29.

21 Quoted in ibid., 35.

22 Hirschauer, "Manufacture," 300.

23 Walter Benjamin, "The Work of Art in the Age of Mechanical Reproduction," trans. Harry Zohn, in *Illuminations: Essays and Reflections,* ed. Hannah Arendt (New York: Schocken, 1969), 233.

24 Hirschauer, "Manufacture," 301, 299.

25 We might contrast this wound that refuses to cicatrize with the visible scar of Odysseus, which provides the basis for Erich Auerbach's discussion of realism in Western literature (Auerbach, *Mimesis: The Representation of Reality in Western Literature* [Princeton: Princeton University Press, 2003]).

26 Jonathan Crary, *Techniques of the Observer: On Vision and Modernity in the Nineteenth Century* (Cambridge: MIT Press, 1992), 4.

27 Jacobs, *Eye's Mind*, 28.

28 Ibid., 27.

29 Jean Toomer, "To Horace Liveright, January 11, 1923," in *The Letters of Jean Toomer, 1919–24*, ed. Mark Whalan (Knoxville: University of Tennessee Press, 2006), 118.

30 See Mary Louise Pratt's discussion of landscape descriptions in written travelogues. Quoted in Rony, *The Third Eye*, 82.

31 Jacobs, *Eye's Mind*, 19.

32 Julia Kristeva, *Powers of Horror: An Essay in Abjection*, trans. Leon S. Roudiez (New York: Columbia University Press, 1982), 3.

33 Abel Meeropol, "Bitter Fruit," *New York Teacher*, January 1937, 17.

34 Quoted in Smith, *Photography on the Color Line*, 43.

35 W. E. B. Du Bois, "The American Negro at Paris," *American Monthly Review of Reviews*, November 1900, 577.

36 See Smith, *Photography on the Color Line*.

37 W. E. B. Du Bois, "The Souls of White Folk," in *Darkwater: Voices from within the Veil* (1920; New York: Dover Thrift, 1999), 17.

38 W. E. B. Du Bois, "Strivings of the Negro People," *The Atlantic*, August 1897, 194.

39 Benjamin, "The Work of Art," 234.

40 As Smith notes, Du Bois was not the singular author of the exhibit. It was produced in collaboration with students and graduates of Atlanta University, and many of the photographs were taken by Thomas E. Askew, the first African American photographer in Atlanta (*Photography on the Color Line*, 4).

41 See Goldsby's different interpretation of this section; she argues that *Cane* "stages lynching's passage from being a literal threat to a malaise that infuses the whole of American institutions from the cane fields of Georgia to the university metropolis of Chicago" (*Spectacular Secret*, 290).

42 Tom Gunning, "The Exterior as Intérieur: Benjamin's Optical Detective," *Boundary 2* 30, no. 1 (Spring 2003): 107. Gunning comments here upon Benjamin's discussion of the new nineteenth-century *intérieur*.

43 Quoted in ibid., 107.

44 Edmunds argues, in contrast, that Toomer uses the grotesque in order to critique African American adherence to white, bourgeois morality ("The Race Question").

45 See Susan L. Blake, "The Spectatorial Artist and the Structure of *Cane*," in *Jean Toomer: A Critical Evaluation*, ed. Therman B. O'Daniel (Washington, D.C.: Howard University Press, 1988). Blake argues that *Cane* is unified by a creative persona, which progresses from detached viewer in the first section to embodied artist in "Kabnis" (207).

46 Peter Brooks, *Body Work: Objects of Desire in Modern Narrative* (Cambridge: Harvard University Press, 1993), 88.

47 Jean Toomer, "To Waldo Frank, 12 December 1922," in *Cane*, ed. Turner, 152.

48 Du Bois, "American Negro," 576–77.

3. Sutures and Grooves

1 N. Katherine Hayles, *How We Became Posthuman: Virtual Bodies in Cybernetics, Literature, and Informatics* (Chicago: University of Chicago Press, 1999), 2.

2 Hans Moravec, abstract to "The Senses Have No Future," http://www.frc.ri.cmu .edu/~hpm/project.archive/general.articles/1997/970128.nosense.html.

3 Hans Moravec, "The Senses Have No Future," in *The Virtual Dimension: Architecture, Representation, and Crash Culture,* ed. John Beckmann (New York: Princeton Architectural Press, 1998), 88.

4 Ibid., 87.

5 Ibid., 88.

6 John S. Belrose, "The Development of Wireless Telegraphy and Telephony, and Pioneering Attempts to Achieve Transatlantic Wireless Communications," in *History of Wireless,* ed. Tapan K. Sarkar, Robert J. Mailloux, Arthur A. Oliner, Magdalena Salazar-Palma, and Dipak L. Sengupta (Hoboken: Wiley, 2006), 415.

7 George C. Schoolfield, *Young Rilke and His Time* (Rochester: Camden House, 2009), 143; and Carolyn Burke, *Becoming Modern: The Life of Mina Loy* (New York: Farrar, Straus and Giroux, 1996), 77.

8 Burke, *Becoming Modern,* 77.

9 I am indebted to Friedrich A. Kittler both for introducing me to Rilke's extraordinary essay and for his compelling theorization about sound recording and technical reproduction of the voice. As my chapter progresses, however, my reading of "Primal Sound" markedly deviates from Kittler's use of it, focusing on the male privilege embedded within Rilke's auditory experiments (Kittler, *Gramophone, Film, Typewriter,* trans. Geoffrey Winthrop-Young and Michael Wutz [Stanford: Stanford University Press, 1999], 40).

10 Quoted in ibid., 41.

11 Mina Loy, "Incident," in *Stories and Essays of Mina Loy,* ed. Sara Crangle (Champaign, Ill.: Dalkey Archive Press, 2011), 39. Hereafter cited parenthetically by page number.

12 Quoted in Luigi Russolo, *The Art of Noises,* trans. Barclay Brown (New York: Pendragon Press, 1986), 57.

13 Quoted in Kittler, *Gramophone,* 39.

14 Ibid.

15 Ibid., 40.

16 Ibid., 40, 39.

17 Ibid., 40.

18 Manuel De Landa, *A Thousand Years of Nonlinear History* (Boston: MIT Press, 2000), 27.

19 See Kittler's discussion of the phonautograph as well as his discussion of the relation between death and sound media more generally *(Gramophone).* See also Douglas Kahn's discussion of death and phonography (Kahn, "Death in Light of the Phonograph: Raymond Roussel's Locus Solus," in *Wireless Imagination:*

Sound, Radio and the Avant-Garde, ed. Douglas Kahn and Gregory Whitehead [Cambridge: MIT Press, 1992], 69–103).

20 Quoted in Kahn, "Death in Light of the Phonograph," 93.

21 And, perhaps reversing Rilke's desire to play the skull like a record, a British company called And Vinyly offers to press cremated remains of loved ones into a vinyl disc (along with a recorded message or favorite song).

22 Russolo, *Art of Noises*, 49.

23 Ibid.

24 Ibid., 27.

25 Quoted in Kittler, *Gramophone*, 39, 40.

26 Ibid., 42, 41.

27 Ibid., 41.

28 Charles Grivel, "The Phonograph's Horned Mouth," in Kahn and Whitehead, *Wireless Imagination*, 36.

29 Mina Loy, *The Sacred Prostitute*, in *Stories and Essays*, 199–200.

30 Ibid., 196.

31 Quoted in Russolo, *Art of Noises*, 57, 26.

32 Filippo Tommaso Marinetti, *Zong Toomb Toomb*, in *F. T. Marinetti: Selected Poems and Related Prose*, ed. Elizabeth R. Napier (New Haven: Yale University Press, 2002), 57.

33 Quoted in Kittler, *Gramophone*, 41.

34 Kittler, *Gramophone*, 54.

35 Ibid., 51.

36 Kittler does mention Laurie Anderson, but her voice is "distorted as usual on *Big Science* by a vocoder"; he also claims that this distortion is not Anderson's own artistic choice but that she "follow[s] a very practical piece of advice" from William Burroughs (*Gramophone*, 111).

37 Mina Loy, "The Library of the Sphinx," in *Stories and Essays*, 257.

38 Kittler, *Gramophone*, 44.

39 Ibid., 83.

40 Gilles Deleuze and Félix Guattari, *A Thousand Plateaus: Capitalism and Schizophrenia*, trans. Brian Massumi (Minneapolis: University of Minnesota Press, 1987), 248.

41 Mina Loy, "Letters of the Unliving," in *The Lost Lunar Baedeker: Poems of Mina Loy*, ed. Roger L. Conover (New York: Farrar, Straus and Giroux, 1996), 129–32.

42 Mina Loy, "Aphorisms on Futurism," in *The Lost Lunar Baedeker*, 149.

43 While Donna Haraway's "A Cyborg Manifesto" specifically distinguishes between the cyborg and *Frankenstein*'s monster, my citation of her here does consider the technological creature of Hollywood film (as distinct from the literary creation) to be a cyborg (Haraway, "A Cyborg Manifesto," in *Simians, Cyborgs, and Women: The Reinvention of Nature* [New York: Routledge, 1991], 151.)

44 James A. W. Heffernan notes, "While film is a wholly artificial product, the creature consists entirely of natural body parts, so that he is closer to an actual human being with one or more transplanted organs than he is to the mechanical men

constructed by futurist designers in the 1920s or to the cyborg of present-day science fiction" (Heffernan, "Looking at the Monster: *Frankenstein* and Film," *Critical Inquiry* 24, no. 1 [Autumn 1997]: 141).

45 Ibid., 139.

46 Scott J. Juengel, "Face, Figure, Physiognomics: Mary Shelley's *Frankenstein* and the Moving Image," *Novel: A Forum on Fiction* 33, no. 3 (Summer 2000): 354.

47 Slavoj Žižek, "'I Hear You with My Eyes'; or, The Invisible Master," in *Gaze and Voice as Love Objects*, ed. Renata Salecl and Slavoj Žižek (Durham: Duke University Press, 1996), 92.

48 Quoted in Susan Laxton, "*Flou*: Rayographs and the Dada Automatic," *October* 127 (Winter 2009): 38–39.

49 While Laxton's article does not address these rayographs in particular, her discussion is useful for my understanding of Man Ray's technique. Laxton also usefully describes "flou" not only in relation to Man Ray but also as a "blurred" moment between defined modernist art movements: "*Flou*, 'blur' in French, is the name that has been given to this period that belonged to neither Dada nor Surrealism, and yet belonged to both" (ibid., 30).

50 Ibid., 28.

51 Jacques Derrida, *Specters of Marx: The State of the Debt, the Work of Mourning, and the New International*, trans. Peggy Kamuf (New York: Routledge, 1994), 10.

52 Ibid., 157–58.

53 Irene Gammel and Suzanne Zelazo explicitly compare the Baroness's bodily performance to Haraway's cyborg in their introduction to *Body Sweats: The Uncensored Writings of Elsa von Freytag-Loringhoven* (Cambridge: MIT Press, 2011), 11. Alex Goody also insightfully discusses the Baroness as a cyborgian figure, although she argues that this role is often projected onto her by male contemporaries; the Baroness thus ultimately functions, in Goody's view, "as a means of reproducing an acceptable version of modern femininity rather than a challenge to the humanist and masculinist process of individuation" (Goody, "Cyborgs, Women, and New York Dada," *The Space Between: Literature and Culture, 1914–1945* 3, no. 1 [January 2007]: 100).

54 Irene Gammel, *Baroness Elsa: Gender, Dada, and Everyday Modernity—A Cultural Biography* (Cambridge: MIT Press, 2002),182.

55 Gilles Deleuze and Félix Guattari, *Anti-Oedipus: Capitalism and Schizophrenia*, trans. Robert Hurley, Mark Seem, and Helen R. Lane (Minneapolis: University of Minnesota Press, 1983), 1.

56 See Bruno Latour, "Pragmatogonies: A Mythical Account of How Humans and Nonhumans Swap Properties," *American Behavioral Scientist* 37, no. 6 (May 1994): 791–808.

57 Quoted in René Steinke, "My Heart Belongs to Dada," *New York Times*, August 18, 2002.

58 Quoted in Gammel, *Baroness Elsa*, 191.

59 Ibid., 192.

60 Ibid., 207.

61 Quoted in ibid., 155. In "Love—Chemical Relationship" the Baroness refers to herself not as a futurist but as a "future futurist" (*Body Sweats,* 253).

62 Elsa von Freytag-Loringhoven, *Body Sweats,* 242.

63 The Baroness writes in defense of James Joyce, claiming that he was an "engineer" of the body, rather than a pornographer (ibid., 286).

64 Ibid., 170.

65 Elsa von Freytag-Loringhoven Papers, Special Collections and University Archives, University of Maryland Libraries.

66 See Irene Gammel and Suzanne Zelazo's discussion of "Klink—Hratzvenga (Death-wail)" as a "mourning cry" for the losses of World War I; their attention to both the sonic and semantic aspects of this poem informs my own approach to the Baroness's sound poetry (Gammel and Zelazo, "'Harpsichords Metallic Howl—': The Baroness Elsa von Freytag-Loringhoven's Sound Poetry," *Modernism/modernity* 18, no. 2 [April 2011]: 255–71).

67 Elsa von Freytag-Loringhoven, *Body Sweats,* 184.

68 Georges Bataille, *Erotism: Death and Sensuality,* trans. Mary Dalwood (San Francisco: City Lights Books, 1986), 56.

4. Love and Corpses

1 Djuna Barnes, *Ryder* (Elmwood Park, Ill.: Dalkey Archive Press, 1990), 119.

2 Ibid.

3 Ibid., 121.

4 Emmanuel Levinas, *Ethics and Infinity: Conversations with Philippe Nemo* (Pittsburgh: Duquesne University Press, 1985), 86.

5 Roland Barthes, "The Great Family of Man," in *Mythologies,* trans. Annette Lavers (New York: Farrar, Straus and Giroux, 1972), 100.

6 Ibid., 101.

7 Quoted in Neil Badmington, *Alien Chic: Posthumanism and the Other Within* (New York: Routledge, 2004), 37.

8 Warner defines "reprosexuality" as "the interweaving of heterosexuality, biological reproduction, cultural reproduction, and personal identity" (Warner, "Introduction: Fear of a Queer Planet," *Social Text* 29 [1991]: 9).

9 Dana Luciano and Mel Y. Chen, "Introduction: Has the Queer Ever Been Human?" *GLQ: A Journal of Lesbian and Gay Studies* 21, no. 2 (May 2015): 190.

10 Djuna Barnes, *Nightwood,* introduction by T. S. Eliot, preface by Jeanette Winterson (New York: New Directions, 2006), 41. Hereafter cited parenthetically by page number.

11 Jeffrey J. Cohen and Todd R. Ramlow, "Pink Vectors of Deleuze: Queer Theory and Inhumanism," *Rhizomes* 11–12 (Fall 2005–Spring 2006), www.rhizomes.net /issue11/cohenramlow.html.

12 Leo Bersani, "Is the Rectum a Grave?" *October* 43 (Winter 1987): 221.

13 Lee Edelman, *No Future: Queer Theory and the Death Drive* (Durham: Duke University Press, 2004), 31.

14 Cohen and Ramlow, "Pink Vectors of Deleuze."

15 Judith Butler, *Undoing Gender* (New York: Routledge, 2004), 35.

16 Luciano and Chen, "Has the Queer Ever Been Human?" 186.

17 Approaching the relation of death and sexuality from an ethical perspective, David Sherman argues that "the problem of the other's death is an erotic problem" in *Nightwood*. Pairing Barnes and T. S. Eliot, Sherman argues that both authors "imagine mortal obligation at the heart of desire, and as the principle of its queering" (Sherman, *In a Strange Room: Modernism's Corpses and Mortal Obligations* [New York: Oxford University Press, 2014], 147.

18 Cohen and Ramlow, "Pink Vectors of Deleuze."

19 Cary Wolfe, *What Is Posthumanism?* (Minneapolis: University of Minnesota Press, 2009), xvi.

20 Carl Sandburg, prologue to *The Family of Man: 60th Anniversary Edition*, ed. Edward Steichen (New York: Museum of Modern Art, 2015), 2.

21 Cohen and Ramlow, "Pink Vectors of Deleuze."

22 Donna Haraway, "A Cyborg Manifesto," in *Simians, Cyborgs, and Women: The Reinvention of Nature* (New York: Routledge, 1990), 150.

23 See J. Jack Halberstam's influential discussion of queer temporality and space (Halberstam, *In a Queer Time and Place: Transgender Bodies, Subcultural Lives* [New York: New York University Press, 2005]).

24 Gilles Deleuze and Félix Guattari, *A Thousand Plateaus: Capitalism and Schizophrenia*, trans. Brian Massumi (Minneapolis: University of Minnesota Press, 1987), 272.

25 Carrie Rohman, "Revising the Human: Silence, Being, and the Question of the Animal in *Nightwood*," *American Literature* 79, no. 1 (March 2007): 66.

26 Deleuze and Guattari, *A Thousand Plateaus*, 275.

27 Ibid., 273.

28 See, for example, Bonnie Kime Scott, "Barnes Being 'Beast Familiar': Representation on the Margins of Modernism," *Review of Contemporary Fiction* 13, no. 3 (Fall 1993): 41–52; and Karen Kaivola, "The 'Beast Turning Human': Constructions of the 'Primitive' in *Nightwood*," *Review of Contemporary Fiction* 13, no. 3 (Fall 1993): 172–85; and Rohman, "Revising the Human."

29 Stefan Herbrechter and Ivan Callus, "What Is a Posthumanist Reading?" *Angelaki* 13, no. 1 (April 2008): 95.

30 Jami Weinstein, "Posthumously Queer," *GLQ: A Journal of Lesbian and Gay Studies* 21, no. 2 (May 2015): 237.

31 See Rohman's discussion of blood and family lineage in *Nightwood* ("Revising the Human").

32 Deleuze and Guattari, *A Thousand Plateaus*, 10.

33 See Dana Seitler's discussion of atavism in this final scene (Seitler, "Down on All Fours: Atavistic Perversions and the Science of Desire from Frank Norris to Djuna Barnes," *American Literature* 73, no. 3 [September 2001]: 525–62).

34 Teresa de Lauretis is one of the few critics to distinguish the "actual, diegetic animals" from the metaphorical use of animals in *Nightwood*, but she still regards the dog from a Freudian perspective, as a difficult textual inscription of the death

drive, which is by definition that which is unrepresentable (de Lauretis, "*Nightwood* and the 'Terror of Uncertain Signs,'" *Critical Inquiry* 34, no. 5 [Winter 2008]: 117–29).

35 See also Sherman's discussion of Edelman in relation to *Nightwood (In a Strange Room)*. Michael Davidson's discussion of *Nightwood* also draws upon Edelman's notion of "reproductive futurism," but he uses Edelman to consider the figure of the pregnant male and his relation to an "uncanny futurity" (Davidson, "Pregnant Men: Modernism, Disability, and Biofuturity in Djuna Barnes," *Novel: A Forum on Fiction* 43, no. 2 [Summer 2010]: 209.)

36 Edelman, *No Future*, 31.

37 Weinstein, "Posthumously Queer," 237.

38 Jussi Parikka, *Insect Media: An Archaeology of Animals and Technology* (Minneapolis: University of Minnesota Press, 2010), xxiii.

39 See Brian Glavey's different discussion of the possibilities of a "queer reading of spatial and other ekphrastic forms" in *Nightwood;* Glavey revises Joseph Frank's discussion of modernist spatial form as aspiring toward a "timeless unity," rather than a linear progression through time (Glavey, "Dazzling Estrangement: Modernism, Queer Ekphrasis, and the Spatial Form of *Nightwood*," *PMLA* 124, no. 3 [May 2009]: 751; Frank, "Spatial Form in Modern Literature," *Sewanee Review* 53, no. 1 [1945]: 221–40).

40 See Davidson's discussion of the doctor's "verbal grotesquerie" as a kind of textual equivalent of male pregnancy ("Pregnant Men," 215).

41 Matthew O'Connor has been the subject of much critical discussion. Jane Marcus argues that the doctor offers a parody of Freud (Marcus, "Laughing at Leviticus: *Nightwood* as Woman's Circus Epic," *Cultural Critique* 13 [Fall 1989]: 143–90). Ann Kennedy expands upon this point of view, suggesting that he is "a perfect parody of the great male modern narrative makers—Freud, early sexologists, and Barnes's male counterparts, Eliot, Pound, and Joyce" (Kennedy, "Inappropriate and Dazzling Sideshows: Interpellating Narrative in Djuna Barnes's *Nightwood*," *Post Identity* 1, no. 1 [Fall 1997]: 100). Joseph Frank and Alan Singer compare him to Tiresias of *The Waste Land* (Frank, "Spatial Form"; Singer, "The Horse Who Knew Too Much: Metaphor and the Narrative of Discontinuity in *Nightwood*," *Contemporary Literature* 25, no. 1 [Spring 1984]: 66–87). Victoria Smith compares his role to Dante's in the *Commedia* (Smith, "A Story beside(s) Itself: The Language of Loss in Djuna Barnes's *Nightwood*," *PMLA* 114, no. 2 [March 1999]: 194–206).

42 Barnes modeled the doctor on Dan Mahoney, by all reports a remarkable figure of Parisian life, but the dense verbal patterning and intertextual allusions in his speeches in *Nightwood* also exceed biographical reference.

43 Kennedy, "Inappropriate and Dazzling Sideshows," 112.

44 George Biddle offers the following description of her New York loft: "It was crowded and reeking with the strange relics which she had purloined over a period of years from the New York gutters. Old bits of ironware, automobile tires, gilded vegetables, a dozen starved dogs, celluloid paintings, ash cans, every conceivable horror,

which to her tortured, yet highly sensitized perception, became objects of formal beauty" (quoted in Lynn DeVore, "The Backgrounds of *Nightwood*: Robin, Felix, and Nora," *Journal of Modern Literature* 10, no. 1 [March 1983]: 81).

45 Butler, *Undoing Gender*, 25, 19.

46 Ibid., 18.

47 Ibid., 30.

48 Ibid., 35.

49 For other discussion of *Nightwood*'s treatments of darkness and "night worlds," see Martin Bock, *Crossing the Shadow-Line: The Literature of Estrangement* (Columbus: Ohio State University Press, 1989); Karen Kaivola, *All Contraries Confounded: The Lyrical Fiction of Virginia Woolf, Djuna Barnes, and Marguerite Duras* (Iowa City: University of Iowa Press, 1991); and Catherine Whitley, "Nations and the Night: Excremental History in James Joyce's *Finnegans Wake* and Djuna Barnes' *Nightwood*," *Journal of Modern Literature* 24, no. 1 (Fall 2000): 81–98.

50 See Marcus's discussion of Bakhtin and the bodily grotesque in *Nightwood* ("Laughing at Leviticus").

51 Judith Scherer Herz, "Under the Sign of Donne," *Criticism* 43, no. 1 (Winter 2001): 29–58.

52 Butler, *Undoing Gender*, 35.

Coda

1 B. L. Reid, *Art by Subtraction: A Dissenting Opinion of Gertrude Stein* (Norman: University of Oklahoma Press, 1958), 172.

2 Diana Fuss, "Corpse Poem," *Critical Inquiry* 30, no. 1 (Autumn 2003): 30.

3 Catharine R. Stimpson, "Gertrude Stein: Humanism and Its Freaks," *boundary 2* 12, no. 3–13, no. 1 (Spring–Autumn 1984): 301.

4 Jane Bennett, *Vibrant Matter: A Political Ecology of Things* (Durham: Duke University Press 2010), 50.

5 Gertrude Stein, *Tender Buttons* (San Francisco: City Lights Books, 2014), 41. Hereafter cited parenthetically by page number.

6 Gertrude Stein, "Poetry and Grammar," *Lectures in America* (Boston: Beacon Press, 1985), 242.

7 Carl Van Vechten, "How to Read Gertrude Stein," in *Gertrude Stein Remembered*, ed. Linda Simon (Lincoln: University of Nebraska Press, 1994), 47.

8 See also Pamela Hadas's discussion of "kind" and cattle as *kine* (Hadas, "Spreading the Difference: One Way to Read Gertrude Stein's *Tender Buttons*," *Twentieth-Century Literature* 24, no. 1 [Spring 1978]: 64).

9 Upton Sinclair, *The Jungle* (New York: Penguin, 2006), 119. Hereafter cited parenthetically by page number.

10 Bennett, *Vibrant Matter*, 46.

11 William Faulkner, *As I Lay Dying* (New York: Vintage, 1990), 57.

12 Bennett, *Vibrant Matter*, 49.

13 Quoted in Catharine R. Stimpson, "The Somagrams of Gertrude Stein," *Poetics Today* 6, nos. 1–2 (1985): 68.

14 Gilles Deleuze and Félix Guattari, *A Thousand Plateaus: Capitalism and Schizophrenia*, trans. Brian Massumi (Minneapolis: University of Minnesota Press, 1987), 86.

15 Jacques Derrida, "Eating Well," trans. Peter Connor and Avital Ronnell in *Points . . . : Interviews, 1974–1994,* ed. Elisabeth Weber (Stanford: Stanford University Press, 1995), 282.

16 Sianne Ngai, "The Cuteness of the Avant-Garde," *Critical Inquiry* 31, no. 4 (Summer 2005): 831.

17 Derrida, "Eating Well," 285.

18 Patricia Keenan and James Cargill, "Tender Buttons," *Tender Buttons* (Warp Records, 2005).

INDEX

Page numbers in italics refer to illustrations.

36–38, 54–61, 186; decomposition in, 23, 38, 39–61, 62; gaze in, 41–42, 43, 50; generative assemblages of, 63; language of, 23–24, 39, 41, 47–54, 203nn30–31; life–death mediation in, 37; material transfers in, 189; models of body, 41–47; mutation in, 41, 44, 45, 52, 61; the nonhuman in, 56, 158; the posthuman in, 40, 42, 61; public self in, 203n36; reconceptualization of the human, 38; reconfiguration of body in, 37, 57–59; the senses in, 47–48, 49–50, 51, 52–53; space in, 56, 202n20, 203n29; and technological determinism, 54–61

Askew, Thomas E., 208n40

audition. *See* sound

Auerbach, Erich, 207n25

autopsy: acoustic, 116, 132; alternatives to, 13, 146, 182–83, 194; and Christian salvation, 43; and critical practices, 110, 194; and epistemology, 82; and film, 80, 84; knowledge of body through, 80, 83; metaphysical, 88; and metempsychosis, 182; as model of looking, 183; and modernism, 86; and photography, 24, 95; retrospective process of, 83, 107–8; and viewership, 82, 84, 91, 95, 102, 103, 183

Badmington, Neil, 14; on *Family of Man*, 156

Bakhtin, Mikhail: and the grotesque, 102, 215n50; on heteroglossia, 48–49, 203n31

Baldanzi, Jessica, 203n41

Banks, Kimberly, 206n7

Barnes, Djuna: on Baroness Elsa, 144. See also *Nightwood*; *Ryder*

Barthes, Roland: on *Family of Man*, 156, 163

Bataille, Georges, 149–50

Bell, Alexander and Melville, 192; talking machine of, 120, 136

Belrose, John S., 209n6

Benjamin, Walter, 24, 84, 97, 100

Bennett, Jane, 15; on agency, 66; on edible matter, 187, 189; on "thing-power," 198n16

Bersani, Leo, 163; "Is the Rectum a Grave?," 160; on queer sexuality, 172

Biddle, George, 144, 214n44

Bielawski, Tim, 204n59

bios, 164; and *zoë*, 18–19, 20, 164

blackness, 22, 25, 77, 79–80, 94–95

Blade Runner (film), 15

Blake, Susan L., 208n45

Blanchot, Maurice: on the corpse, 35–37

Bleikasten, André, 203n39, 204n43

Bock, Martin, 215n49

body, the: acoustic life of, 115; American history of, 105; autopoetic, 190; biopolitical control over, 17, 23; black, 24, 77, 79–81, 90, 206n9, 206n11; in Cartesian space, 44; construction from absence, 56; disarticulation of, 30–31, 33, 52, 123; dualism with mind, 4, 40; in Faulkner, 37, 39–40, 41–47, 57–59, 60, 63–64; fluid passages of, 180; gendered topographies of, 146; grotesque, 102, 104; ideological constructions of, 104; machine assemblages of, 31, 116, 120, 125, 127, 135–36, 142–43, 146–47, 151; as material other, 39; micropolitics of, 40; mineralized structure of, 65–66, 68; mutation of, 40, 41; photographic perspectives on, 24; in poststructuralism, 39; rationalist control over, 3; and technical media, 3, 29, 46–47, 102–3, 115, 119, 134, 158; as text, 185; transcendence of, 4, 112, 171; visual penetration of, 50, 85; white social, 91

bones, 9, 120; in *Absalom, Absalom!*, 64–65, 69, 70; in *Tender Buttons*, 188; as veil of decency, 149–50. *See also* skeleton; skull, human

Bontemps, Arna, 206n13

Braidotti, Rosa: on bare life, 18–19; on becoming-earth, 2; on conceptual creativity, 10–11; on decomposition, 2; on human–posthuman boundary, 9; on modernist technology, 28; reconceptualization of death, 5, 9, 18–19, 21

Broadcast (band): *Tender Buttons*, 194–95

Brooks, Peter, 45, 107

Brown, Bill, 33

Brown, William: lynching of, 77–79, 98, 106

Burke, Carolyn, 209n77

Burroughs, William, 210n36

Butler, Judith, 10, 171; "Beside Oneself," 179–80, 182; on Foucault, 39–40; on heteronormativity, 160

cadavers: history of, 13, 199n34; and images, 37, 40; and materiality, 40, 51, 80; medical, 6, 12, 40, 42, 82–84; philosophy and, 12, 39, 43. *See also* corpses

Callus, Ivan, 11, 33

Cane, 79–82; African Americans in, 24, 79, 88, 89; artificial man in, 82, 105, 106, 107; autopsy in, 88, 103; autoptic gaze in, 81, 116; the body in, 84–85, 93; "Bona and Paul," 206n11; "Box Seat," 99–102; childbirth in, 91–92; corporeality in, 90, 92, 94, 98; dehumanization in, 1, 23; "Esther," 90–91; "Fern," 86–90; gaze in, 80, 86–91, 99–103, 106, 107, 116; the grotesque in, 102, 208n44; "Her Lips Are Copper Wire," 103, 116; the human/nonhuman in, 80, 92; imagery in, 98, 100, 103; "Kabnis," 104–8, 208n45; "Karintha," 91–93, 94; landscape in, 87–88, 92; literary form of, 107, 108, 109–10, 206n13; lynching in, 89, 90, 94, 106, 107, 158, 206n7, 208n41; narrators of, 86–88; the North in, 82, 98–99, 104; photography in, 24, 81,

88–89, 105–6; "Portrait in Georgia," 79–80, 85, 89, 103, 158; "Reapers," 92–93; retrospection in, 107–8, 110; "Seventh Street," 98–99; the South in, 86–94, 104–8; spiritual entity of, 109–10; technological gaze in, 86, 102; theatrical performance in, 100, 101–2; viewers in, 80–81, 86–87, 90–91, 102, 208n45; vision in, 87, 104, 105, 107; visual techniques of, 104, 108, 116

Cargill, 216n18

Chafe, Chris, 120

Chaplin, Charlie: *Modern Times*, 9, 27–28, 29, *29*

Chen, Mel Y., 157; "Has the Queer Ever Been Human?," 160

circulation: bodily, 52, 98, 103, 125, 144, 175–76, 180, 182; urban, 99, 181

Civil War (American), 38–39, 62, 67, 68–71

Cohen, Jeffrey Jerome, 159–62

colonialism, 20

consciousness: and embodiment, 41, 43, 46, 51, 56, 123; in modernism, 149, 166; and the senses, 47, 48, 58; and transhumanism, 4

coronal suture, 28–29; and Frankenstein, 133, 136; in "Incident," 115, 124, 125, 132, 142; in "Primal Sound," 115, 117, 119, 121, 142; and recording grooves, 114–15, 119–24, 142; as sound source, 115, 116; and technical media, 115, 132. *See also* skull

corporeality: ambient, 52, 61; of cadavers, 83; disavowed, 12, 80, 88, 90, 99, 107; fluid, 98; liminal, 56, 101; and modernism, 33; posthuman, 42; spectral, 60; and vision, 51, 92, 105, 183, 203n37

corpses: agency of, 5–6, 38, 198n15; appearance of, 20, 23, 37, 80; and artistic corpus, 185; in *As I Lay Dying*, 36–38, 54–61, 186; becoming, 54–61; becoming-earth of, 176; black, 24, 78, 80; celebrities', 6, 198n18;

epistemology of, 11, 42, 82; examination of, 6, 7, 11–12, 13, 14, 146, 183, 194; gaze of, 94–103, 104; killing of, 77; language of, 48; life of, 5, 8, 34; materiality of, 39, 113, 117; modernist, 2, 8, 54–55; Native American, 20–21; nonhuman, 3, 33, 185–95; ontology of, 6, 35–36; photographs of, 1, 197n3; posthumanist, 3, 4, 5, 39; as prosthetic body, 3, 50, 120, 187; reanimation of, 1, 2, 10, 21, 115, 124, 125, 136; temporality of, 3, 6–7. *See also* cadavers; exquisite corpse; zombies

Crary, Jonathan, 13, 85

Cullick, Jonathan S., 204n56

Cunningham, Christopher J., 204n53

cyberspace, 46, 112

cyborgs, 3, 29, 133, 210n3, 211n44, 211n53

dadaism, 114, 116, 121, 194, 211n53

Davidson, Michael, 214n35, 214n40

dead, the: ancestral, 91; boundary with living, 1, 35, 92, 139, 166–67, 186; metaphorical, 9; reanimation of, 25, 133–34; speech of, 48, 120, 124, 185; trench cities of, 1

death: of the author, 26, 46, 186; and birth, 27, 156, 162–63, 177, 180, 193; and blackness, 79–80; extending horizon of, 5, 19, 28, 174; incorporation of, 167, 174; in modernism, 14; of others, 80, 174, 213n17; as passage, 35, 42; and racialization, 22–23; and sexuality, 213n17; social, 2, 136, 168, 172; and technical media, 25, 130

decomposition: into ecological networks, 2, 7, 37, 73; and humanism, 23, 38, 62; and language, 39, 41, 53, 130; material processes of, 3, 48, 149–50; and mutation, 50, 52, 54; and temporality, 8, 16

dehumanization: and humanism, 194; and lynching, 78, 79; of other, 2, 20, 38, 157; and queer subject, 160; racist,

1, 21, 23, 24, 38, 62, 66, 74, 90, 99; and technology, 27, 82; and war, 71

De Landa, Manuel, 65; on bone, 68, 119

de Lauretis, Teresa, 213n34

Deleuze, Gilles, 57–58, 162, 174

Deleuze, Gilles and Félix Guattari: on assemblages, 7–8, 35, 54, 143, 165; on authorship, 44, 59; on becoming, 58–60, 131, 168–69; on intermingling of bodies, 6, 30–31, 187, 191; on molarity/molecularity, 61, 204n51; on wasp and orchid, 168, 176; on "wolf-children," 58–59; on zombies, 9

Derrida, Jacques: on eating, 191, 193; on "ends of man," 7; on "hauntology," 141–42

Descartes, René: and mind–body dualism, 40; and space, 44, 47; and subject, 4; and thought, 13; on visual objectivity, 12, 183

disembodiment: of cognition, 41, 149; and ghosts, 142; and realism, 46; and technical media, 112–13, 120, 123, 130; of texts, 15, 186, 190, 195; transhuman, 5, 14, 112, 130; "triumphant," 14, 200n42; and vision, 12, 25, 45, 80, 90–91

Donne, John: *Infinitati Sacrum,* 182

Du Bois, W. E. B.: double consciousness theory, 96, 97; on viewership, 107. *See also* "Georgia Negro Exhibit"

Duchamp, Marcel, 145

Duncan, Bowie, 207n13

Edelman, Lee, 160, 173, 214n35

Edison, Thomas Alva, 120

Edmunds, Susan, 101, 208n44

electroencephalograms, 120

Eliot, T. S.: "The Love Song of J. Alfred Prufrock," 86, 110; on *Nightwood,* 159; *The Waste Land,* 1, 8, 86, 128, 129, 214n41

Elsa, Baroness, 25, 214n44; costumes of, 142–45; on gender, 29, 142, 143,

151, 212n63; influence of, 114, 178; machine/body performances of, 142, 145, 211n53; poetry of, 146–47, 148, 212n66; representation of Old Europe, 144, 145; skull of, 142–43, 144, 145, 150–51; sound poetry of, 117, 144, 145–48; street performances of, 117, 142, 143–45

embalming, 3–4, 197n8, 204n59

embodiment, 14, 47, 67, 71, 72, 82, 106–7, 200n42; of enunciation, 111, 148; and posthumanism, 5, 24, 46, 47, 136, 141; and reading, 73, 189; technical media as, 113, 116–17; and vision, 12–13, 51, 102, 104

Enlightenment, 11, 12–13, 28, 115

Ethnographic Exposition, 84

ethnography, 83, 84, 86, 88, 90, 94, 104, 207n20

exquisite corpse, 31–33, *32*, 194

Family of Man: gendered norms of, 30, 163; myth of, 156–57; and queer love, 159, 171, 181; and reproduction, 158, 167; universalism of, 159, 161, 163, 180

Family of Man (exhibition), 156, 162

Faulkner, William: and incest, 205n62; literary corpus of, 74; racial dehumanization in, 23. See also *Absalom!, Absalom!*; *As I Lay Dying*; *Sound and the Fury, The*

film: corpses in, 2, 80, 84, 85; objectivity of, 88–89; visual techniques of, 81, 84, 85, 87–89, 101, 104, 135. *See also* Chaplin, Charlie; *Frankenstein*; zombies: cinematic

Fitzgerald, F. Scott, 1, 9

Foucault, Michel: on autopsy, 82; *The Birth of the Clinic*, 11; on the corpse, 11–12, 23, 42, 199n34; on death, 13–14, 53, 112; on erasure of man, 7; on inscribed body, 39; on medical power, 41; on "micro-physics" of the body, 40, 60

Frank, Joseph, 214n39, 214n41

Frankenstein (film, 1931), 2, 114, *133*, 134, 135–36, 151, 192

Frankenstein's creature: coronal suture of, 115, 133, 136; immaturity of, 134; reanimation of, 115, 125, 133–34, 142, 147, 210n44; voice of, 135–36

Frazer, James: *The Golden Bough*, 86

Freud, Sigmund: *Civilization and Its Discontents*, 47; on dreams, 9; and *Nightwood*, 213n34, 214n41; on vision, 47, 202n28

Freytag-Loringhoven, Baroness Elsa von. *See* Elsa, Baroness

Friedrich, Ernst: *War against War*, 197n3

Fuss, Diana, 30, 194; and "corpse poems," 185–86; on speaking corpse, 190

futurism, 114, 116, 121–22, 126, 127, 132

Gammel, Irene, 143, 145, 211n53, 212n66

gaze: African American, 94–98; autoptic, 81, 84, 116, 125; in *Cane*, 80, 86–91, 99–103, 106, 107, 116; clinical, 41, 80, 82, 84, 193; corpses', 13, 42, 94–103, 104; upon corpses, 11, 13, 80; Descartes on, 12, 183; humanist, 112; upon queer body, 182; technological, 80, 86, 104; viewer/viewed binary of, 98; white, 12, 90–91, 95–98, 100, 107. *See also* vision

gender: in Barnes, 154–55, 157, 163, 179–80; and Baroness Elsa, 142–46; binary, 162; and the body, 6, 146; boundaries of, 163; centrality for family, 56, 157–58, 163, 171–72; and crossdressing, 178–80; in *Gramophone, Film, Typewriter*, 128; and humanism, 157; ideological construction of, 81; in "Letters of the Unliving," 129–32; as mode of dispossession, 179; posthuman escape from, 165, 175, 182; queering of, 174, 179; in *The Sacred Prostitute*, 125–27; transgression of, 142, 143, 180

Krasny, Michael, 207n13
Krause, David, 205n63
Kristeva, Julia: on the corpse, 13, 90
Kurzweil, Ray, 4

Larsen, Nella: *Passing,* 1
Latour, Bruno, 211n56
Laxton, Susan, 140, 211n49
Levinas, Emmanuel, 154
Lieber, Todd, 207n13
Lippit, Akira Mizuta, 203n30
Liveright, Horace, 86
love, 26, 29–30, 126, 154–183; association
    with death, 174, 176; and molecular-
    ity, 174–75; queer, 158–61
Loy, Mina: "Aphorisms on Futurism,"
    132; artistic identity of, 113–14; and
    futurism, 126, 127, 132; "Incident,"
    115, 123–27, 128, 132, 142; "Letters
    of the Unliving," 129–32; *The Sacred
    Prostitute,* 125–26; on technical
    media, 29, 116
Luciano, Dana: "Has the Queer Ever Been
    Human?," 157, 160
Luhan, Mabel Dodge, 190
lynching, 77–79, 205n2; and the black
    body, 81; William Brown's, 77–79, 95,
    106; in *Cane,* 81, 89, 90, 93–94, 106,
    107, 158, 206n7, 208n41; NAACP
    pamphlets on, 78; photographs of,
    1, 77–79, 94; as protection of white
    femininity, 78, 158; during Red
    Summer, 77, 79; Southern history
    of, 105–6; Emmett Till's, 156; Mary
    Turner's, 106, 107

Mahoney, Dan, 214n42
Man Ray, 25, 29, 31, 114, 136. *See also*
    rayographs
Marconi, Guglielmo, 111–12, 113, 117
Marcus, Jane, 214n41
Marinetti, F. T., 116, 132, 148; Loy's sati-
    rization of, 126; *Zong Toomb Toomb,*
    126–27

materiality: authorial engagement with,
    31; becoming of, 189; of corpses,
    13, 24, 39, 82, 113, 117; and cultural
    performance, 178; and food, 187; of
    inscription, 129–30; of modernism,
    15, 19; primal sound of, 120, 127; of
    signs, 69–72; of sound recording, 118;
    and technical media, 113, 118, 129,
    132, 137; transcendence of, 5
matter: animation of, 40; "dead," 10, 30,
    66; edible, 187, 189; and flat ontology,
    8; futurist relations with, 132; and
    humanism, 5; and information, 41,
    112, 136, 193; molecular processes of,
    8; queer ecology of, 179; reorganiza-
    tion of, 46, 61, 147; signifying proper-
    ties of, 71–72; temporal difficulty of,
    141
Matthews, John T., 203n38
McAlister, Elizabeth, 21
Meeropol, Abel: "Strange Fruit," 94
Michaels, Walter Benn, 69–70, 74, 200n58,
    204n53; on lynching, 79, 206n9
Mitchell, W. J. T., 3
modernism: anoptic, 86; antirepresen-
    tational, 20; authorship in, 33;
    autopsy in, 86, 110; consciousness in,
    149; corpse in, 2, 3, 8, 10, 13–14, 20,
    54–55; corpus of, 194; death in, 14;
    experimental techniques of, 15, 33,
    39, 47, 85, 110, 137, 194; interiority
    in, 85, 149; and media archives,
    197n4; mourning in, 14; newness in,
    17; nonlocal transmission of, 114;
    penetrative gaze of, 86; photography
    in, 89; and posthumanism, 5, 59, 194;
    signs in, 70; skull in, 149–51; sound
    art of, 122; spatial form in, 214n39;
    and technical media, 15, 25, 28; trans-
    atlantic currents of, 113; and vitalism,
    8; in the wake of the human, 15–20
modernity, 8, 18, 85–86, 121
Moglen, Seth: *Mourning Modernity,* 14
molarity, 3, 7, 14, 50, 61, 204n51

molecularity, 3, 7, 8, 14, 21, 24, 37, 44, 60–61, 164, 165, 175, 204n51

Moravec, Hans, 4, 112–13, 150

Morse code, 111–12, 113

mutation: in *As I Lay Dying*, 41, 44, 45, 50, 52, 54, 60, 61; biological, 40, 41, 200n42, 201n12; in *Nightwood*, 166, 167, 169; and technical media, 113, 115, 120, 136

Native Americans, 20–21, 64

necrophilia, 6

necropolitics, 9

Ngai, Sianne, 193

Nietzsche, Friedrich, 199n38

Nightwood, 157–83; the animal in, 30, 154, 158–61, 164, 165–66, 168–71, 180, 213n34; autopsy in, 182–83; becoming-earth in, 161, 176; *bios* and *zoë* in, 164, 176; birth and death in, 162–63, 165, 177; bodily materiality in, 166, 178; burial in, 171–72, 175; circus lioness of, 169–70; corpse in, 158, 160; darkness in, 180–81, 215n49; desire in, 30, 158, 160, 165–68, 174, 177, 179, 213n17; deterritorialization in, 174, 175–76; doctor character of, 177–83, 214nn41–42; doll in, 173–74; eland-bride of, 165–66, 169–70; family in, 157, 171, 213n31; family grave in, 171–74; and *Family of Man*, 167, 171; gaze in, 182–83; gender in, 157, 163, 179, 180, 214n40; heteronormativity in, 158, 165, 171, 173, 174; and humanism, 167; human–nonhuman exchanges in, 169–70, 171, 181; life cycle, 163, 164; marginalized bodies of, 181; networks of circulation in, 176–77, 181; the nonhuman in, 159, 164, 165, 167–70; nonprocreative sexuality in, 173; otherness in, 183; "The Possessed," 170–71; the posthuman in, 29, 158, 161, 166, 167, 168, 175; the posthumous in, 167, 171,

179; queerness in, 30, 161, 158–60, 168, 170, 173–75, 177–78, 179, 214n39; reading against self in, 166–67; self-replication in, 167; setting of, 162; spatiotemporal shifts in, 163–64; "Town of Darkness," 180–81; transformation in, 157–58, 161; transgression in, 166, 179, 180; transmaterialism in, 178; trans-specied birth in, 171; "Watchman, What of the Night?" 177–78, 180

noise: futurist, 116, 121, 126–27; of life, 122; and signal, 111–12, 135

other, the, 14, 180; death of, 80, 174, 213n17; dehumanization of, 2, 38; visual invasion of, 12, 80–81

otherness: 33, 36, 39, 127, 167, 174, 197n7

Parikka, Jussi, 176

Parvizi, Josef, 120

Pearson, Erin, 205n65

Pettey, Homer B., 202n24

Phillips, Michelle H., 206n12

phonograph: reanimation of the dead, 120, 124, 209n19; Rilke's construction of, 28, 114–15, 117–23, 132, 134, 137; stylus of, 122–23; in *The Waste Land*, 128. *See also* sound recording

photographs: 1, 24, 25, 84–85, 88–89, 95, 97, 137, 141, 197n3. *See also* "Georgia Negro Exhibit;" Man Ray; Steichen, Edward

Poe, Edgar Allan: *The Narrative of Arthur Gordon Pym*, 9

posthuman, the: bodily forms of, 4, 28, 57, 59, 82, 107, 115, 124–25, 134, 144, 161; cosmological, 197n7; destructive, 10; in Faulkner, 40, 41, 61, 62, 63, 67; generative, 10; in *Nightwood*, 161, 166, 167, 168, 175; paradoxes of, 11; in *Spring and All*, 16; technological representation of, 141; thematic representations of, 33; *zoë* in, 19 posthumanism: in *As I Lay Dying*, 54, 62; "bad," 20, 21, 63, 126; corpses and, 3, 4, 5, 39–40; critical, 10–15; embodied, 5, 24, 136; emergent, 194, 195; human and other in, 3; and modernism, 194; mutation in, 40; and the nonhuman, 197n7; posthumous, 3–10, 198n14; and queerness, 158–62; reading practices of, 14, 33, 166–67, 194; and technological determinism, 54, 81

posthumous, the: continuum with living, 3, 136; in *Nightwood*, 167, 171, 179; and posthumanism, 3–10, 198n14; redefinition of the human, 35; sensorium of, 47; and Gertrude Stein, 186; versus transhumanism, 4

Pound, Ezra, 15, 136, 201n6

Pratt, Mary Louise, 208n30

"Primal Sound," 28, 117–23; coronal suture in, 115, 117, 119, 121, 125 142, 150; as extension of senses, 122, 127; phonograph exercise in, 114–15, 117–23, 132, 134, 137; the voice in, 121, 127

prostheses, 4, 134, 178

race: in *Absalom, Absalom!*, 63–67, 68–72; as binaristic difference, 81, 98, 105, 199n36; and corpses, 6; and kinship, 68–72; and miscegenation, 38, 70, 72; and personhood, 69, 72. *See also* blackness; lynching; whiteness; white supremacy

radio, 111–13, 123–4, 146–7. *See also* sound; technologies

Ramlow, Todd, 159–62

rayographs, 115, 136–42, *138, 139*, 151, 211n49

RCA dog, 128

reading, 33, 73, 161, 166–67, 194–95

realism: epistemological commitments of, 45–46; visual techniques of, 43, 48, 51, 85–86, 207n25; window as trope of, 45–46, 202n24

Red Summer, 77, 79, 95, 98

Regnault, Félix-Louis, 84

Reid, B. L.: *Art by Subtraction*, 185, 186, 190–91, 194

Renard, Maurice: "Death and the Shell," 128

Rilke, Rainer Maria: anatomical studies of, 114, 118, 125; female audience of, 127, 150; gendered flesh tropes of, 150. *See also* "Primal Sound"

Rohman, Carrie, 164

Rony, Fatimah Tobing, 83–84

Russolo, Luigi, 121–22

Rutsky, R. L., 40–41

Ryder, 153–58, *155*, 161–62

Sandburg, Carl, 162

Sarraute, Nathalie, 61; on Proust, 204n51

Saunders, Rebecca, 205n60

Saussure, Ferdinand de, 202n20

Scandura, Jani, 6; on the corpse, 54–55

Schérer, René, 58

Schlabach, Kyle, 203n41

Schoolfield, George C., 209n7

Schwartz, Margaret, 198n18

Scott, Bonnie Kime, 213n28

Seitler, Dana, 213n33

Seltzer, Mark, 204n53

senses, the: and Enlightenment, 12–13; Freud on, 47; prosthetic extension of, 28, 112, 115, 122, 126, 144; synesthetic experience of, 44, 50, 122, 127, 137, 139

sensorium: limitations of human, 33, 121, 141, 181; of posthumanism, 47, 49; technologically mediated, 142

sexuality: in *Cane*, 88, 89; and death, 213n17; as dispossession, 179; ontology of, 160, 190; queer, 158–62

Sherman, David, 198n15, 201n4; on death of other, 213n17; *In a Strange Room*, 14

Shildrick, Margrit, 198n14

Simon, John K., 201n15, 202n26

Tobin, Patricia, 204n54
transhumanism, 4–5, 112, 150
Traubeck, Bartholomäus, 120
Troyer, John, 197n8
Turner, Mary: lynching of, 106, 107

Van Vechten, Carl, 187
Verdery, Katherine, 198n18
Vernon, Alex, 204n55
viewership: embodied, 12–13, 51, 102, 104; racialized, 24, 78–82, 86, 90, 95–98, 102, 104–8. *See also* gaze; vision
viscera, 12
vision: in *As I Lay Dying*, 41–47, 50–52; autoptic, 24, 81, 84, 98, 104, 116, 193–94; in *Cane*, 86–94; panoptic, 43, 51; penetration of body, 50, 85–86; technologically mediated, 13, 46, 82. *See also* gaze; viewership
vitalism: of the corpse, 5, 8, 10, 21, 30, 149, 188, 198n14; Deleuze and Guattari on, 7–8; of language, 39, 49, 131; and mechanism, 7, 117; and mortalism, 5, 6, 8, 82; of the nonhuman, 14, 48, 54, 62, 182
voice: disembodied, 48, 147–48, 186, 190; in entertainment, 135, 148; and gender, 116, 127–28; interpenetration with machine, 127, 129–32; nonhuman, 49, 71; recorded, 116, 118, 120. *See also* phonograph; sound recording

Waldby, Catherine, 43
Warner, Michael, 157, 212n8
Watkins, Patricia, 207n13
Webb, Jeff, 21

Weinstein, Jami, 167, 175, 198n14
Whalan, Mark, 206n11
Whale, James, 25, 29, 115. See also *Frankenstein*
White, Christopher T., 203n30
whiteness, 67, 74; association with life, 22, 25, 79–80; ideologies of, 78; production through violence, 98
white supremacy: in *Absalom, Absalom!*, 38, 62–64; and lynching, 78; and technology, 82; and viewership, 92
White Zombie (film, 1932), 21, 22
Whitley, Catherine, 215n49
Whyde, Janet, 207n13
Wiegman, Robyn, 199n36
Wilks, Jennifer M., 207n13
Williams, William Carlos, 1, 15, 200n58; *In the American Grain*, 20–21; *Spring and All*, 15–20
Winterson, Jeanette, 159
Wolfe, Cary: on embodiment, 47, 200n42; on Freudian vision, 202n28; on mutation, 201n12; on posthumanism, 14–15, 21, 161; on transhumanism, 4
Wood, Amy Louise, 205n4
World War I: corpses of, 1, 8–9; soundscape of, 121–22, 212n66; and technology, 117, 121, 123, 145–46; and temporality, 25, 27, 122–23, 164
Wright, Richard: *Native Son*, 1

Zelazo, Suzanne, 211n53, 212n66
Zender, Karl F., 205n62
Žižek, Slavoj, 135
zoë, 19, 164; and *bios*, 18–19, 20, 164, 176
zombies, 9; cinematic, 2, 21–22; in *Modern Times*, 9; social punishment of, 21; and colonialism, 22

ERIN E. EDWARDS is associate professor of English at Miami University.